ROMANS

A Bible Commentary in the Wesleyan Tradition

CLARENCE L. BENCE

CONTENTS

EDITOR'S PREFACE

This book is part of a series of commentaries seeking to interpret the books of the Bible from a Wesleyan perspective. It is designed primarily for lay people, especially teachers of Sunday school and leaders of Bible studies. Pastors will also find this series very helpful. In addition, this series is also for people who want to read and study on their own for spiritual edification.

Each book of the Bible will be explained paragraph by paragraph. This "wide angle lens" approach helps the reader to follow the primary flow of thought in each passage. This, in turn, will help the reader to avoid "missing the forest because of the trees," a problem many people encounter when reading commentaries.

At the same time, the authors slow down often to examine particular details and concepts that are important for understanding the bigger picture. Where there are alternative understandings of key passages, the authors acknowledge these so the reader will experience a broader knowledge of the various theological traditions and how the Wesleyan perspective relates to them.

These commentaries follow the *New International Version* and are intended to be read with your Bible open. With this in mind, the biblical text is not reproduced in full, but appears in bold type throughout the discussion of each passage. Greater insight will be gained by reading along in your Bible as you read the commentaries.

These volumes do not replace the valuable technical commentaries that offer in-depth grammatical and textual analysis. What they do offer is an interpretation of the Bible that we hope will lead to a greater understanding of what the Bible says, its significance for our lives today, and further transformation into the image of Christ.

David A. Higle
Editor

AUTHOR'S PREFACE

Writing a commentary on Paul's letter to the Romans offers moments of both agony and ecstasy. The agony of this past year has come from wrestling with the deep thinking and complicated writing style of this brilliant theologian of the first century in the Christian church. My agony has been intensified by frequent feelings of inadequacy to accomplish the task—feelings that surfaced when scanning bookshelves filled with commentaries authored by the likes of St. Augustine, Martin Luther, John Calvin, John Wesley, Karl Barth, and almost every other New Testament scholar. What contribution could a professor of church history, who devotes much of his energies to the ministry of preaching, offer to this great legacy?

I have decided to approach this task more as a student-turned-teacher than a biblical scholar. Although I have consulted the original text in my studies, I make no claim to expertise in pointing out the subtle meanings of words or grammatical structures in the Greek language. I have endeavored to place Paul's letter in its historical and cultural setting, but I in no way consider myself an authority on the world of the first-century church. I have simply endeavored to let Paul be my teacher, and then to pass on the insights he has generated, in a way that might be understandable to a layperson, Sunday school teacher, or pastor who is unfamiliar with both New Testament Greek and the cultural setting of ancient Rome.

If there is a unique element to this commentary, it is my love of theology—the basic doctrines of the Christian faith—particularly as they have developed over two thousand years of church history. I am intrigued by the ways in which different followers of Christ, equally sincere in their passion to follow His commands, interpret the teachings of this letter. These differing opinions are not to be seen as distortions of God's Word by devious minds; rather, they are serious endeavors to unpack the deep truths that the book of Romans offers about God, human nature, and salvation from sin.

My digressions from the biblical text will most often take the form of theological dialogues, in which several divergent approaches are presented regarding some issue Paul has presented to his readers. This is not an attempt to ignore the plain words of Scripture, nor to elevate human reasoning above the revelation of God in His Word. It is my attempt to sort out the complex issues with which Paul wrestles, in a way that does not impose a sole answer to each question raised by the text, and also does not brush over the options available to committed believers who study Romans.

I confess to reading the text through the spectacles of my own theological heritage, the theology of John Wesley. But this is not a "Wesleyan" commentary, so much as a personal engagement with the Scriptures. I am seeking to expound the truth of God's Word, while retaining my loyalty to a particular tradition of the faith. Where there have been tensions between historical tradition and Scripture, I have allowed my conscience to ask, "What does the Bible say?" rather than, "What would my church want it to say?" In such cases, however, I have been more inclined to make tentative suggestions than to impose dogmatic assertions upon the holy mysteries of God's Word to us. The agony of the commentator is to live up to Paul's expectation to be one "who does not need to be ashamed and who correctly handles the word of truth" (2 Timothy 2:15).

There have been personal agonies as well. Attempting to include this project in the busy life of work, family, and ministry has resulted in strains upon all three. My wife and children, as well as my students, have demonstrated their own form of perseverance during this endeavor. My editor, David Higle, has alternately created and relieved my agony at points along the way. Our friendship will long outlast this book.

Enough of agony. The ecstasy of studying God's Word and then sharing it with others makes all the anguish of writing worthwhile. The gospel explained in this commentary is Paul's understanding of the Christian faith—but it is no less mine. I, too, have been encountered by Christ and sense my debt to preach the gospel "both to the wise, and to the unwise" (Rom. 1:14 KJV). After years of proclaiming the message from the pulpit, this opportunity to put my thoughts in written words is a unique joy.

No one can spend extended time in the book of Romans without being reminded of the gift of grace God has offered in His Son. My ecstasy goes beyond sharing God's Word with others; the ultimate joy is to be confronted by the Word and, in "the renewing" of my mind, to experience the transformation of life that Paul describes in Romans 12:2. The agonies of this task will fade quickly; my prayer is that the joys of this endeavor will be eternal.

Clarence L. Bence
Marion, Indiana
September 1995

INTRODUCTION

God has offered to humanity the clearest revelation of himself in the life, death, resurrection and teaching of His Son, Jesus Christ. It is not surprising that the written record of that gift comes to us in the form of narratives, or stories—four Gospels written by individuals who either traveled with Jesus or heard first-hand reports from those who did. From these accounts, we can grasp a clear picture of the mission of Jesus, and how His words and actions completed the work given Him by His Father.

The Gospels very clearly reveal that Jesus came to save His people from their sins (Matthew 1:21). But *how* that salvation is accomplished is not clearly defined in the Gospel narratives. The explanation of how God saves us in Christ, and what being a disciple of Jesus entails, is found in a group of letters sent out by early-church leaders to their followers. We do not gain our understanding of the apostles' faith from minutes of church councils. We cannot turn to lecture notes of classes taught by the disciples to their congregations. We do not even have access to great books or essays on the Christian faith. Instead, we find our principle teachings buried in correspondence between early believers. Their letters are not, however, casual jottings; they deal with the weighty matters that confronted the community of faith during its first two generations of existence. Many of these issues still confront the church today.

Yet, for all the serious issues these writers addressed, none of them could have envisioned that two thousand years later, followers of their Master, Jesus Christ, would be scrutinizing their "mail" to gain a richer understanding of salvation and the life of faith. No, more likely these authors simply sat down, with pen in hand, to share insights, advice, and correction to clusters of believers who were still endeavoring to flesh-out the full meaning of the good news as it related to life in Christ and life in the world.

Although the writers of these letters did not grasp the full significance of what they were doing, they wrote with a sense of their authority to speak a clear word to the church. After all, each of them had spent considerable time with the Master. They had been eyewitnesses to His death and resurrection. They had experienced the power of the Spirit's presence in the church on the Day of Pentecost. They could assert, "That which . . . we have seen with our eyes, which we have looked at and our hands have touched—this we proclaim concerning the Word of life" (1 John 1:1).

They could all say this, that is, with one notable exception. The person who wrote the most letters found in our New Testament came late to the scene. His encounter with Christ was not in Galilee or even Jerusalem. He met the Master on a highway, miles north of Palestine, on the route leading to Damascus. It happened several years after the great events described in the Gospels and the opening chapters of Acts.

This writer's understanding of the significance of Jesus and the meaning of salvation did not arise out of conversations with Jesus or the disciples. His ideas were shaped instead by his own careful analysis of what he had studied in the Jewish Scriptures under the instruction of devout rabbis. Thus, his understanding of Jesus the Messiah was hammered out during hours of lonely reflection in the deserts of Arabia. His revolutionary message was then proclaimed through a remarkable mission to the people considered the most unlikely recipients of God's love—the pagan Gentiles.

This writer of New Testament epistles was the Apostle Paul. His letters to churches and pastors in the first years of Christianity give us the clearest insights into the meaning of salvation and the practice of the Christian life. And in no writing does Paul give us a more complete picture of God's eternal purposes for humanity than his letter to the believers at Rome. One could imagine a New Testament without the book of Romans, but how limited our grasp of salvation by faith would be without this masterpiece! It forms the theological framework around which the superstructure of Christianity is built.

At pivotal moments in the history of the church, Paul's letter to the Romans has called the people of God back to the heart of the gospel. Augustine, the great bishop of Africa in the third century, came to grips with his sin and God's righteousness by reading from this letter. Martin Luther's study and lectures on the book of Romans transformed his students, and thousands of believers during the Reformation era. John Wesley's heart-warming experience and heart-changing ministry stemmed from hearing Paul's words to the Romans explained one night on Aldersgate Street in London. In our own century, German theologian Karl Barth's *Letter to the Romans* (1919) called a bland Protestantism back to a God of grace, who is encountered by faith, not human reason.

Every generation of believers must return to this letter and rediscover Paul's great insight concerning God's righteousness, which comes to sinful humans by His grace . . . and through our faith. We step back through two thousand years of history to enter a world that politically, socially, and religiously is quite different from our own. However, Paul's description of the human condition of sin and the grace of our Lord Jesus Christ are as relevant now as they were in the days of the Roman Empire. In Paul's letter, we discover again the good news of God's righteousness to "everyone who believes" (Rom. 1:16).

THE OCCASION OF THE LETTER

Paul wrote his letter to the Romans several decades after his encounter with Christ on the road to Damascus. During that intervening time, Paul spent several years sorting out his own understanding of the relationship between his Jewish heritage and the new covenant revealed in God's Messiah, Jesus of Nazareth. Before Paul's public ministry, he lived in solitude in Arabia and in his home city of Tarsus.

Barnabas found Paul in Tarsus and offered him an opportunity to minister to believers in Antioch. Here was a location far enough away from Jerusalem to allow Paul freedom to proclaim the gospel without threats from his former associates, who still sought to silence followers of Christ. Paul also could avoid the suspicion and criticism of believers who openly questioned his right to apostleship due to his previous hostility toward the faith.

Antioch also provided Paul with a broader vision of the good news than he might have developed in Jerusalem. The congregation was a mixture of Jewish believers, Gentile converts who had converted first to Judaism and then to Christ, and pagans who were drawn to the gospel but remained detached from its Jewish underpinnings. In this diverse congregation, Paul grasped an understanding of God's righteousness that grew out of Jewish roots, but beyond them into a message of salvation to all persons, both Jew and Gentile.

An opportunity to spread this good news of Christ across Asia Minor (present-day Turkey) and then into Greece became the passion and joy of Paul and his comrades. For about a decade, Paul preached Christ from town to town along the coastline of the Mediterranean Sea. At the time he wrote this letter, he had completed a first missionary trip to Asia Minor and a second trip reaching farther westward to Greece. At the close of the second tour, he was called upon to defend his mission to the Gentiles before the Jewish leaders of the church in Jerusalem (Acts 15). Despite their hesitation to accept his more universal understanding of salvation for all, the apostles gave Paul the authority to continue preaching the gospel.

On his third expedition, Paul retraced the path of his earlier travels, encouraging the congregations he had planted, and adding new converts to the faith. During his journey, Paul became aware of the serious plight of believers in Jerusalem who were at the point of starvation because of a famine in that region. He organized a relief fund to be collected from the Gentile congregations that would serve two purposes. It would demonstrate Christ's "law of love" in doing good to those within "the family of believers" who were in great need (Galatians 6:10). The offering would further reconcile the Jewish believers to the Gentiles, who were still considered "far away" from the faith (Ephesians 2:17) by the more conservative members of the body.

Paul's references to this offering and his impending trip to deliver the funds to Jerusalem (Rom. 15:25-28) allow us to date the letter and its point of origin with considerable accuracy. The letter was sent from the city of Corinth at the conclusion of Paul's third missionary trip, just prior to his return to Jerusalem via Asia Minor. Scholars therefore assign the date A.D. 58 to this letter.

THE RECIPIENTS OF THE LETTER

The destination of Paul's epistle was the believers in Rome. The earliest origins of this congregation (or congregation*s*, as Romans 16:5, 10-11 suggest) are lost in history. The Roman Catholic tradition which says that Peter founded this church seems unlikely, since Paul makes no mention of Peter in the list of persons he greets. Peter's arrival and probable martyrdom in Rome would have occurred at some later date.

The first suggestion of a group of believers in Rome comes from a New Testament reference combined with the historical records of Rome. The book of Acts reports that the "[Emperor] Claudius had ordered all the Jews to leave Rome" (18:2). The chronicles of Suetonius, an early Roman historian, include a passing reference to this same edict of Claudius banishing the Jews (c. A.D. 52) because of arguments instigated by one called "Chrestus."[1] We might imagine that the historian incorrectly spelled "Christ" and assumed that this man was the perpetrator of the dispute, rather than the topic of disagreement among the Jews. Therefore, although the evidence is not clear-cut, there is good reason to think that the gospel had already arrived in Rome years before Paul's letter was sent. The fact that the letter was delivered in person to a group of individuals, whom Paul could identify by name, indicates that the government's opposition of Jews (and Christians) had largely subsided by that time.

Little else is known about these believers in Rome, except what can be gleaned from the letter itself. It is clear that the church was composed of both Jews and Gentiles, and that disagreements on matters of doctrine and practice divided them. Paul himself had not yet been to Rome, although he expressed great eagerness to minister to them (Acts 19:21; Rom. 1:11). The church did include a significant number of Paul's personal acquaintances (Rom. 16), who had migrated to that city from other places where Paul had ministered previously.

THE PURPOSE OF THE LETTER

Even a casual comparison of Paul's letter to the Romans with his other writings reveals the more logical and theological character of this work. In all his letters, Paul follows the standard form for correspondence in his day. After a greeting identifying both sender and destination, Paul offers a prayer for God's grace upon the recipients. The letter then proceeds to the main body, where truths about the faith are explained and followed by practical application to Christian living or particular problems in the congregation. A final section offers personal greetings and a prayer of benediction.

In his letter to the Romans, Paul uses an extended and rather continuous progression of thought to develop the theme of God's righteousness and its availability to humans through faith. Readers have wondered why Paul would be so meticulous in this letter, when on other occasions he moves rather quickly to dealing with problems in the church.

Some scholars think Paul wrote the letter to the Romans as a final defense of his ministry in the face of threats to his life. They point to the conclusion of the letter (15:23-33), in which Paul indicates that he is traveling to Jerusalem, where he faces some danger from unbelievers as well as the (Jewish) saints in the city. (Paul did, in fact, encounter strong opposition and threats to his life when he arrived on his mission. His arrest eventually led to his one and only trip to Rome.) Anticipating such dangerous circumstances, Paul used the occasion of this letter to write a theological "last will" spelling out the essential ideas of the gospel.

However, Rome seems an unlikely place to direct such a final word. Paul had never been to this city, and many of the believers there were strangers to his message. Furthermore, this letter clearly indicates that there would be opposition to Paul's ideas in this church. If Paul wanted to leave a written legacy for the early church, one would expect him to direct such a letter to his home base of Antioch, or at least to one of the churches he had established and visited.

A more plausible explanation for the purpose of this letter is found in Paul's final remarks concerning an anticipated mission to Spain with a stopover visit in Rome. Even though the region of Spain was far to the west of Paul's main theater of operations, it represented a glorious opportunity for the further spread of the gospel. Culture and learning were thriving in this region during the first century, and no doubt Paul's sense of indebtedness to the "non-Greeks" (1:14) extended all the way to the shores of the Atlantic Ocean.

But if Paul was planning to travel so far from his sending congregation in Antioch, he would need a new base of operations. Rome offered an ideal spot for this base. It was the capital city of the Empire, and a core of believers already existed there, including several of Paul's close friends and faithful workers in the cause of Christ. Thus, Paul would have written a careful exposition of the gospel as his own letter of commendation to the church in Rome. He could demonstrate his deep compassion for both Jews and Gentiles in the hopes of winning their mutual support for his bold enterprise into the regions beyond.

There is much to commend this view. But one wonders why the simplest explanation could not suffice to explain this letter. Paul is writing to a congregation for which he feels a deep responsibility, even though he had not planted the church, nor had he visited it by the time he wrote this letter. He certainly had heard good reports of the faith (1:8) and obedience (16:19) of the believers in Rome. Given his close friendships with several members of that congregation, Paul no doubt was aware of the tensions within the body as well. These conflicts appear to have arisen between Jewish believers who retained their deep reverence for the law—perhaps to the point of "works righteousness"—and a larger majority of Gentile converts who struggled with understanding how the ancient covenant of God with the children of Israel related to the gospel they had received.

Paul, ever seeking to bring about unity between the two branches of faith in the early church, uses this letter to deal with a very real problem in the Roman church, just as his other letters deal with specific issues in those congregations. The tone of Romans is more theological than Paul's other letters because the problem in Rome was more doctrinal in nature. If this latter view is valid, we can be grateful for the disagreements among the believers in Rome. Their disagreements have afforded us the opportunity to study Paul's own understanding of righteousness in a direct manner, rather than speculating about it from shorter treatments in his other letters.

THE THEME OF THE LETTER

Although the contention between Gentile and Jewish believers is the immediate problem facing the church in Rome, Paul's appeal for unity in the body is not the central or direct focus of the book (cf. Eph. 4:1-16; Colossians 3:11-15). Instead, he presents a more basic concept that forms the *foundation* for unity in the church—the righteousness of God. The disagreement among Christians in Rome centered upon two different views of righteousness. Both Jewish and Gentile believers worshiped the God whose very character was holiness, justice and truth. Both groups understood also that God expected those who worshiped Him to be righteous individuals.

The primary point of disagreement was how righteousness, which was a reflection of God's character, was to be attained. Jewish believers considered righteousness to be a moral accomplishment, attained by observing rituals and obeying the law. Persons who thus became righteous could expect the blessings (grace) of God to be bestowed upon them.

What the Gentile believers in Rome thought about righteousness is more difficult to determine. Some no doubt assumed that righteousness was inconsequential to salvation. They had come to Christ seeking eternal life, and they rejoiced in their salvation without giving much thought at all to God's moral character and His desire for a reflection of that character in the lives of those who followed His Son. These believers assumed they were righteous, without giving thought to what righteousness might mean in terms of a transformed life.

Other Gentiles probably had heard Paul's gospel and understood righteousness to be God's gracious gift to those who trust in Him. In Paul's view, righteousness does not qualify one for God's grace; grace is a gift that enables one to be righteous before God. In either understanding of grace, the Gentile believers rejected the moralism and legalism that characterized the Jewish understanding of righteousness.

To clear up the misconceptions in this congregation, Paul takes them back to the starting point of salvation—the realization that all persons, whether Jew or Gentile, have no innate righteousness to offer God as a ticket to a right standing with Him. All humans are sinners and "fall short" of what God desires (Rom. 3:23).

To attain a right standing with a righteous God, one must, according to Paul, exercise faith and *faith alone*. Like Abraham, who believed God, we must trust God's promise and receive the gift of *His* righteousness, rather than trusting in any righteousness of our own. Having trusted in His grace, however, we must then live out the righteousness that comes from above by considering ourselves dead to sin and alive to Christ. Thus, one not only accepts Christ by faith and is *declared* righteous, but also *lives* Christ by faith and *becomes* righteous.

This righteousness that is both a gift (God's righteousness) and a new nature (our righteousness) results in a transformed life that impacts our everyday encounters and relationships with believers and nonbelievers. Paul not only deals with the great concepts of justification and sanctification, but he also demonstrates how righteousness operates in the realities of life.

Thus, from his opening affirmation of the gospel to his final benediction, Paul exalts the holy character of God and rejoices in the grace which offers sinful humans access to that righteousness through God's Son. The gift is righteousness, the means is faith, and the end result is eternal life through Jesus Christ our Lord.

ENDNOTE

[1]Henry Bettensen, ed., *Documents of the Christian Church,* (New York: Oxford University Press, 1967), p. 2.

ROMANS OUTLINE

I. RIGHTEOUSNESS REJECTED: THE NATURE OF SIN (1:1–3:20)
A. The Gospel in Rome (1:1-17)
    1. 1:1   Paul's Title
    2. 1:2-7   Paul's Greeting
    3. 1:8-17   Paul's Gospel
B. The Path to Depravity (1:18-32)
    1. 1:18-20   The Clear Revelation
    2. 1:21-23   The Foolish Exchange
    3. 1:24-27   The Shameful Perversion
    4. 1:28-32   The Depraved Mind
C. The Divine Judgment (2:1–3:20)
    1. 2:1-5   The Condemnation of Sin
    2. 2:6-11   The Coming Judgment of God
    3. 2:12-16   The Inner Law of the Gentiles
    4. 2:17-24   The Written Law of the Jews
    5. 2:25-29   The Meaning of Circumcision
    6. 3:1-8   The Objections of the Jews
    7. 3:9-20   The Accountability of Everyone

II. RIGHTEOUSNESS REVEALED: THE ACT OF FAITH (3:21–4:25)
A. Faith: The Condition for Justification (3:21-31)
    1. 3:21-26   Righteousness Comes From God
    2. 3:27-31   Justification Comes Through Faith
B. Abraham: The Father of the Faithful (4:1-25)
    1. 4:1-8   Faith Rather Than Works
    2. 4:9-15   Faith Rather Than Circumcision
    3. 4:16-25   Faith Rather Than Unbelief

III. RIGHTEOUSNESS RESTORED: THE GIFT OF GRACE (5:1–7:25)
A. The Blessing: Reconciliation With God (5:1-21)
    1. 5:1-5   A New Perspective
    2. 5:6-11   A New Relationship
    3. 5:12-21   A New Identity
B. The Result: New Life in Christ (6:1-23)
    1. 6:1-13   Dead to Sin
    2. 6:14-23   Slaves to Righteousness
C. The Antagonists: Sin and the Law (7:1-25)
    1. 7:1-6   Sin Brings Bondage to the Law
    2. 7:7-13   The Law Brings Awareness of Sin
    3. 7:14-25   Sin and Law Bring Inner Conflict

Part One

RIGHTEOUSNESS REJECTED:
The Nature of Sin

Romans 1:1–3:20

P aul opens his letter to the believers at Rome with his usual pattern of salutation, but wastes no time with social amenities (one of my friends calls it "porch talk"). He moves directly to his primary purpose of clarifying how the gospel is "good news" for all. The gospel not only reveals the righteousness of God, which previously was revealed to humanity by other means, but also provides the way for making this righteousness a reality in one's life through the response of **faith from first to last** (1:17).

Righteousness, for Paul, is a given in the equation of salvation. He does not offer a lengthy definition of what the righteousness of God means, nor does he explain how the content of that moral standard is embedded in the minds and hearts of human beings. He is, however, deeply concerned with establishing that although the *knowledge* of righteousness is available to all persons, the *attainment* of such righteousness by any human means is an impossibility. To experience the righteousness of God, one first must come to grips with the unrighteousness (sin) that pervades one's human existence.

The insidious character of sin affects humanity in two dimensions. First, the personal dimension of unrighteousness worms its way down into the deepest recesses of the human soul. In chapter 1, Paul traces this downward spiral of ungodliness from its first subtle influences upon our spiritual lives to its fullest expression in the thoughts and sordid behavior of degenerate unbelievers. One cannot help but be sobered by the far-ranging effects of unrighteousness upon the human soul as they are described in this opening chapter.

But, the second dimension of unrighteousness is equally important to Paul's understanding of the gospel. Not only does sin spread downward into all areas of the human soul, but it also spreads outward to embrace every descendant of Adam. Unrighteousness is not merely the problem of a few moral outcasts (the wicked); it is also a serious problem for those who judge themselves to be righteous by any standard other than faith in the righteousness that comes from God. Paul devotes the remainder of this first section to a sharp criticism of the erroneous thinking of his own people, the Jews, who had come to consider themselves righteous for all the wrong reasons. He shatters their assumption that being the recipients and protectors of the divine law qualifies the Jews as righteous in the eyes of God.

In this opening section, Paul moves toward a familiar, yet disturbing conclusion: **all have sinned and fall short of the glory of God** (3:23). Neither Paul's specific indictment against the righteousness of the law, nor the objections to which he responds, addresses our status today (the post-Jewish era of the church). Nevertheless, we must listen closely to Paul's graphic description of the corrupting nature of unrighteousness— upon both a fallen society *and* those who claim a right standing with God based on human standards of morality and spirituality.

1

THE GOSPEL IN ROME

Romans 1:1-17

Paul addresses his letter to **all in Rome** (v. 7)—that is, to everyone associated with the body of believers residing in that city. The original Greek includes an extra word for emphasis that is omitted by most modern translations. The literal text reads "to all those *being* (Greek, *ousin*) in Rome." We hardly can imagine what it meant for these new believers to be in this place. Rome was the capital city of the Empire, the hub of Western civilization in Paul's day. If a person living in the first century, or even today, were to think of political power or cultural elegance, the eternal city where the Caesars ruled certainly would come to mind. The Roman Empire was the standard by which everything else was judged. Historians describe this particular era in history using the words *Pax Romana,* "the peace of Rome." Military legions of the Caesars established a political stability that extended from the ocean shores of Spain to the foothills of the Himalayan mountains in India. Although many conquered nations resented the ever-present soldiers and the high taxes they imposed, who could deny that Rome was the power to be reckoned with in every aspect of life.

Yet here in this most strategic place, at this pivotal moment in history, a small cell of followers were *being* in Rome. Paul is rightfully concerned that the corrupting influences of Rome might have a detrimental impact upon these believers. For that reason, he expresses his eagerness to come and **make [them] strong** (v. 11). But Paul is equally confident that the presence of these Christians in Rome can have a powerful impact for good upon the Empire (and history records that they did!). So he boldly asserts, **I am not ashamed of the gospel,** and then proceeds to lay out clearly what that gospel is and how it brings about **the salvation of everyone who believes: first for the Jew, then for the Gentile** (v. 16), including the Romans!

1. PAUL'S TITLE 1:1

The opening salutation of this letter follows the pattern of Paul's other letters, indicating who the author is, the recipients of the letter, and an opening word of blessing. In this letter, Paul uses his Greek name and two distinct designations to identify his role in the Kingdom—**a servant of Christ Jesus, called to be an apostle.** The first title speaks of Paul's lowly status and submission to the Master; the second describes his authority and role of leadership in the church.

All believers must be servants of Jesus Christ, first and foremost. Paul even goes beyond the frequently used "servant" *(deaconos)* to use the word for "slave" *(doulos)*. With only one exception (2 Timothy 2:24), Paul uses only this word to describe persons who are actually owned by human masters, or to describe *himself,* bound in a similar relationship to his Lord.

This word and the relationship it describes are unsettling to our modern patterns of thought. We place high value on our personal freedom and our inalienable human right to liberty. We are tempted, therefore, to explain the use of this word as a cultural limitation of Paul, who lived in a time and society where almost one-third of the inhabitants of the Empire were slaves. But any contemporary substitute that we might suggest reduces the deep sense of ownership and obligation implied in the word *slave*. Paul does not hesitate to describe himself as having been purchased and, therefore, owned by Christ (1 Corinthians 6:20). And, while the Master is good to His slaves—even identifying himself as both a Master and a friend (John 15:15)—He nonetheless demands our full obedience and loyalty. If the Lord of life, who shares equality with God, was willing to empty himself and take on the form of a servant (Philippians 2:6-7, using the same word Paul uses here!), how could we, as Christ's followers, do anything less?

But, lest this humility in the presence of Paul's Master be misconstrued by his hearers and critics, Paul immediately asserts his right to speak with authority to the Roman Christians by reminding them of his call to be an apostle. During his ministry, Paul repeatedly had to counter challenges to his leadership in the church. There were those who questioned his authority because of his earlier sins of persecuting the church. Some claimed that by these actions, Paul had forfeited his right to assume a position of leadership. Others challenged him because of his unconventional approach to evangelism, in which he bypassed the rituals and traditions of Judaism to preach the good news of salvation by faith directly to Gentiles. Still others wanted to reserve the highest authority for those apostles who were a part of the Twelve and had been called by Jesus during His ministry in Galilee. Paul addresses all of these objections in his letters, but here he does not spend time justifying his apostleship; he simply declares that he, too, was called and that, like the disciples, he has been given a specific mission on behalf of the One who called him.

So Paul positions himself between two equally destructive threats to effective ministry. There is the danger of pride and arrogant flaunting of power in the name of being the messenger of God. In order to resist such a temptation—whether a pastor, board member, teacher, or gifted parishioner—we must always remember that we are slaves of Christ, purchased at great cost for His purposes, and not for our own dreams of superiority. But, there is also the danger of doing little or nothing for the Kingdom, which we justify with an appeal of humility. Resisting the temptation to let others take the initiative requires us to remember that we are children of the King and are called to be His message bearers to the world. We are slaves, called to be apostles.

2. PAUL'S GREETING 1:2-7

Paul does not claim the title of apostle in order to gain status or power in the early church. His commission and authority center on the *message* of the church (the gospel) rather than the *structure* of the church. In later centuries, the very church in Rome to which Paul is now writing will use the concept of apostleship to justify a hierarchy of leadership, to the neglect of Paul's proclamation that "'the righteous will live by faith'" (1:17).

In this opening paragraph of his letter, Paul gives a clear summary statement of the gospel he proclaims. First, it is rooted in the history of God's chosen people, the Jews. It is not just another "mystery religion" among the many spiritual movements that were springing up in Paul's day. This gospel had been promised centuries ago by God's messengers, the prophets. Second, the gospel is revealed in a person, Jesus Christ. Paul clearly spells out one of the core beliefs of Christian faith: that Jesus of Nazareth was truly human, **a descendant of David** (v. 3), and truly divine, **the Son of God** by means of the Spirit (v. 4). Paul does not give detailed explanations of this profound idea of the God/man here nor elsewhere in his writings. Along with the early church, he simply accepted the truth of the Incarnation (God in the flesh) as essential to the divine plan of salvation.

In this flash picture of Jesus, Paul highlights only two aspects: Jesus' birth and His resurrection from the dead. The birth of Jesus (which is implied by referring to Jesus as **a descendant of David**) brings to mind all we know of the significance of Christmas. These few words call up recollections of the virgin birth, the humble shepherds, and the eternal Word in diapers. Jesus is never quite so human as he appears in Bethlehem's manger.

But then the second picture: The rising Son on Easter morning, appearing as the conqueror of death and Satan, the breakthrough runner of all those who would follow him in the race! Here is the essential moment of His divinity. No mention of the cross, which Paul will speak of later as the key to salvation. We will have to wait until later in this letter to see how Paul unfolds his understanding of grace through the death of Christ. For now, we only see the bookends of the Master's life: a natural birth and a supernatural resurrection.

After pointing out the gospel's roots in the prophets, and its manifestation in Christ, Paul finally takes us in verses 6 and 7 to the third feature of the gospel: It is demonstrated in the transformation of human lives. Sorting out the intricacies of messianic prophecies and explaining the mystery of the Incarnation do not finally make the gospel "the power of God for the salvation of everyone who believes" (1:16). Only when a person receives grace, and then alters the priorities of life to match God's agenda, does the good news become a reality. For Paul, the call of God on one's life includes the grace and power to obey the "follow me" of the Master.

By this call and response, the gospel spreads. Paul heard the call, and in obedience became the messenger of the good news to the Gentiles, including the believers in Rome. Having responded to the message, they are now embraced by grace and also belong to Christ (v. 6). Now a call comes to these Romans as well. They, too, are **called to be saints** (v. 7). When individuals are loved by God—and that includes everyone—He calls them to himself and then, **for his name's sake** (v. 5), calls these converts to a life of faith that leads to obedience, and the final outcome of holiness. (**Saints** in the Greek *[hagiois]* literally means "holy ones.") And how is this accomplished? Through the grace (chap. 4), peace (chap.

5), and new life (chap. 6) of the God who is our Father, and the Son who is our Lord.

3. PAUL'S GOSPEL 1:8-17

Having offered a preamble to the letter, Paul now turns to the specifics of his communication to the Romans. But even here his writing style sets the agenda. In these opening verses, as in almost all of Paul's letters, he begins with a reference to his prayers of thanksgiving for his readers (see also 1 Corinthians 1:4-9, Ephesians 1:15-19a, Philippians 1:3-11, and Colossians 1:3-12). Paul makes special reference in this letter to the faith of the Romans and the worldwide reputation they have attained (v. 8). Again, Paul is drawn to the strategic nature of the capital city and this congregation that exists in the shadow of Caesar's palace and the Roman Senate. His fascination with this place is expressed in his desire to visit this church in person (v. 10).

Paul's purpose in visiting them is twofold (vv. 11-13): to **impart to [them] some spiritual gift;** and to minister in such a way that they **may be mutually encouraged**—something that occurs when believers come together for work and worship. Paul also envisions a twofold result of such a ministry. One anticipated outcome is **to make [the church] strong** (v. 11; literally, "to establish you"). The other is to produce **a harvest** (v. 13)—visible evidence of God's work among the people.

What a powerful statement about ministry in the body of Christ! Paul desires to visit Rome, not to see the grandeur of the city, nor even to make a cameo appearance in the church. His purpose is to be a channel of spiritual gifts—gifts designed to strengthen the body and produce Kingdom results, rather than to impress or entertain the saints. And the fringe benefit of such a ministry style is that Paul himself will be encouraged and strengthened in the work to which He has been called by God.

Paul returns to his passion for ministry as he closes his introduction (vv. 14-17). The bondservant of Christ is under obligation not only to his Master, but also to other believers whom he serves as well. Paul writes to (and eventually visits) Rome because He senses that God is directing him to the task of sharing the gospel to every possible audience. Having shared the gospel in various ethnic, religious and intellectual contexts across the regions that comprise modern-day Greece and Turkey, Paul is now eager to take on the ultimate challenge of proclaiming his message to Rome without embarrassment or apology.

The response to Paul's preaching throughout Asia and Europe had been mixed. In places, he had encountered vehement opposition. Paul bore on his body "the marks of Jesus" (Galatians 6:17). What reception would He receive in the capital city of the Empire? What would Christianity mean to Caesar? What would being a follower of Jesus mean to the movers and shakers of the Senate and Forum? What would a Jewish scribe-turned-evangelist have to proclaim, in comparison to the edicts that issued from the imperial city?

Certainly Paul knew the context in which he was living and preaching. In another letter (see 1 Corinthians 1:20-25), he would acknowledge that to the philosophically inclined Greeks, the gospel appeared to be foolishness. Even the Jews, who had waited expectantly for the Messiah to appear, took Paul's message of a Suffering Savior who reconciled humanity to God through the *cross* as a scandalous offense. If the Jews and the Greeks took such little notice, how could the Romans ever switch their allegiance from the Caesars, who were promoted to divine status by the Senate, to a carpenter-turned-rabbi who was condemned to crucifixion by a no-name governor named Pilate? How could they switch from proclaiming, "Caesar is Lord," to declaring, at the risk of their lives, that "Jesus Christ is Lord"?

Yet Paul boldly asserts, **I am not ashamed of the gospel** (v. 16). Certainly this statement is more than an appeal to his ethnic or religious heritage. Paul does not say, "I am proud to be Jewish," nor even, "I am a follower of Christ." To the believers in Rome, and through them to all the citizens of that empire and all empires to come, Paul declares he is not ashamed of what—or, more correctly, *whom*—he believes (see also 2 Timothy 1:12). He is convinced that this gospel can hold its own against all challengers.

First, Paul is not ashamed even when skeptics reject the gospel. There have always been scoffers who point out what they see as logical absurdities, scientific fallacies, and practical difficulties of the Christian faith. Paul's ability to anticipate and answer all of the objections raised against the gospel demonstrates his awareness of these potential problems of the story and teachings of Jesus of Nazareth. Without burying his thinking cap in the sand or appealing to blind faith, Paul stands his ground and claims that the gospel is **the power of God** himself (v. 16). In the face of skeptics, Paul's response is, "I am not ashamed."

Nor is Paul ashamed of this gospel even when so-called followers of Christ discredit it. From the very beginning, some individuals have claimed allegiance to this gospel, but their actions have brought embarrassment to the church. In Samaria, Simon sought to purchase the gift of the Spirit as a marketable commodity (Acts 8:9-24). In Corinth, a man lived in flagrant immorality with a close relative and appealed to Christian "truths" as a warrant for his infidelity (1 Cor. 5). Paul encountered those who would distort his ideas to their own desires; others would take advantage of the generosity of the community of faith, rather than doing their part in the work of the Kingdom (2 Thessalonians 3:10). By the end of his ministry, Paul could have drawn up quite a list of those who had brought shame upon the cause of Christ. Like the comic-strip character Pogo, Paul might have been tempted to say, "We have met the enemy . . . and they is us!"

Despite these "horror stories" of the faith, Paul can tell the Romans, **I am not ashamed.** For all the flawed individuals associated with the church, Paul believes that persons can, and actually do, become new creatures in Christ. The gospel is not just power; **it is the power of *God* for the salvation of everyone who believes** (v. 16, italics mine). Having seen jail keepers, idol makers, fornicators and hypocrites all set free from their sins, Paul has no reason to be embarrassed about the gospel he is proclaiming to Rome.

Finally, Paul is not ashamed of the gospel even when the powers of darkness test it. Paul would not hesitate to describe the conflict in which he was engaged in terms greater than politics and "culture wars" with Rome. There were "powers of this dark world" and "spiritual forces of evil" behind the flesh-and-blood encounters of this life (Eph. 6:12). Paul would find ample opportunity in his own life to question precisely what God was doing in countering the dark forces of the Evil One. Despite hardships, opposition and discouragement, Paul is not ashamed because the gospel **is the power of God for the salvation of everyone *who believes*** (italics mine). Ultimately, one's faith relationship with God defines the Christian life. Although there are strategies for countering the criticisms of the skeptics, or compensating for the failures of less-than-perfect believers, or coping with spiritual adversaries, faith is the key to experiencing the good news of salvation in one's life. Paul's overwhelming confidence in God's power to save motivates him to share the gospel everywhere, particularly in Rome.

What is that gospel message? For the next eight chapters, Paul lays out the core of his beliefs about sin and salvation. The gospel is the good news that **a righteousness from God is revealed** (v. 17). As we shall see, Paul connects a right relationship with God to moral accountability. It is the divine standard of what is right and wrong that defines the operation of God's work of salvation. Not that God is bound to some law higher than himself, but rather His own character of justice and holiness sets the standard by which all other moral agents—be they angels, humans, or whatever—relate to Him.

For Paul, the critical question then is, "How can a less-than-righteous person ever enter into a relationship with a perfectly holy God?" And that question is as pertinent to us today as it was to the Romans two thousand years ago. And the answer, spelled out in this letter, is both simple and complex: First to last, **The righteous will live by faith** (v.17). The ongoing experience of righteousness, attained by a daily walk of faith, is the theme of this letter to the Romans.

2

THE PATH
TO DEPRAVITY

Romans 1:18-32

At no place in his introductory remarks does Paul hint of what he intends to do in this letter, which is to lay out the case for salvation by faith in a logical argument. Although it is his pattern to begin most letters with doctrinal themes, and then proceed to the matters related to practical living, Paul outdoes himself in this letter by spelling out both the need for salvation and the plan of grace that makes this salvation accessible to his own people, the Jews, and to all other persons who receive it by faith. But to lay the foundation for the universality of God's grace (for "everyone who believes" [v. 16]), Paul must establish the universality of unrighteousness ("for all have sinned" [3:23]).

Paul begins with the obvious expressions of unrighteousness—the immoral conduct of those who know what is right, but choose instead to do what is wrong. The approach he uses is both subtle and profound. He avoids listing all the horror stories of Roman culture—the gladiatorial games, the blatant obscenities of the royal family, the crudities of the lower classes in Rome. Instead, he traces for his readers the pilgrimage of spiritual disintegration.

He opens this section with God's disclosure of His moral standard for the human race, and ends the chapter describing the moral cesspool of those who **deserve death** (1:32) for the deeds they practice and approve. His focus throughout is the deliberate actions of persons who have **exchanged the truth of God for a lie** (v. 25). According to Paul, there should be no question that these sinners stand accountable and condemned for their rejection of righteousness. In subsequent verses, he will move to the more problematic dimensions of sin—self-righteousness and the sinful nature.

1. THE CLEAR REVELATION 1:18-20

From the high pinnacle of the gospel, which reveals the righteousness of God, Paul plunges us immediately into the depths of wickedness where godless persons **suppress the truth by their wickedness** (v. 18). Paul offers no convenient "out" for this type of conduct. He will not let the ungodly appeal to ignorance as a justification for their actions. God has revealed truth about himself in the infrastructure of His creation, and **what may be known about God is plain to them** (v. 19).

Here we enter into one of the classic discussions of Christian theologians through the centuries: What is the *content* of this knowledge of God, and how, if at all, can one use this truth to come into a right relationship with God?

We might start with the most obvious truth that comes to us through creation—a supernatural being (the Creator) exists. Contemporary secularists would reject this assumption as a starting point, claiming that we know nothing of the first causes of our present universe. They take us back to a "big bang," but, beyond that, shrug their shoulders in puzzlement. "No reason to introduce God," they claim, "even to explain the origins of the primordial matter and energy that brought our world into being."

But the biblical and innate human assumption is that this universe did not just happen into existence. Reality, as we perceive it, is the result of the thought and purposeful action of a divine Creator.

But, the awareness that "Somebody bigger than you and me" exists is not very helpful when it comes to developing a personal relationship with God. And standing on the rim of the Grand Canyon does not help one to know how to live a moral and holy life. Paul certainly would affirm that a basic awareness of the existence and creative energy of a divine being exists almost universally in the human race. In fact, Paul speaks specifically of humanity's ability to see **God's invisible qualities—his eternal power and divine nature** (v. 20).

But the case Paul is building here is not a case for God's existence. Paul argues that humans are *morally* accountable and that God's anger against their unrighteousness is justified, because violators of His righteous standard should have known better.

Paul argues for a moral as well as a philosophical knowledge of God. He will explain this further in his discussion of the human conscience in chapter 2. For now, he simply declares that no person can claim ignorance of right or wrong as justification for ungodly behavior.

In C. S. Lewis's most popular writing, *Mere Christianity,* he explains that although the specifics of this moral revelation appear to differ in various cultures, there seems to be a "moral sense" which is universal to all human beings. Without any sophisticated training in ethical theory, individuals—whether in primitive cultures or in the early stages of childhood development—still seem to know when an injustice is being imposed upon them, and will voice their objection with the protest, "That's wrong!"

Those persons who stand under God's wrath might use another defense to excuse their immoral conduct. They might argue that the forces of evil are so pervasive and powerful that they are unable to prevent themselves from sinning. In all of Paul's writings, he never addresses the ancient question of the origins of evil. But, it is clear that he rejects the prevailing view of dualism, proposed by almost all the religions (except Judaism) that competed for converts in his day.

The Jewish understanding of reality, drawn largely from the Genesis account of Creation, begins with a "monism"—a belief in one supreme being who is all-powerful and good. The created order is a product of that goodness and power. God's repeated assessment in Genesis of what He had made, including His capstone creation of the human race, was that "it was good" (Genesis 1:10, 12, 18, 21, 25; cf. v. 31).

Evil entered the creation, not as some competing deity or force of "non-good," but as a distortion or flaw from *within* the system. In the Garden of Eden, evil manifested itself as a serpent, one of "the wild animals *the LORD God had made*" (Gen. 3:1, italics mine). As difficult as it becomes to account for how this flaw appeared in God's good creation, the biblical account will not allow for some divine power to exist apart from God's sovereign power and authority.

Dualism, on the other hand, explains sin in terms of two eternal and opposing forces. Sometimes dualism gave these supernatural powers the names of mythological gods. At other times they described them in terms of light and darkness. At the root of this pagan theology was the assumption that good and evil are locked in a never-ending conflict, and that one can attribute good and bad acts or events in our world to the ups and downs of this struggle. A more contemporary expression of this mind-set would be the passing off of immoral behavior by the flippant comment, "The devil made me do it."

It is remarkable that in this passage, which deals with the moral depravity of human hearts, Paul makes no mention of Satan or any other evil agent. He focuses instead on the thoughts and resulting actions of *humans*—persons like you and me—who are deceived by whatever means, and then stray from the truth. Furthermore, when we stray, we are not so likely to chase after the demonic and the occultic as we are to be tempted to worship the things of God's good creation, rather than God himself.

This understanding of sin as the consequence of a wayward will, rather than forces of fate, was one of the great contributions of Augustine, one of the church fathers who lived in the fourth century. But the idea of a willful decision to reject truth—and, consequently, human accountability for sin—is already present in Paul's description of the unrighteous.

While there is a dark side of reality to be reckoned with, we probably become fascinated and overwrought by the small minority who dabble in the demonic, while remaining oblivious to the hundreds of ways we substitute the creation for the Creator in our own value systems and worship. Without denying or minimizing the reality of the Evil One, from whom we need to be delivered daily (Matthew 6:13), we will discover in this opening argument of Paul's case for grace that there is plenty enough depravity in the human mind to explain the fallen nature of our world, and to justify God's righteous wrath against all those who participate in this distortion.

2. THE FOOLISH EXCHANGE 1:21-23

Having established that persons should know better than to sin, Paul now describes the downward path the human race has taken in its departure from the righteousness of God. As we have noted, nothing is said of the negative influence of the dark forces of evil in this rejection of holiness. But Paul does suggest an interplay between human and divine activity in this process. In the next few verses, he alternates between the actions of humans ("They did not . . . retain the knowledge of God" [v. 28]) and the puzzling description of God's role ("God gave them over" [vv. 24, 26]).

The starting point of this path to ungodliness begins with an action by humans, not God. Paul's description of sin here in chapter 1 echoes the same themes we find in James 1:13-15: "When tempted, no one should say, 'God is tempting me.' For God cannot be tempted by evil, nor does he tempt anyone; but each one is tempted when, by his own evil desire, he is dragged away and enticed. Then, after desire has conceived, it gives birth to sin; and sin, when it is full-grown, gives birth to death."

Like James, Paul contends that human beings are the ones who ignore—even reject—the innate knowledge of God and His moral expectations. The first step is not some dastardly deed; it is simply one of disregard—**they neither glorified him as God nor gave thanks to him** (Rom. 1:21). Here we see the sobering consequences of placing spiritual matters on the back burners of our lives. Individuals who lose their God-awareness, who no longer attribute the gift of life and the blessings of daily living to the generous bounty of God, will soon find themselves easy prey for much more serious spiritual problems.

The immediate consequence of this neglect of God is not flagrant immorality; it is the subtle altering of one's mind-set and heart-set. With a mind that is no longer being renewed (12:2), the foolish preferences of the heart begin to dominate one's moral sense. It is not that these individuals park their brains altogether; something far more unsettling happens. They use their thinking capacities to justify what they really want to do.

In contrast, Christians are "alert and self-controlled" individuals (1 Thessalonians 5:6) whose desires and actions are controlled by the indwelling mind of Christ (Philippians 2:5). They do not rationalize their less-than-moral conduct by logical arguments of whatever sort. Nor do they drift obliviously into a disregard for Kingdom affairs.

The product of such spiritual neglect is a "wise" fool. A comedian who flaunts his foolishness on purpose and is recognized as a buffoon may be quite harmless. But persons who act irrationally, yet present themselves as scholarly about what they do, are extremely dangerous. The cult leader who draws believers into error by using big words and quoting Scripture is a much greater threat to the church than the person who openly ridicules the gospel in the name of entertainment. So it is with the persons Paul describes in this passage. In the name of *religion,* these individuals transfer their loyalties from the immortal God to lesser images (Greek, *icons*).

In ancient times and in more primitive cultures, this exchange of deities often resulted in idolatry, the actual fashioning of artistic representations of animals (like the golden calf of Exodus 32) or humans (like the goddess Diana/Artemis of Acts 19). But we certainly can find those today who claim to find spiritual "highs" in lesser realities—be it a love of nature, the use of hallucinogenic drugs, obsession with body physique, or, as Paul will point out shortly, a preoccupation with the erotic dimension of human existence.

The heart of the problem is that most humans do not begin their journey away from God by rejecting religion altogether. The process is much more subtle. Instead, while retaining the innate sense of worship placed in their hearts by the Creator (Ecclesiastes 3:11), they have **exchanged the glory of the immortal God** (Rom. 1:23) for lesser objects of devotion.

Note that in Paul's description of the destructive process of unrighteousness in the ungodly, sin is a condition of the heart *before* it becomes an overt action of the body. Sin begins with an internal deception that causes individuals to reject truth and choose a lie instead. In all the attention and media hype we give to the evil behavior exhibited in our society, Paul's attention to the internal dynamics of sin must never be forgotten.

Jesus observed that the outward conversation of the Pharisees was nothing more than "the overflow of the heart." He explained the comment with these words: "The good man brings good things out of the good stored up in him, and the evil man brings evil things out of *the evil stored up in him"* (Matthew 12:35, italics mine). The path to ungodliness begins in the dark recesses of the soul.

3. THE SHAMEFUL PERVERSION 1:24-27

Although this disregard of God has its beginning in human hearts, God is not oblivious or indifferent to this turning away. At three strategic points in this path to degeneracy, Paul indicates a divine response to human unrighteousness. **Therefore God gave them over in the sinful desires of their hearts** (v. 24). Underlying these words is one of the classic disagreements between Christians who take the Scripture and doctrine seriously. Who ultimately determines the salvation or destruction of a human being—the individual or God? Whichever position one selects, there are difficult questions to be resolved.

Many Christians align themselves with the tradition of John Calvin, who developed his theology at the time of the Protestant Reformation, from the earlier writings of Augustine. This group of believers emphasizes the great truth rediscovered by Martin Luther in his studies of Paul's Epistle to the Romans: that salvation comes only by the grace of God revealed in His Son, Jesus Christ.

Developing their ideas from this starting affirmation, Calvinists deny that individuals can choose to save themselves. Proposing even the tiniest toehold of human endeavor to begin the move back to God is an offense to the Cross and the incredible grace that calls, draws, and forgives the sinner. God does not need any help, thank you, from human beings, who in their hearts are inclined to boast, "I did it my way," when that salvation becomes a reality.

But, if one's salvation depends *totally* upon God, how can we explain the reality of hell and the possibility that a considerable number of human beings will find their destiny in condemnation and eternal punishment? One would expect God to either damn us all to hell for our sinful ways, or, in His great mercy, redeem us all. Staunch Calvinists propose that God, in His sovereign and incomprehensible wisdom, has predetermined those who will be saved as a demonstration of His grace and mercy. These believers must then conclude that the damnation of those who were not predestined for salvation is a demonstration of His justice and holy wrath against all sin.

In this view, free will does not exist, and human action has nothing to do with deciding who is redeemed and who is damned. As difficult a concept as this is to swallow, Calvinists would argue that it affirms the sovereignty of God and protects the great biblical truth that salvation is a total act of God's grace.

Most Calvinists move away from this strong position and point out that God does not *send* people to hell; all persons are under God's wrath and "without excuse" (1:20) because of their sinful condition. As sinners, *all humans deserve to be condemned* (3:23), but God in His mercy reaches out and rescues some (the "elect" or "called ones") by His grace. Again, we cannot probe the mind of God to know whom He chooses or why, but by His grace we are saved.

This view avoids the distasteful idea of a loving God decreeing that some persons go to hell for His glory, but it still raises the question of why God would not choose to rescue all of His creation, rather than just a part. If a person dashes into a burning building to rescue those inside and is able to bring out only a few, we praise his heroism and do not hold him accountable for those who might not be rescued. If that same person has the opportunity to bring everyone out alive, but stops after rescuing one person, we are likely to be very angry. And so the tough issue for all those who say that salvation is *only* by God's grace, apart from any human response, is "How can you account for those who are lost without reducing God's power and love?"

The alternative is to grant the individual *some* role in determining his or her ultimate destiny. (To suggest that humans are *totally* responsible for saving themselves, and are capable of doing so, is not a Christian option.) In this view, first proposed by the sixteenth-century Dutch theologian, Jacob Arminius, and later popularized by John Wesley's Methodists, the sinner cannot come into a relationship with God without the work of the Spirit and the saving work of the Cross; but neither can that person find eternal life without making specific responses to God's call. At the very least, a person must exercise faith in God.

Most Wesleyans consider obedience to God's commandments to be a natural corollary to placing one's trust in God. The familiar gospel song "Trust and Obey" describes quite well the basic assumption of this view.

This assigning of some responsibility to the individual certainly reduces the questions about why there is a hell and who will end up there. From the Wesleyan-Arminian view, persons who do disobey God's laws and do not accept His gracious offer of heaven have every reason to be condemned to hell. God does not predestine persons to damnation. Nor does He allow them to remain in their lost state without reaching out to them. Instead, God is the righteous Judge who reveals His moral code and then holds His creation accountable to that standard.

The problem with the Wesleyan perspective is not so much in accounting for those who are eternally lost as it is accounting for those who are delivered from sin. For now the possibility that human beings can, to some degree, save themselves is introduced into the formula. If a person obeys God's commandments, then it would appear that those good works are the deciding factor. And even if the human response is nothing more than reaching out to God and receiving the salvation He offers in Christ, there is still the suggestion that the believer, and not God, plays the pivotal role in obtaining eternal life.

For centuries, Christians have walked a theological tightrope, endeavoring to counter-balance human freedom and responsibility with divine sovereignty and grace. This tension will surface throughout Paul's letter to the Romans.

Even here in this first chapter we can see how it influences our understanding of Paul's view of sin. Paul has asserted that godless and unrighteous individuals are accountable ("without excuse") for their behavior because God has revealed His moral character in creation. If these wicked persons had been predestined to destruction, they would have the ultimate "excuse" for their behavior—God made them do it! Although Paul does not specifically state that they could have acted otherwise, he builds a strong case for God's wrath and judgment upon those who reject His ways. From a Wesleyan perspective, such condemnation can result only from some deliberate choice and act on the part of the sinner.

Now we can address the phrase, **God gave them over** (v. 24). Calvinists would view this as a direct action of God, which increases both the sin and the divine condemnation. Having determined (or at least having foreknown) that these wise fools have turned from Him, God intensifies their falling away by directing them to more and more degrading practices. He turns these people toward wickedness because He sees ahead to their ultimate destiny and, in effect, sets up the "end game" of their lives in such a way that condemnation is a logical consequence.

Wesleyans, on the other hand, understand this phrase as God *allowing* human freedom to run its course in these wicked persons. The "giving over" is a reluctant letting go of the rebelling sinner by a Heavenly Father. While He is "not wanting anyone to perish" (2 Peter 3:9), He nevertheless does not *force* individuals to be righteous. Neither does He always interfere to restrain their "bent to sinning," when their inner desires are to reject the truth and turn to evil.

Given over by God, these persons continue in their path of degradation. Having begun with spiritual neglect and then moved to false worship of lesser gods, these unrighteous persons now become focused upon their own desires and passions. The religious aspects of their behavior are being replaced by **sexual impurity** (v. 24)—the self-gratification of physical desires. There is no suggestion here that these sexual relationships are the wholesome expressions of the marriage bond established by God in the Garden; instead, Paul speaks of **the degrading of [the] bodies** (v. 24) of those who engage in such practices. The digression from worshipping the things of creation to sexual perversion would appear to be a major shift to our twentieth century way of thinking. We must remember, however, that in Paul's day, many of the pagan religions were "fertility cults"—the abundance of food and the growth of crops was associated with the reproductive activities of the gods and goddesses. Furthermore, it was not uncommon for worship practices at the pagan temples to include ritual acts with temple "virgins," who were little more than prostitutes—male and female—offering their services in the name of religious passion. From Paul's Jewish background, any association of sexual activity with worship of God would be as counterfeit as a three-dollar bill.

Truth has been exchanged for a lie, and for these individuals the divine extends no further than their own passions. Having chosen to worship the "deity" of themselves, they distort and degrade human nature by excess and perversion in order to create a sense of ecstasy and the spectacular in what they do.

One of the further consequences of this pornographic pursuit is the shift from using sexual relationships for the purposes designed in creation—the bonding of a woman and a man in a relationship that provides a suitable context for child-raising—into one that focuses upon unnatural relationships between same-sex partners (vv. 26-27).

We have heard much in recent years concerning this passage in chapter 1. Our contemporary society is clearly re-orienting its thinking about sexual codes and personal relationships in a direction that condones and, in some cases, advocates homosexual relationships as an acceptable social practice.

There are several detailed studies of the biblical view toward homosexuality. Some scholars suggest that Paul only condemns the pagan practice of incorporating homosexual prostitution in sacred rituals. Others suggest that Paul is referring to the "degrading" practices of overt promiscuity between lesbians and gays. At best, these scholars can only suggest that Paul is silent about "meaningful" same-sex relationships. There is no place in his writings (nor in all Scripture) where one can find approval for homosexual acts.

On the contrary, Paul appears to give a clear-cut condemnation of homosexual practices. These words appear in a passage that describes the degrading effects of sin upon human nature. Paul condemns the practice, not because it is a pagan ritual, but because those who practice it have **exchanged natural relations for unnatural ones** (v. 26). The descriptions of these activities clearly mark them as sin: **shameful lusts, inflamed with lust, indecent acts, perversion** (vv. 26-27). Paul expresses the long-standing view of both Jews and Christians that homosexual acts are contrary to the order of creation and are, therefore, subject to the wrath of God.

But we must not allow Paul's comments here to lead us into full-blown homophobia. If Paul is describing a progression of sin in this passage, we must conclude that there is even worse behavior than the perversions of lesbians and gays. In his analysis of unrighteousness, Paul is giving one illustration of what happens when individuals turn to self-worship and self-gratification. He describes that exchange of truth for a lie in the area of human sexuality; he is not making statements about one class of persons who are more despicable than everyone else. One might imagine what illustration Paul might have used in describing persons who center their lives on greed . . . or power . . . or fame.

There is much in our society's exploitation of sex that is shameful and abhorrent. But moral depravity is far more widespread and devious than this one aspect of human personality. There are countless ways in which the ungodly repeatedly abandon what is God's intended plan for nature, and instead choose the unnatural.

4. THE DEPRAVED MIND 1:28-32

Finally, Paul brings us to the bottom of the moral cesspool. We see individuals who have not merely neglected God, nor even substituted created things for worship of the divine Creator. Here are those who no longer consider it worthwhile to hold on to the knowledge of God. A mutual withdrawal has taken place; these persons have given up on God and have "served created things rather than the Creator" (v. 25). God, for His part, has given them over to what they think they really want—the right to live a lie and control their own destiny.

The result of this rejection of God is **a depraved mind** (v. 28). Paul describes a moral wasteland where every quality that holds the fabric of society together is shredded. With the exception of the act of murder, Paul concentrates on *attitudes* that spill over into broken relationships and deep wounds to the victims of those who operate with such mind-sets. Who would ever want to be on the receiving end of encounters with persons like this?

Paul concludes this list of despicable qualities with a set of single words, which in the Greek all begin with the prefix *a-*, which signifies the negation of the word that follows (as in our English word *atheist*). The translators of the NIV capture the same idea by using the suffix *-less*. **They are senseless, faithless, heartless, ruthless** (v. 31). Sin, at its worst, is not what a person *is;* it is what he or she *is not*.

John Wesley described the consequences of Adam and Eve's original disobedience as "the loss of the image of God." Humanity was created in God's image, stamped in some remarkable way with the moral and spiritual imprint of God. When we decide to turn to our own way, we do not create another identity as a substitute for God's image in us. Rather, we lose our one true identity and become something less than real to ourselves, to others, and to God.

In one sense we might look at the unrighteous as "non-persons" in the eyes of God (vv. 25-26). With four descriptive words in verse 31, Paul indicates that the unrighteous eventually lose their moral bearings (**senseless**), their integrity (**faithless**), their capacity for love (**heartless**), and their ability to respond to those in need (**ruthless**). When an individual has lost these qualities, there is not much left of what we would consider to be human. Apart from a re-creating work of God, there is nothing here that would make a person qualified to be a citizen of the eternal kingdom; and who would ever want to live forever with such an individual!

But Paul points out that, even in this degraded sinful condition, at least one moral truth still penetrates the darkened mind of these unrighteous persons: they are the objects of divine wrath (v. 18), and **they know . . . that those who do such things deserve death** (v. 32). Having lost their moral compass, they still retain the awareness that they are lost and doomed.

In that moment of inner despair, do they turn to God? Do they share their concern and fear with others? No. In their misery, they look for companions to share in their shameful deeds and **approve of those who practice them** (v. 32). Like the story of the long-ago emperor, these wise fools try to convince each other that what they think and do is acceptable behavior. And in doing so they perpetuate the lie that ultimately leads to their exposure and destruction on the Day of Judgment.

Paul offers the Romans a most sobering opening to his treatise on the good news of God. But we can never grasp the meaning of grace or experience the power for salvation until we take a hard look in the mirror and see how corrupting sin can be. The pattern described here is not that unusual or atypical of human nature. Some of the primary truths from this passage that we can apply to our lives today have to do with avoiding a path of destruction in our relationship with God:

    a. Neglecting to acknowledge God and to show gratitude for His work in our lives

    b. Choosing to worship the good *things* of the creation instead of the One who created all things

    c. Turning from God to a preoccupation with our own desires and needs for self-gratification

    d. Exchanging conformity to God's plan for creation for the thrills of what is perverse and unnatural.

    e. Abandoning all sensitivity to God and others for a totally self-centered mind-set

    f. Justifying our own sinfulness by tolerating and approving those actions in others

The wrath of God is being revealed from heaven against all the godlessness and wickedness of men who suppress the truth by their wickedness (v. 18).

3

THE
DIVINE JUDGMENT

Romans 2:1–3:20

Paul's description of sin in chapter 1 is sobering indeed. He has already indicated that such wickedness will not go unnoticed or unpunished by God. His wrath is already being revealed against such godlessness (1:18) and He has decreed that "those who do such things deserve death" (1:32). Now Paul will spell out in detail the judgment that awaits those who do not measure up to God's high standard of righteousness and, more disturbing yet, he will demonstrate that everyone—both Jew and Gentile—falls into that category.

When caught in a situation where blame is assigned to a group, one of the natural tendencies of human nature is to find some defense that would warrant receiving special consideration or even exemption from the punishment that is to be administered. Students remind the teacher that they were not the ones who were talking. Tax dodgers point out to the Internal Revenue Service that they know others who do the same thing. Americans appeal to their United States citizenship when apprehended in a foreign country.

Paul is not ignorant of this tendency. He perceives at least three categories of special status in which his readers might want to place themselves, in order to exempt themselves from God's wrath and condemnation upon the unrighteous. The first defense one might offer is ignorance of the moral standard, the second involves comparing oneself with others and the final strategy is to appeal to special consideration.

First there are those who might argue that they never received any information on moral conduct. This would particularly apply to the Gentiles who never received the written law of God. But Paul will develop a case against them by pointing to the revelation of God in creation and to the law of conscience, written on their hearts. One cannot plead ignorance to escape the judgment of God.

Second, there are some who compare themselves with those around them and quickly point out that they are not nearly as bad as someone else. They justify their own behavior by judging the behavior of others.

Jesus told the story of a Pharisee whose Temple prayer was little more than a listing of all the things he did or did not do in contrast to a less respectable tax collector in the crowd. The Pharisee assumed that his relative goodness should count for *something* in the eyes of God. Jesus concluded the story by affirming that it was the tax collector, through an honest confession of his sinful condition, who "went home justified before God" (Luke 18:14), rather than the Pharisee who engaged in comparative piety.

A final strategy for escaping judgment is the assumption that a particular group of people holds a special status with God. This was the case of Paul's own race, the Jews. As God's chosen people, they thought they were exempt from the judgment that would fall upon all godless Gentiles. Jesus also had to deal with this thinking. He warned those who were "Abraham's children" that such biological relationships would profit them nothing on the Day of Judgment (John 8:39-44). Neither will the special rituals of circumcision or observing the ceremonial law help them secure a right standing with God.

Paul states it clearly and bluntly—**God does not show favoritism** (Rom. 2:11). In this passage, Paul argues for a universal accountability before God, based only upon one's response to the revelation of God's righteousness given to all. Everyone will have to give a personal account for his or her behavior. Diverting attention away from one's unrighteousness by pointing out the faults of others or by appealing to some special status (being American, Protestant, clergy, etc.) is an exercise in futility.

The ultimate question will be, "What did *you* do with the revelation of truth that *you* received?" And, at that point, apart from faith in the saving power of the Cross, all will be found guilty according to the moral standards of God.

1. THE CONDEMNATION OF SIN 2:1-5

The pronoun shift between the close of chapter 1 and the beginning of chapter 2 holds great significance. To this point, Paul has been describing the downward spiral of ungodliness in the third person—"they." Now he becomes much more direct and refers to a group of persons with the pronoun "you." To whom is he addressing these comments?

The believers in Rome might be one option. Paul already has spoken directly to them in his introductory remarks. But, after praising them for their faith (1:8), and expressing his great desire to be encouraged by them (1:12), Paul's words of rebuke would be inappropriate. Later, he will address the subject of judging one another as it relates to the church in Rome (Rom. 14). But the issue he deals with in that passage is Roman *believers* judging the conduct of *other believers,* not the judging of unbelievers in order to justify oneself, which is the focus of this passage.

Paul might be referring to the Jews who looked down upon the Gentiles for their failure to keep the commandments. As a Pharisee, Paul himself knew first-hand the temptation to arrogance and superiority that comes by maintaining a higher moral code than others. There is no specific reference to the Jews here, even though Paul is not reticent to rebuke them elsewhere in this letter.

We assume, then, that Paul is using the term "you" inclusively, directing his charge at all those persons—Christian, Jewish or pagan— who claim to be in harmonious relationship with God on the basis of comparing themselves favorably with others. John Wesley describes this attitude well when speaking of his spiritual state as a young university student before his conversion: "What I now hoped to be saved by, was, 1. Not being so bad as other people. 2. Having still a kindness for religion. And, 3. Reading the Bible, going to church, and saying my prayers."[1] And that description of being "saved" would characterize a host of religious persons in our churches today!

Paul's purpose in rebuking those who judge others is not to condemn their pride and superiority, but to point out the illegitimacy of anyone other than God presuming to determine who is righteous and who is not. Paul has stressed that ungodly and unrighteous persons are "without excuse" (1:20), and has given a rather sordid picture of what these persons are like.

One can imagine the response of some of Paul's audience after being presented with a description of such despicable behavior: "Well, I have never murdered anyone. I have never committed homosexual acts!" All of us at some point are tempted to elevate our spiritual status by looking with disgust on those who are "more depraved" than we are.

"Wait a minute!" Paul declares. **"You . . . have no excuse, you who pass judgment on someone else** (2:1). Anyone who claims to be more righteous than others also stands condemned by the absolute moral standard of God. And in some sense you are even more guilty. Guilty because you do not conform to God's standard for the very faults you condemn others; **you who pass judgment do the same things"** (v. 1).

Perhaps those of us who condemn others have not committed the more despicable acts mentioned in chapter 1. But which of us has *never* failed to give God glory and thanks? Which has not chased after spiritual reality by adoring lesser things? Which of us has not experienced episodes of mindless, faithless, loveless or insensitive behavior?

Once we presume to use some moral code to establish our righteousness before God, we must allow ourselves to be judged by the *whole* code . . . and none of us can claim perfection against the standard of God's holiness and purity. Having failed at *one* point, we stand guilty of failing the *entire* standard God has established (James 2:10).

These self-proclaimed judges stand condemned for another reason. They are guilty not only because they are offenders themselves, but because they also have assumed a divine prerogative in making assessments about who is guilty and innocent. They have made themselves both judge and jury of their own case, when that right belongs to God alone. One might look with pity upon those with depraved minds who seem to have lost all moral sense. But here Paul is addressing *moral* persons, who use their ability to discern right from wrong as measuring sticks to decide who is righteous and who is wicked. And you can guess where they will categorize themselves!

And so we see the irony of these self-righteous legalists. In protecting the moral code—even the standards of holiness established by God— they overlook the purpose of God's righteousness, which, according to Paul, is not His wrath and condemnation, but rather **the riches of his kindness, tolerance and patience** (2:4). They incorrectly assume that God is tough on sinners—at least on sinners who do things that these self-righteous persons don't. The self-righteous declare His wrath against ungodliness without any sense of their own need for repentance, or any attempt to proclaim the good news **that God's kindness leads [sinners] toward repentance** (v. 4).

How strange! These self-proclaimed guardians of righteousness are labeled by Paul as the ones who **show contempt for [God's] riches** (v. 4). The consequences of this attitude are sobering. Not only are they "without excuse" like the ungodly, but they are also **storing up wrath against [themselves]** (v. 5)—the same wrath that God has revealed against the wicked (1:18), who the self-righteous delight in condemning.

This warning applies to Christians today as much as it did to self-righteous Gentiles and Jews in Paul's day. We, too, can be tempted to substitute abhorrence of evil for a genuine repentance of our own spiritual failures and turning toward God for salvation. Someone has said, "Loving what is right is not the same as hating what is evil and feeling good about it." The prophet Micah reminds us that God's requirement is for us "to act justly and to love mercy and to walk humbly with [our] God" (Micah 6:8).

2. THE COMING JUDGMENT OF GOD 2:6-11

Having eliminated those seeking exemption from God's judgment by using their own moral yardsticks to determine who is righteous, Paul now makes his point directly: God judges each individual on the basis of his or her response to *His* standard. Paul begins this passage by quoting the Jewish Scriptures (cf. Psalm 62:12; Proverbs 24:12), and closes by restating the concept in his own words.

But in emphasizing the accountability of each person to God, Paul, the apostle of grace, appears to introduce a very un-Pauline idea, namely that a person's works have a direct bearing on his or her eternal destiny: **God "will give to each person *according to what he has done"*** (v. 6, italics mine). Paul speaks first of **those who by persistence in doing good** [Greek, "good works"] **seek** the treasures of heaven (**glory, honor and immortality**), and therefore are given **eternal life** (Rom. 2:7). By contrast, those who do (or work) evil, rejecting the truth and obeying unrighteousness, will be the objects of God's indignation and wrath. Their "reward" will bring trouble and distress.

Here Paul repeats a common theme found throughout the Old and New Testaments—the concept of two ways. It is found in the blessings and curses that Moses spells out to the children of Israel as they enter the Promised Land (Deuteronomy 28; 30:19-20). The book of Psalms opens with a description of the ways of the righteous and the ungodly (Ps. 1:6). Jesus describes two paths: a broad way "that leads to destruction," and a narrow path that leads to eternal life (Matthew 7:13-14); and houses built on both unstable and lasting foundations (Matt. 7:24-27). Paul certainly has good support for describing a contrast between **those who by persistence in doing good seek glory** (Rom. 2:7), and those **who reject the truth and follow evil** (v. 8).

In fact, we would have little argument with Paul's statement that those who do evil works are deserving of God's wrath (1:32). But what is more puzzling is the promise of eternal life to those who do what is good, without any reference to divine grace or even faith as a necessary condition of such eternal blessings. Is this the same Paul who declares we are saved "by grace . . . through faith . . . not by works, so that no one can boast" (Ephesians 2:8-9)?

We might explain this passage in Romans by recalling where we are in the argument Paul is building. In these early chapters of his letter, Paul is laying the foundation for his proclamation of the gospel. He is describing human accountability to God prior to the revelation of God's Son, Jesus Christ. In fact, Paul has not even addressed the provision for salvation under the old covenant given to Abraham and his descendants. His isolated references to the Jews have always been related to his primary focus on the Gentiles, and make the point that God is not a respecter of persons.

One might argue that obedience to the commandments was the requirement for salvation under the old covenant. In his preamble to the giving of the law, Moses declared, "Hear now, O Israel, the decrees and laws I am about to teach you. Follow them so that you may live. . . . Keep his decrees and commands, which I am giving you today, so that it may go well with you and your children after you and that you may live long in the land the LORD your God gives you for all time" (Deuteronomy 4:1, 40).

Certainly by the time of Jesus and Paul, the understanding of most of the Jews, and surely the Pharisees, was that righteousness before God could be equated with strict compliance to His law. When Paul states that God **"will give to each person according to what he has done"** (Rom. 2:6), perhaps he is conceding a theological point for the time being, in order to introduce the good news of God's grace at a later point in his argument.

The possibility exists, however, that Paul is not speaking just about earlier eras (some Christians call these "dispensations") before the law of Moses or the incarnation of Christ. He also might be speaking of the *present* spiritual status of millions of human beings who are born, and who live and die with only minimal knowledge of the Creator and His invisible qualities of holiness and righteousness. In holding every person "without excuse" for their ungodliness, Paul allows for the theoretical (and perhaps real) possibility that there are those who do seek the eternal, and who, in their persistent endeavor to do what they judge to be right, become qualified for eternal life.

Must we assume that the only persons who **seek glory, honor and immortality** (v. 7) are those who have heard the good news of Jesus Christ? Or are there still those individuals, like Abraham, who follow the leading of a God they do not fully comprehend, and whose response to that faint call of the divine Spirit is counted as righteousness to them as well?

At this point, we must return to our earlier discussion of how we can affirm that God holds individuals accountable for their actions, while also maintaining that salvation is only by God's grace through Christ. If one leans too far toward the Calvinist doctrine of predestination, then eternal life is simply determined by the divine decree of God long before the individual even exists as an unborn child.

In that case, Paul's quotation from Psalm 62:12 that God **will give to each person according to what he has done** (v. 6) would be at worst a lie and at best a puzzling charade in which persons are rewarded for what they could not help doing or not doing! No, to make sense of this passage, we must make every individual accountable for his or her compliance with the moral standard of God's righteousness.

But there is an equal danger of taking Arminianism too far and asserting that eternal life is the reward one earns for living a good life. In such a view, self-righteousness replaces the gracious gift of God in Christ.

Wesleyan theologians endeavor to resolve this dilemma by introducing a different dimension to God's grace—a grace that alerts sinners of their moral accountability, calls them to righteousness, and enables them to turn toward God. This grace is not *saving* grace; that is, it does not force one to turn to God against that person's free will. Instead, it is *enabling* grace in that the sinner cannot begin to sense a need of God or make the appropriate response toward Him without it.

John Wesley called this grace "preventing grace," from the Latin meaning "to come before." Since the word *preventing* means something quite different in English usage today, the term has been altered to "prevenient grace."

The term *prevenient* never occurs in the Bible, nor is it even described in exactly the terms used by Wesley and his followers. But it is a concept which cuts through the endless debates about divine election and free will, offering an explanation of how God can be the one who offers and accomplishes our redemption, while humans are still held accountable for their actions.

How does this concept of prevenient grace help us to understand this passage? Once again, Paul quotes from the Old Testament, asserting that even in the age of grace, God **will give to each person according to what he has done.** The works that he describes in the next two verses are not specific behaviors, but responses to some pre-existing awareness of the moral expectations of God.

The persons receiving eternal life are those who **seek glory, honor and immortality,** and, with that objective in mind, are persistent in doing what they judge to be good. No mention here of persons who don't steal, cuss or chew. The persons who stand under God's wrath are those **who reject the truth and follow evil.** One must assume there is an awareness of truth and falsehood, right and wrong in this person, in order for a deliberate act of rejection to occur.

Paul is not claiming that salvation comes by works; he is declaring that God is righteous and will hold each person accountable for the light they have received (John 1:5, 9). It is one's *response* to the divine initiative (in whatever form that call comes), and not some universally applied code of conduct, which gives content to the phrase **what he has done** (v. 6). Any endeavor of respectable persons to claim salvation on the basis of comparisons with others will not succeed in the presence of the righteous Judge, **for God does not show favoritism** (v. 11).

3. THE INNER LAW OF THE GENTILES 2:12-16

In verse 9, Paul introduced the categories of **Jew** and **Gentile,** but only to stress his point that these distinctions do not determine who is righteous and who is wicked. But that statement about God's impartiality provides the transition to Paul's next point, namely that the judgment of God has little, if anything, to do with one's religious heritage.

The children of Israel had long assumed that they were God's covenant people, the true children of God, based on the simple fact that their genealogical roots originated in Abraham. While there were occasional episodes of God's grace upon Gentiles (e.g., the Moabite woman, Ruth; or the Syrian general, Namaan), persons of other ethnic backgrounds were not given "most-favored status" by God. This idea had already been challenged by the Old Testament prophets (Jonah 3–4), and was openly refuted by Jesus (Matthew 8:11; John 8:39-40).

Paul, who at one time boasted of his status as a Jew, now reinforces the prophets and Jesus by declaring that a right relationship with God does not depend on one's ethnic identity. In arguing this point, Paul refutes three different arguments the Jews might offer in order to claim righteousness with God:

    a. *The Jews are the only people who have the law.* Paul counters this by proposing that the Gentiles also have access to God's moral code through **the law . . . written on their hearts** (Rom. 2:15).

    b. *The Jews carefully observe the law.* Paul counters that they **dishonor God by breaking the law** (v. 23).

    c. *The Jews have received the special covenant seal of circumcision.*

Paul counters by saying that true **circumcision is circumcision of the heart, . . . not by the written code** (v. 29).

This claim to special status for the Jews was not simply ethnic prejudice; the Jews had good reason to think that they were a people particularly blessed by God. Had not God revealed His moral character more fully to these people than He had to others? The Jews were the "people of the law." They had received the commandments of God through a divine encounter with Moses. Certainly, as persons who revered and, to a large degree, obeyed this law, they were eligible for special consideration on the Day of Judgment.

"Not so," replies Paul, "for God does not show favoritism" (v. 11). He opens verse 12 by declaring that **all who sin apart from the law will also perish.** One can almost hear the "amens" coming from those who pride themselves in being people of the law. Condemnation is what those ungodly heathens deserve. Things get strangely quiet, however, when Paul asserts that **all who sin *under* the law** (v. 12, italics mine) are equally accountable. A right relationship with God does not come merely by hearing or protecting the law. Righteousness is a matter of obedient response to the law in whatever form it is revealed to the individual.

Paul uses the distinction between those **apart from the law** and those **under the law** as an opportunity to spell out in more detail the nature of the law that exists apart from the commandments given to Moses. While most Christians today are familiar with Paul's distinction between the law and the gospel, they often limit their understanding of law to the Jewish code spelled out in the first five books of the Old Testament.

Paul does devote his primary attention to that Jewish law, as he develops his case for justification by faith. But here he speaks of a more basic law that is imbedded into the structure of creation itself and is accessible in some way to all human beings. And it is the response to this *creational* law that determines the destiny of those who are born and die apart from the revealed law of Scripture.

I prefer to speak of this as *creational,* rather than *natural* law. Theologians have long acknowledged that there are moral qualities built into the very fabric of nature. These laws can be logically deduced from observing the order and dynamics of the world around us. However, there are two dangers in building ethics upon this concept of natural law.

First, the moral "laws" of nature are in many cases ambiguous. Although one can observe maternal affection in the way some animals treat their young, one can also find terrible examples of child rearing (even cannibalism) in nature. Can one justify homosexual activity in humans because this practice occurs in some animals? Nature, at best, provides mixed signals for determining right and wrong in human relationships.

A more serious flaw to be reckoned with is that natural law reduces morality (or, more correctly, *righteousness*) to principles drawn only from nature, and thus rejects any direct engagement of God in dealing with humans. To suggest that all one needs to know of right or wrong can be found in nature is a dangerous assumption. It comes close to the perversion we previously discussed of substituting worship of the creation for the Creator (see comments on 1:23).

Beginning in the late seventeenth century, the deists developed a false understanding of Christianity based upon their confidence in the laws of nature. They claimed that God created the world as an intricate system of precise order and then allowed it to operate on its own principles without divine interference. Deists claimed that one did not need to turn to religious teaching or even Scripture to find moral truths; all moral truth was imbedded in nature, and a person of reason could figure it out with common sense.

One of the popular books of this era was *Christianity As Old As Creation,* in which Matthew Tindal argued that all the basic truths of Christianity could be discerned apart from any reference to the life and teachings of Jesus Christ or even the accounts of God's dealing with humanity in the Old Testament! Although this sounds similar to what Paul is suggesting in this passage, the natural theology of the deists eliminates any active role of the Holy Spirit in revealing truth. The spiritual sensitivity that the Bible associates with one's heart and conscience is reduced to common-sense thinking.

The deists of previous centuries have been replaced largely with a secular mind-set in our present time. Although the idea of the universe as an intricate machine governed by precise laws has given way to far more complex understandings of reality, the assumption that morality can be based upon observations of the natural order still persist. However, our confidence in reason as an absolute referee of morality is lost.

Now we use even more obscure criteria, like community standards, majority rule or congressional legislation, to define what is right and wrong. But, lurking under the surface of all our cries for "law and order" is the old deistic assumption that one can define morality without God. All such endeavors are bound to fail.

But, if one takes the concept of prevenient grace seriously, God is operating at every moment within His creation. His Holy Spirit is continually convicting persons of sinful conduct and is drawing them toward righteousness. This sense of law is more universal and basic than the specific revelation given to the Jews or the full disclosure of God in the incarnation of Jesus Christ. In that sense it is creational, but it should never be reduced to some cold, Spirit-less process of reason by scholars and politicians.

Paul declares that there are individuals (**Gentiles**) who meet the requirements of God's moral standards without any conscious awareness of what the Jewish law contains. They do this **by nature** (v. 14). Some translations (NASB and Williams) render this to read "instinctively," introducing the idea that Gentiles do good either by chance or because it is imprinted in their genes. But Paul gives this a much more spiritual focus, outlining three aspects of moral accountability for humans.

First, **the requirements of the law are written on their hearts** (v. 15). In ways we cannot explain fully, God reveals His moral standard to the inner core of individuals. Second, **their consciences also [bear] witness.** It is one thing to be aware of right or wrong; it is another thing to be *sensitized* to those actions or thoughts that violate this standard.

One group of Native Americans describes the conscience as an inner triangle whose points prick the heart when a person violates the law. Repeated disregard of those jabs tends to wear off the corners of the conscience until one's sense of right and wrong is dulled. The human heart not only knows what should be done, but feels the discomfort of a guilty conscience when sin occurs.

The final aspect of moral accountability is a rational process and decision of the will—**their thoughts now accusing, now even defending them** (v. 15). We frequently speak of guilty feelings, but only when these feelings can be sorted out rationally can we really choose to do what is right or wrong. Hence the parent's rebuke to the child, "You should have *known* better than to do that!"

Because these three aspects—a moral sense, a conscience, and a rational decision of the will—all are internal and precede the outward act of sin, it is impossible for human beings to judge the righteousness or unrighteousness of another person. Two individuals might behave in identical ways, but for very different reasons and with very different moral criteria influencing their decisions. That is why judgment is reserved for God, who at the appropriate time **will judge men's secrets through Jesus Christ** (v. 16). Among those secrets are the content of one's moral understanding and the motives which prompted one's actions.

We cannot pass by these verses without raising another complex question for Christian doctrine: Is there a possibility of eternal life for those who have only this dim light of creational law and prevenient grace to guide them? How do we reconcile this passage with Peter's claim before the Sanhedrin that "salvation is found in no one else [i.e., Jesus Christ], for there is no other name under heaven given to men by which we must be saved" (Acts 4:12)? We will deal with this matter more fully later.

But, note that Romans 2:12-16 seems to suggest a route to eternal life for those who have never heard the gospel; Paul inserts that God's judgment of the Gentiles is **through Jesus Christ** (v. 16). And Paul's purpose in discussing the Gentiles living apart from the law is not to propose alternative routes to heaven, but to stress the fact that every person—whether Jew, Gentile or Christian—stands accountable for his or her actions as they relate to God's standard of righteousness. Paul is building toward the climactic verse in the next chapter, where he will declare that "all have sinned and fall short of the glory of God" (3:23).

4. THE WRITTEN LAW OF THE JEWS 2:17-24

Paul certainly must be aware that he is charting a different course than traditional Jewish theology with his argument that Gentiles might qualify for the kingdom of God by being "a law for themselves" (v. 14). He concludes his thoughts on the law and the Gentiles with the bold disclaimer, "As my gospel declares" (v. 16), suggesting that there might be opposing views on this matter.

Paul's training in Jerusalem under the best rabbis of his day prepared him well for making an airtight case. He realizes that proposing a righteousness for Gentiles apart from the law does not close all the loopholes in his argument that God shows no favoritism in His judgment of unrighteousness. His critics—most likely Jews—might concede that some Gentiles could be judged righteous apart from the law, but only as rare exceptions. And these exceptions only confirm the rule that those who are the recipients and protectors of the divine law retain a special status which qualifies them for entrance into the eternal kingdom.

An illustration from the present day might be helpful. One could argue that there are immigrants who have become citizens of the United States by declaring their allegiance to the Constitution and by complying with the laws of the land. On the other hand, there are *natural-born* citizens who have that status by birthright. And these citizens-by-birth retain that status even if they are bad citizens and break the law! One might even be charged with treason against the government, yet claim rights as a citizen.

Similarly, the Jews might grant that some Gentiles enter the kingdom of heaven under special circumstances. But those born into the covenant relationship—even those who do not keep all the commandments—remain citizens of the Kingdom that is to come.

"No!" declares Paul. Not only is it possible for non-Jews to enter a right relationship with God through their obedience to the law they do not have, but there are also Jews who forfeit their right standing with God by violating the law which they do have. And these transgressors of the law deceive themselves when they think they are more righteous than the Gentiles who seek the Kingdom through the law written on their hearts.

Paul probably had in mind the sect of Jews to which he belonged before his conversion, and who were meticulous in their loyalty to the law and their compliance to its smallest demands. These Pharisees strained at gnats (see Matthew 23:24) and tithed even from their herb gardens in a public display of devotion to the law. If being born a descendant of Abraham did not automatically qualify one as righteous, then certainly observance of all the commandments should count for something!

Paul will not allow the defenders of the Mosaic Law to use their piety and devotion to the law as substitutes for faith. In what appears to be a rhetorical setup, Paul leads the self-proclaimed protectors of the law step-by-step toward a stinging accusation:

    a. **You call yourself a Jew** (v. 17).
    b. **You rely on the law and brag about your relationship to God** (v. 17).
    c. **You know his will . . . because you are instructed by the law** (v. 18).
    d. **You are convinced that you are a guide for the blind, a light for those who are in the dark, an instructor of the foolish, a teacher of infants** (vv. 19-20).
    e. **You have in the law the embodiment of knowledge and truth** (v. 20).

Then Paul levels his charge—you who claim to be the instructors of righteousness are not paying attention to what is being taught. You violate the very law you use to argue that you have a right relationship with God. Rather than the law of Moses being your unique heritage among the nations, it is your greatest embarrassment! You discredit the integrity of God by your disregard of His moral standard (vv. 23-24).

The concept of God protecting His reputation, associated in Jewish culture with one's name, recurs throughout the Old Testament. God, whose very essence is holiness, chose the descendants of Jacob (Israel) to model that holiness to the Gentile nations. His command to them was direct: "Be holy, because I am holy" (Leviticus 11:44). When the children of Israel did not live up to that mandate, God continually called them back to the covenant.

Although numerous texts suggest that God did this for the sake of His steadfast love, a passage in Ezekiel indicates that God acted on behalf of His people to preserve His name and reputation: "It is not for your sake, O house of Israel, that I am going to do these things, but for the sake of my holy name, which you have profaned among the nations where you have gone. I will show the holiness of my great name, which has been profaned among the nations" (Ezek. 36:22-23).

Certainly Paul has this text in mind when he accuses the Jews of discrediting God's name among the Gentiles. But Paul's audience is different than Ezekiel's. Paul is not addressing rebellious and overtly wicked persons (he treated their case in chapter 1). Here he speaks to persons who give outward indications of being lovers of God's law, but whose life-service does not measure up to their lip-service.

It is the hypocrisy of the Jewish Pharisees that is so damaging to God's reputation. Paul even quotes a passage in Isaiah (52:5) which says that they have gone beyond profaning God's name: **God's name is blasphemed among the Gentiles because of you,** he charges (Rom. 2:24). Rather than the law being a "free ticket" to righteousness, it becomes the noose that will hang those who treat lightly the sacred things of God.

5. THE MEANING OF CIRCUMCISION 2:25-29

Paul now has refuted two of the arguments Jews might use in claiming to be righteous in the eyes of God. He has described a revelation of the divine law in the hearts of Gentiles, thus undermining the claim that Jews are the only ones who have received the law of God. In response to boasts about the Jews' special relationship with God, based on their devotion to the law, Paul has exposed their hypocrisy by citing specific violations of the commandments. The Jews' inconsistent devotion has discredited both them and the God they worship. Paul now proceeds to the very core of Jewish identity—circumcision.

God established this sign of the covenant with Abraham centuries earlier (Genesis 17:9-14). Circumcision was the biological passport that every Jewish male carried on his person. From birth he was marked as a member of God's covenant community in a way that he could not ignore in the routines of daily life, nor conceal in times of challenge and persecution. The logic Paul challenges here is relatively simple: (1) the Jews, God's chosen people, are in good standing with God; (2) circumcision is the identifying mark that makes one a Jew; (3) therefore a circumcised Jew is in good standing with God.

Paul could see the flawed logic in this argument. One is not right with God because he is circumcised. Nor can righteousness be attained by surgical procedures. The physical marking of a Jewish male gives evidence that he knows the law and is accountable to it. But this does not suggest at all that he has kept the law and is considered righteous in the eyes of God, any more than carrying a passport proves that one has a clean record in his home country.

The passport defines the country to which a person belongs and the laws to which he is ultimately accountable. In that sense, a passport is of value in determining one's identity, but not one's patriotism or legal standing. In a similar way, circumcision marks the identity of the Jewish people, but does not in itself make them righteous before God.

When a Jew breaks the law, circumcision does not excuse that person or exempt him from divine justice. It only confirms that the offender has acted contrary to the covenant, and in that act has nullified the meaning of his circumcision. If a right relationship with God based upon obedience to one's knowledge of truth is the primary issue, then the Gentile who conforms to God's moral standard is closer to the covenant relationship than the Jew who breaks the law. Paul wonders aloud, **Will they not be regarded as though they were circumcised?** (Rom. 2:26).

The question of how circumcision relates to one's salvation seems archaic and irrelevant to twenty-first-century Christians. But we might pause and think of all the "markers" that human beings still use to convince others (and ultimately themselves) that they are in a right relationship with God: bumper stickers and baptismal certificates, church membership and tithing—things we do and things we don't do! Paul does not scorn any of these things. They have great value as ways of expressing who we are to others. But they are *signs* of who we are— they do not *make us* who we are.

And so Paul brings us back to his main point: **A man is not a Jew if he is only one outwardly** (v. 28a). There is an *inner* focus that determines one's relationship with God—the condition of one's *heart*.

God has given a witness of His moral standard to the hearts of all persons (v. 15) whether Jew or Gentile. A right standing with God originates, then, out of an inner identity, which Paul terms the **circumcision of the heart** (v. 29).

Obviously Paul intends to transfer a concept from his Jewish heritage over to the gospel of the new covenant in Christ. He does not reject the ideas that underlie this ritual, but neither does he choose to make it a literal one-for-one exchange. He vehemently opposes the idea that an outward marking is necessary for Gentiles who believe. His entire letter to the Galatians is a sharp criticism of the Judaizers—Christians who declared that salvation required one to both believe in Christ *and* keep all the Jewish rules. But Paul does see validity in speaking of an inner circumcision.

How do we grasp what is being described, particularly since most of us today have not been immersed in the cultural and religious thinking of Judaism? Without straining the metaphor Paul uses here, we might suggest several aspects of circumcision of the heart.

First, it is a *painful* experience. Circumcision involves the cutting and removal of human flesh. The "surgery" may be minor, but the significance of shedding blood, of removing a part of what a person has been given "by nature," cannot be ignored. Zipporah, the wife of Moses, had not been raised in the Jewish culture and, therefore, found the procedure offensive for those very reasons. After her husband had circumcised their firstborn, Zipporah accused him of being a "bloody husband" (Exodus 4:24-26 KJV).

Circumcision of the heart does not entail any bloodshed. But the principle remains that no person comes into a right relationship with God without some painful separation from their fallen nature (see the discussion of "flesh," or "sinful nature" in Romans 8:3). In most cases, that "cutting away" involves some discomfort or pain.

Circumcision is also an *intimate* experience. Other cultures in ancient and modern times have marked the body in religious rituals. But circumcision involves very sensitive and private aspects of one's anatomy and personhood. Speaking of this rite, a Jewish rabbi once commented to me, "You Christians can conceal or even ignore your religious identity, if you choose. But a day does not pass but what a Jewish man has to face the reality of who he is." In marking His people, God wanted them to confront their identity on a constant and deeply personal basis. Even persons with circumcised hearts must make their relationship with God a deeply personal and intimate aspect of their daily lives.

Above all else, circumcision is a *distinguishing* mark. Circumcision is an act which establishes that this individual is bound to God his Creator. The sign was not a creative idea thought up by Abraham, or copied from other religions (although it was not unique to the Israelites). The Scripture clearly indicates that the covenant and its sign of circumcision were initiated by God (Genesis 15, 17). But God's covenant called for a human response—obedience to the law. Circumcision was both an act and a sign—an *act* of obedience and a *sign* of a deeper commitment and accountability to God.

And so Paul speaks of an inner circumcision **by the Spirit** (Rom. 2:29). This divine act involves a cutting away from human nature that which is sinful, even at the cost of some discomfort and pain. It involves a deeply personal and intimate covenant act between the believer and God, and leaves its distinguishing mark on the soul that identifies a person as one who is in a right standing with God. And all of this, Paul reminds us, is for God's praise. We can no more boast in our right standing because of this divine act of the Spirit, than a Jew can boast of his status as one of the chosen people.

6. THE OBJECTIONS OF THE JEWS 3:1-8

When making a case for Christianity, one always encounters the nay-sayers. They listen—sometimes politely, sometimes with hostility. But sooner or later they interrupt with the words we encounter in this chapter of Romans: Why? What value . . . ? What if . . . ? Before examining the specific objections Paul feels compelled to answer, we need to think for a few minutes about the issue of our natural tendency to question the ways of God.

No one wants to think that the truths of Christianity are unreasonable and must be accepted only by blind faith. Job encountered a difficult experience when he lost his possessions and family. He and his friends sat down together and tried to sort out how his calamity fit into their understanding of a loving and all-powerful God. Some of the answers that surfaced were not good ones, but we should not condemn Job's comforters for trying to find a reasonable explanation for their faith commitments.

David struggled with the question of "the prosperity of the wicked" (Psalm 73:3-17). The writer of Ecclesiastes presents a fairly pessimistic view of life when he comes to the end of the matter: "This is the evil in everything that happens under the sun: The same destiny overtakes all. The hearts of men, moreover, are full of evil and there is madness in their hearts while they live, and afterward they join the dead" (Ecclesiastes 9:3).

But the fact that these struggles of the soul are found in the inspired Scriptures—in some cases involving entire books—certainly suggests that asking the tough questions of God is not inappropriate for persons seeking to find God's truth.

One danger of such questioning, however, is that we assume all the answers are simple, direct and reasonable. But perhaps God operates at a different level of thinking than our laptop computers. Speaking through the prophet Isaiah, God reminds us, "'For my thoughts are not your thoughts, neither are your ways my ways. . . . As the heavens are higher than the earth, so are my ways higher than your ways and my thoughts than your thoughts'" (Isaiah 55:8-9).

When we assume that God has to answer every question to *our* satisfaction, we are **using a human argument** (Rom. 3:5) and have lost our perspective about who we are in relationship to the all-knowing God. Blaise Pascal, the great mathematician of a few centuries ago, stated it well when he wrote in his spiritual diary, "The heart has its reasons which reason knows nothing of."

A second danger is that we assume God is obligated to answer all the objections we raise. God tolerated the questions Job asked, and listened (with amusement, I suspect) at the attempts of Job's friends to provide answers for God. But, in the closing chapters of that book (Job 38–41), God silences Job's questions by informing him that He was able to arrange the constellations in space and shape the earth quite well without any help from human engineers and consultants. Ultimately, in the midst of such wrenching questions, the person of faith has to trust God, even when answers are not forthcoming.

How, then, should we handle the questions that arise as we explore the riches of God's wisdom? First, we must use as much of our intelligence as we can to assist us. If we assume that we were made by a God of order who gave us minds to understand His creation, we can start by sorting out sensible responses as Paul does in this passage. To each "what if," Paul offers a reasoned response.

Second, we must start from a perspective of trust, not skepticism. Long ago, the eleventh century Christian scholar, Anselm, described this path to truth as "faith seeking understanding." Rather than being spiritual hecklers who assume we can stump God or at least the theologians, we should bring our questions to the table, just as children ask their parents for insights to life. "Anyone who comes to him must believe that he exists and that he rewards those who earnestly seek him" (Hebrews 11:6).

Finally, we must allow for elements of our faith that will always be the "unsearchable riches of the wisdom of God," beyond the capacity of our finite minds. The great Christian philosopher, G. K. Chesterton, once said, "The problem with Christianity is not that it is rational, or that it is irrational. The problem is that it is *almost* rational!" We can all identify with that frustrating experience of trying to discern what God is doing in our lives by using our mental faculties. But, about the time we think we have sorted out the solutions to all of life's questions, God inserts one more unexpected variable in the equation. And we are off again on our pursuit of understanding. Finally, we come to the point where we have to leave some of the issues with God in an act of trust. Paul is willing to engage the critics of his gospel, but he is not ashamed of Whom He believes (2 Timothy 1:12), and he is willing to leave the ultimate answers to God.

We might find it helpful to review Paul's argument up to this point. He has boldly declared that the gospel reveals the righteousness of God, which brings salvation to all persons who believe (1:16). The standard of God's righteousness can be discovered in the creation and is written on the hearts of all persons, so that all are "without excuse" (1:20).

Rather than responding positively to God's call to right living, humans have rejected the Creator and, as a result, have degenerated into godless and unrighteous sinners. But the capability of responding to God's call is there—for both Gentile and Jew.

Gentiles can respond in some limited way by following the voice of conscience as it directs them in moral matters. The Jews have a more explicit word in the law, given to them as God's chosen people. But neither status as the people of the law, nor partial obedience to its demands, nor being marked with the covenant sign of circumcision brings the Jews into a right relationship with God. Righteousness comes by an inner testimony of God's Spirit in the hearts of those who live by faith.

These features of Paul's good news would sound like bad news to many in his Jewish audience. His arguments undercut any sense of privilege or favored treatment that God's people might expect at the judgment. It places accountability for one's future blessings upon the individual, and not on God or any other external factor. One could expect objections at this point.

Paul did . . . and he tries to deal with these objections in an organized, logical manner. In modern courtroom procedure, we might describe this section as Paul's "side-bar" conversations. In the course of a trial, various technical matters often arise—usually objections from the opposing legal team. Rather than recessing the trial, the judge calls the lawyers to a side-bar conversation, out of hearing of the jury. When the issues are resolved, the trial resumes with more testimony and evidence.

Paul is eager to address all the protests against the gospel that might arise. But he must digress for a bit to handle these matters. The first few verses of chapter 3 do not contribute *directly* to the case he is building that "all have sinned" (v. 23). He will return to his main line of reasoning in verse 9. But, for these first eight verses, he attempts to silence his critics by the use of a "diatribe"—a literary device that describes an exchange with a hypothetical heckler in the crowd. Let us look briefly at each of the objections Paul addresses.

Objection #1 (3:1-2): If God judges all persons equally, **what advantage, then, is there in being a Jew,** one of God's *chosen* people (v. 1)? One recalls the famous line, "Where ignorance is bliss, 'tis folly to be wise." Why would one need—or want—additional knowledge of God's moral standard, if the only result of such knowledge is greater condemnation for not obeying it? Better to be a pagan with the light of conscience, than a Jew (or Christian) held to a much higher standard of conduct.

Response: Paul wrestles with this issue of Israel's significance in God's plan of redemption, but he postpones the major discussion of the topic until chapters 9 through 11. For now, he gives a one-sentence reply: the Jews have the unique honor of having received a *direct* communication of God's truth. **They have been entrusted with the very words of God** (3:2). We make much of body language in our contemporary society. We describe the subtle ways that we communicate with each other in indirect or nonverbal ways. In some sense, God's revelation in creation is His "body language" to us. But how much clearer and more personal is the *spoken* message that comes through words.

The writer to the Hebrews echoes this idea in his powerful opening sentence: "In the past God spoke to our forefathers through the prophets at many times and in various ways, but in these last days he has spoken to us by his Son" (Hebrews 1:1-2). Granted, Jesus spoke truthfully when He observed, "To whom much is given, of him will much be required (Luke 12:48 RSV). But, to have received this fuller understanding of who God is and how He relates to humanity is not a curse; it is a wonderful blessing.

The thinking that underlies this first objection (Romans 3:1) sometimes surfaces in our discussions of modern missions. Some have suggested that if persons who have never heard the gospel *in words* are still capable of knowing God and finding eternal life, why not leave them in their ignorance-filled bliss? "God forbid!" as Paul would say. First, their sin-darkened lives are anything but blissful. The possibility that a few individuals like Abraham of old might respond to the law written on their hearts does not overcome the fact that millions are lost *because the light they receive is so dim.* The nations of the world need to hear the *words* of God's love in order to respond clearly to the good news.

Furthermore, there is something basically contrary to the Spirit of Christ when those who have been given so much feast on their spiritual blessings while others struggle to survive on the barest essentials of God's revelation. Paul confirms that knowledge of God's character brings a higher accountability, but he will not be moved from his robust confidence that the word of God's love and grace really is good news that needs to be shared. Christians must avail themselves of every opportunity to entrust the message to as many people as possible.

Objection #2 (3:3-4): If responding to God's call is essential for coming into a right relationship with Him, then rejecting God's law (lack of faith) seems to take away God's sovereign control of salvation. If God made promises to Abraham and his descendants, how can one of those descendants, by his or her actions, nullify what God has promised?

This objection takes us back to long-standing disagreements between Calvinists and other Christian denominations. In their zeal to exalt God's sovereignty and, in some sense, His integrity, Calvinists do not allow any human action to interfere with God's eternal decree (predestination) to save individual humans.

Response: The Apostle Paul (along with Wesleyans today) does not want to suggest that God backs away from His promises. However, God's commitment is just in all His dealings. The God who "is not slow in keeping his promise . . . not wanting anyone to perish" (2 Peter 3:9) is the same God who declares, "The soul who sins is the one who will die" (Ezekiel 18:4b). Since God holds humans accountable to His moral standard (an essential component of Paul's argument), He is bound to be faithful to that standard, "[giving] to each person according to what he has done" (Rom. 2:6).

God's integrity is demonstrated by the equity of His judgments (3:4), more than by His obligation to give humans everything they *assume* He has promised. We must believe, then, that God's promises are given conditionally, and are kept to the degree that humans respond in faith to what He has declared.

Objection # 3 (3:5-8): If the disobedience of some Jews proves God's integrity in holding them accountable, how can He then be angry with those who disobey? In some mysterious way, their sin makes God look good! In fact, one might argue that at least some of us should sin boldly in order to be good villains in God's cosmic production! If God needs to condemn sinners in order to make His moral system work well, then **let us do evil that good may result** (v. 8).

Response: Embarrassed to even pose such a ludicrous objection, Paul interjects, **I am using a human argument** (v. 5)—literally, "I speak according to man." Paul wants nothing to do with individuals who attempt to twist human reasoning in order to back God into a corner with some catch-22 argument. His criticism is blunt: **their condemnation is deserved** (v. 8).

The Jews of Paul's day are not the last individuals who have constructed devious excuses for their misconduct. There is still an argument abroad today that suggests God is just too good to punish those who violate His standards. "Somehow God's unconditional love will have to find a way to excuse their sinfulness," goes this line of reasoning. "God will find a way to turn their rebellious attitude into something worthwhile and thus include them in His redemptive plan." Although no true believer rejoices in the destruction of the wicked, we must be wary of those who push God's love into something which absolves us from accountability for our actions.

7. THE ACCOUNTABILITY OF EVERYONE 3:9-20

Paul uses the final "side-bar" objection to draw his readers back to the point he has been making throughout this first section of his letter—no one is without excuse for sin. Before proceeding to a proclamation of the good news of Christ, Paul merges his two opening themes into a sobering conclusion.

The first theme was the downward bent of the human heart to turn from worship of the Creator toward sin and moral degeneration (1:18-32). The second theme was that every individual, whether Jew or Gentile, is accountable to the moral standard of God. The Gentiles cannot plead ignorance of the law written on their hearts; the Jews cannot plead exemption on the basis of their privileged status or their ritual marking of circumcision. **Jews and Gentiles alike are all under sin** (3:9).

It is striking to notice a shift in Paul's method as he comes to the conclusion of this section. Having built much of his case upon his reasoning skills, Paul now turns to the "supreme court" to validate his claim—the Word of God. Paul constantly draws upon his knowledge of the Jewish traditions and Scriptures (usually from the Septuagint, the

Greek translation of the Hebrew text) that shaped his life before his encounter with Christ.

Many issues that we struggle with in our faith can be resolved with common sense or even careful reasoning, as Paul has just demonstrated. But one must always bring reason under submission to the Word of God. When the Devil tempted Jesus to follow his line of thinking, Jesus did not engage in lengthy theological debates. Instead, He quoted the Scripture and, in doing so, silenced the Adversary (Luke 4:1-13).

right to the point

Evangelical Christians have always understood the Old and New Testaments to be the final authority on spiritual matters, "so that whatsoever is not read therein . . . is not to be thought necesary for salvation."[2] We would do well to follow Paul's example and give primacy to God's Word, and not our intellectual speculations or practical considerations, when shaping our understanding of the faith.

Paul might have had in mind another strategy here as well. The Jews understood themselves to be the recipients and defenders of God's special revelation given to Moses. They could always use the Scriptures to defend their beliefs and practices. Paul now turns their own sword upon them, clinching his argument by quoting from the very sacred writings that Jews claimed gave them a special relationship with God. The law itself will confirm Paul's argument that all stand condemned before the moral standard of God.

Look ahead to verse 19 and you will see Paul reminding the Jews **that whatever the law says, it says to those who are under the law, so that every mouth may be silenced and the whole world held accountable to God.** Rather than *exempting* the Jews, the law of God makes them equally, if not more, *accountable* for their failure to measure up to God's holy character.

To avoid any accusation of prooftexting (finding some obscure verse to make his point), Paul quotes no less than six separate passages from the Jewish Scriptures, five from the Psalms and one from the book of Isaiah. His focal point is a passage that can be found in two almost identical Psalms, 14 and 53. Those two Psalms both open with the statement, "The fool says in his heart, 'There is no God.'" Did Paul already have these verses in mind when he referred to the wicked in Romans 1:22 as those who "claimed to be wise," but "became fools"? And again in chapter 3, as in chapter 1, Paul describes a sordid picture of the moral character of humans apart from God.

The remaining verses in this passage echo Paul's own description of the spiritual corruption of humanity apart from grace. His description progresses from those who lack righteousness, understanding and a desire for God (3:10-11) to those who **have turned away** (v. 12), and who practice evil speaking (vv. 13-14), wicked actions (v. 15), and finally a defiant attitude of having **no fear of God** (v. 18), who will ultimately judge them.

Is Paul suggesting that every human being is *this* depraved and godless? Certainly this does not accurately describe the religious or even nonreligious persons we encounter every day. Most of them are decent, law-abiding, friendly people. Why does Paul make them out to be deceitful, bitter, bloody, warring **vipers** (v. 13)?

Because, left to our own inclinations, this is where our fallen hearts will take us. When Christians speak of the *total* depravity of the human race, they do not mean that everyone is as bad as they possibly can be; they mean that there is no divine spark or seed of goodness that can ever grow into godliness and holiness on its own. *Left to ourselves,* we will spiritually degenerate unless God's prevenient grace does its work in our hearts to awaken us to our sinful condition and draw us back to God.

Although these verses describe the reprehensible dimensions of sin, there is another form of ungodliness that looks respectable on the surface, but is equally condemned by God—self-righteousness. When humans assume that their *good behavior,* which for the Jews was equated with **observing the law** (v. 20), qualifies them as righteous before God, they are committing a serious offense. They claim they have no need of God's intervention, being fully capable of achieving salvation for themselves.

And so Paul gives his final and strongest statement on the sinful condition of the entire human race: **No one will be declared righteous in [God's] sight by observing the law** (v. 20a). The law, at its best, only reveals God's high standard of moral character and reveals how far beneath that standard we are. To find a right relationship with God, we must *look beyond the law to faith in the Lawgiver himself.*

ENDNOTE

[1]John Wesley, *The Works of John Wesley,* vol. 1, 3rd edition, (Grand Rapids: Baker Book House, [1872] reprinted 1979), p. 98.

[2]This phrase first appears in the 39 articles of the Church of England (1571) and has been passed down to Methodism and its various branches.

Part Two

RIGHTEOUSNESS REVEALED:
The Act of Faith

Romans 3:21–4:25

A ny doctor, auto mechanic or amateur trouble-shooter knows that diagnosing the problem is only part of the task; discovering the correct remedy for the problem is equally important. In the opening part of his letter to the Romans, Paul has defined the problem of sin in detail. And he has identified several ineffective solutions that humans, particularly his own people, the Jews, attempt in order to gain a right standing with God.

His conclusion is that while everyone—Jew or Gentile—has a natural inclination to violate the laws of Moses and conscience, these same individuals do not have the capacity to make themselves righteous by the law. The law succeeds in making us conscious of sin, but the law in itself is unable to save.

In this section, Paul declares that all **are justified freely by [God's] grace** (3:24). That undeserved gift is offered to us as a promise, which becomes a reality when we respond in faith. We cannot earn this righteousness as compensation for our good works; it is accomplished by the work (sacrifice) of **Christ Jesus** (3:24).

Paul then uses Abraham, the father of the Jewish people, as the model for his new understanding of justification by faith. Apart from any human endeavor or sacred rites of circumcision, Abraham received the promise and its fulfillment by a simple act of trust. Paul will lead us through these verses, reinforcing again and again the heart of his gospel: **Abraham believed God, and it was credited to him as righteousness** (4:3b). We must do the same if we are to attain this right standing with God.

??) Observance of the Law is not the
= justification

4

FAITH: The Condition for Justification

Romans 3:21-31

If "I am not ashamed" (1:16) is the heart of Paul's personal testimony, the heart of Paul's message is 3:22: **righteousness from God comes through faith in Jesus Christ to all who believe.** The good news that Paul proclaims begins with the assumption that the greatest need of human beings is, in the words often used by Billy Graham, "getting right with God." The theological word used to describe this concept is *justification,* which in the Greek is a verb form of the words we have already been translating as *righteous* and *righteousness.* There is some validity in defining being justified by the simple memory device—"just-as-if-I'd" never sinned.

This right standing with God certainly has much to do with correcting the spiritual problem of unrighteousness which Paul has been describing in his letter to the Romans. But it is a far richer and more complex term. Justification might be understood in at least four different ways, and the way one selects says much about how that person understands both God and salvation:

a. *Cosmic Harmony*—One could assume that the goal of human existence is to get it all together by discovering one's perfect place in God's infinite universe. In such a perspective, a strong emphasis is given to God's unity, both with himself and with His creation. The widely accepted Christian teaching on the three distinct persons of the Trinity is minimized, and even the distinction between the Creator and the creation is blurred. Much of Eastern religions and the New Age philosophy builds upon this merging of God with the created order.

In such a view, salvation becomes an inward journey to self-discovery. Since God is in creation, getting right with God is discovering the deity *in me* and in nature, and then bringing all of these elements into harmony with each other. Sin is viewed more as inner discord than a rejection of God's standard of holiness. Since this view is totally alien to the biblical understanding of justification, we can pass over it quickly to more biblical understandings.

b. *Spiritual Appeasement*—There are those who believe that salvation comes when human beings discover the proper ways to appease the wrath of God and "get on His good side." The theology of these persons is also flawed, in that they assume that God (or the gods) is essentially hostile toward human beings. They focus so much on the biblical teaching concerning God's wrath that they continually live under a cloud of fear. Quite often, their view of sin is exaggerated to the point that, in their eyes, even their existence becomes an affront to God.

People with this view assume that they must make enormous sacrifices, sometimes including self-inflicted punishment, like the prophets of Baal on Mount Carmel (1 Kings 18) or even human sacrifice (Leviticus 20:1-5). Although these extreme forms of appeasing the gods are not common in our modern society, there is no lack of misguided Christians who still assume that every misfortune of life is an expression of God's displeasure. They live miserable lives with little awareness of God's love or grace toward them. Furthermore, they often assume that God demands some extreme sacrificial act on their part (martyrdom, denial of legitimate pleasures, self-imposed poverty) to demonstrate their earnest desire to be saved.

Yes, the Bible speaks of God's wrath against all ungodliness and unrighteousness. But the recurring theme of the Bible is God's fatherly love toward His creation and particularly His children, the human race. His instructions to the Israelites concerning sacrifices in the Old Testament were not so much designed to placate His anger as to point to the seriousness of sin and the high price (no less than blood!) that it would take to find redemption for those He loves. Confronted with the deep sin in his own life, King David realized that a right relationship with God could not be guaranteed by sacrifice alone. "You do not delight in sacrifice, or I would bring it; you do not take pleasure in burnt offerings. The sacrifices of God are a broken spirit; a broken and contrite heart, O God, you will not despise" (Psalm 51:16-17).

c. *Legal Acquittal*—We move closer to the biblical understanding of justification when we think of salvation in the terms of the courtroom. In such a view, God is the divine lawgiver and the "Judge of all the earth" (Genesis 18:25), who does what is right. God has revealed His law and expects compliance from those who are subjects of His kingdom. Sin is disobedience of this law; it is a criminal offense against God. Since we are guilty of breaking God's law, we stand condemned before Him, deserving whatever punishment He declares.

Salvation is accomplished when someone (Jesus Christ) pays the penalty and God, the righteous Judge, declares us pardoned. Justification is that act of God which declares the condemned sinner to be righteous before Him and once more qualified for the rights and benefits of a citizen of heaven.

This legal (sometimes called "forensic") view of justification is easily understood and certainly draws upon many biblical passages and themes. The Apostle Paul, a citizen of the Roman Empire that contributed so much to creating the structures of our modern legal system, certainly thinks in these categories when he describes both sin and salvation. Although this view of justification does much to stress the attribute of God's *justice*, it does not enhance the deeper understanding of Scripture concerning the *fatherly love* of God toward His children. While good parents are just and fair in their dealings with their children, few would go so far as to structure their family dynamic like the court system!

In giving God all the legal characteristics He rightly deserves, advocates of this view make His authority *so supreme*, that both His relational characteristics and the significance of faith and love in the plan of salvation are minimized. If God's Word is absolute and final law, then the human response to His decrees is irrelevant.

For example, if the governor or president declares that a prisoner is pardoned, the act is accomplished, no matter how that pardoned convict responds. One would hope that the former criminal would become a model citizen out of gratitude for what had occurred. But, if that person chose instead to scorn the one who had pardoned him, and curse the legal system and become a disgrace to the community, the pardon would still stand. Even human courts could not reverse the pardon and send the scoundrel back to jail for his bad attitude.

A similar danger lurks in the legal understanding of salvation. If we assume that, since Jesus paid the penalty for sin and God has declared sinners to be justified, then our response to the good news is not a relevant issue. Advocates of this legal view argue that we are saved

71

despite what we do, not *because of* what we do. With this understanding of justification, we return to our earlier challenge of maintaining God's sovereign power and right to save humanity, while still holding human beings accountable for how they respond to His work in Christ.

d. *Personal Relationship*—Using the concepts of human relationships, we might be able to develop a view of justification that combines some of the legal understanding of the third option with the more interrelational dynamics between God and His human creation. In this view, sin shifts from being the violation of laws to the *breaking of relationships* through actions that evidence mistrust and disregard for another. To be sure, there is usually the breaking of some agreement (covenant) between two individuals when relationships go awry. But the break doesn't focus so much on what was or was not done, but on the violation of the faith/love relationship that held the two parties together.

Marital infidelity does involve breaking the "rules" of marriage, but the deeper problem is the relational offense. The employee who cheats on the boss has probably violated company policy, but the real anger is often expressed in a statement like, "How could you do that to us after we trusted you with so much?"

God created humans from Adam and Eve to Generation Xers in order to have a love relationship with them. The disobedience of humans is not so much a breaking of God's rules as it is a slap at His very character of righteousness and love. Sin is not merely the disruption of cosmic harmony (although we sense the lack of unity because of sin); nor is it provoking God's wrath by doing what displeases him. And although God holds us accountable for violating His moral standard, it is not our disobedience of the law that is the core of our problem. Sin is our *faithlessness to the relationship.*

Justification, then, is God's marvelous way of bringing us back to a right relationship with Him. The reconciliation that brings estranged humans back to their heavenly Father is made possible by the great sacrifice on God's part—the gift of His only Son (John 3:16). But neither Jesus' death nor God's pardon can *force* rebellious humans to be restored to a right relationship with Him. For this reconciliation to become a reality, we must come to ourselves and return to the Father like the prodigal son in Jesus' well-known parable on forgiveness. We must now discover how these various views merge in Paul's understanding of the salvation events of Jesus' life, and learn the essential response to God's call required of each sinner for a restored relationship.

1. RIGHTEOUSNESS COMES FROM GOD 3:21-26

One could become depressed reading about the sad moral state of the human race in the first few chapters of Romans. One could also get befuddled trying to follow all the logical twists Paul takes in arguing with his imaginary critics. The **but now** that opens verse 21 is like the trumpet fanfare from the *William Tell Overture* announcing that deliverance (or more correctly the Deliverer) is on its way.

It is worth noting that Paul has not mentioned the word *grace* once since his opening prayer (1:5). And there has been only one passing reference to Jesus Christ (2:16) in all this discussion about the sinful condition of the human race. One suspects that Paul forced himself to refrain from any excursion into the gospel territory until he had thoroughly mapped out the furthest borders of the wasteland of unrighteousness. But now, in a few doctrine-packed verses, he announces the theme of the entire letter, the theme of his entire ministry: **A righteousness from God, apart from law, has been made known** (3:21).

Before spelling out the nature of this new righteousness, Paul wants to clarify its relationship to the previous understanding of righteousness under the law. Paul frontloads the sentence (in the Greek, this comes immediately after the **but now**) by emphasizing that *apart* **from law** this righteousness has been revealed (v. 21, italics mine). As wonderful as this proclamation sounds, it is hard to reconcile it with Paul's earlier quotation from Scripture in which we are told that "God 'will give to each person according to what he has done'" (2:6).

Rewarding individuals for what they have done draws up images of God checking our conduct against the rules He has imposed. That certainly appears to be the function of law! How can the righteousness of the gospel be totally distinct from God's law?

The actions by which God judges a person cannot be understood merely as keeping the law. First, it is virtually impossible for a fallen human being to measure up to God's perfect standard of holiness. We could not keep the law at all points even if we wanted to. Second, to do so would be a *self-righteousness* based upon a false assumption that one's good or evil acts determine one's eternal destiny, with God coming along simply to settle the accounts! No, this new righteousness must be understood as an act *originated* by God, *motivated* by His grace, and *accomplished* by His power. Salvation under the law centers upon the obedience of humans; salvation under the gospel centers upon the grace of God.

But Paul does not repudiate his roots in the family of Abraham. And Paul, more than any other human, grasped the foreshadowing of the new covenant in the words and worship of the old. While the gospel is distinct from the law, both the commandments of **the Law** and the visions of **the Prophets** (3:21) *are witnesses* (NIV, **testify,** the same Greek word used in Acts 1:8) to Jesus the Messiah (Christ). Whatever this good news is, it cannot be isolated from the moral character of God—both His holiness and love—which has been revealed to all persons since Creation.

Just as that original revelation had been given to all humans, even so this new word of God's love is universal in its scope. It is available **to all who believe** (v. 22). And the focus of faith is certainly not the created idols of the heathen (1:25), nor even the law of the Jews (2:20). **This righteousness from God comes through faith in *Jesus Christ* to all who believe** (3:22, italics mine).

One of the most frequently quoted verses in the Bible follows. Most often it is used as the first step in a plan of salvation that directs a seeker to faith in Christ. Paul declares, **all have sinned and fall short of the glory of God** (v. 23). One might expect Paul to make this statement at the conclusion to his section on the sinfulness of humanity a few verses earlier. But here it becomes a transition to his present topic, which is the righteousness that God freely offers to all. Paul is saying that just as there are no special categories when it comes to accountability for sin, there are no special categories when it comes to redemption through Christ. **There is no difference** (v. 22)!

One might speculate at great length about the final judgment when all persons stand before God to give an account of the deeds they have done in the flesh. Some people envision a lifelong instant replay of every minute detail of their life projected on a wide-screen monitor for everyone else to see. Others see God like Santa Claus reading through a long list in a big book to see who has been naughty or nice. Still others conceive of a courtroom with a judge's bench, witness stand, and all the paraphernalia of our twentieth-century legal system.

No one knows the details, but this passage in Romans suggests that there will be two essential components of that final encounter with God: First will be the question, "How did you measure up to God's standard of holiness and moral purity?" And all persons will have to acknowledge that, despite incidents of good behavior, they **fall short of the glory of God** (v. 23). The follow-up question will then be, "And what did you do with the knowledge you received—great or small—of God's grace in Jesus Christ, 'the true light that gives light to every man'" (John 1:9)?

All who answer these two questions stand on a level playing field. Accountability for sin is a universal requirement. And so, also, is accountability to God's grace (faith). One's relationship with God is the deciding factor in receiving and experiencing His gift of eternal life.

The significance of Jesus in God's plan of salvation is that He became **a sacrifice of atonement** (Rom. 3:25) on our behalf. The biblical view of redemption is deeply rooted in the concepts of sacrifice established in God's earliest relationships with humankind. Centuries before God gave the detailed instructions for animal sacrifices in the Tabernacle, He commanded those who believed in Him to express that faith commitment by taking the life of living creatures. No doubt Cain, Noah, Abraham and countless others wrestled with the significance and need of such a gruesome act.

God's explanation was vague, but direct: "For the life of a creature is in the blood, and I have given it to you to make atonement for yourselves on the altar; it is the blood that makes atonement for one's life" (Leviticus 17:11). By the New Testament era, the Jews had come to accept sacrifices as essential to their worship and relationship with God. "Without the shedding of blood there is no forgiveness" (Hebrews 9:22).

Paul brings this concept into sharp focus when speaking of his good news about a right relationship with God. He combines the Jewish themes of atonement with first-century ideas of justice to declare that Jesus' death on the cross (His blood) demonstrates God's faithfulness to both His covenant of love and His own standard of justice.

What was the purpose of this sacrifice? We have noted earlier that viewing justification as appeasement of God is an inadequate understanding of both sin and God. In pagan sacrifice, the human offers something to the gods in the hope that the gods' ill feelings will be placated. But here, *God* offers the sacrifice for sin. The sacrifice is the Heavenly Father's action **to demonstrate his justice** (Rom. 3:25), not a human effort to buy off an angry God who would otherwise act destructively toward His creation.

It would not even be appropriate to suggest that Jesus is offering himself to a wrathful Father; such a view pits the persons of the Trinity against each other and discredits Paul's bold assertion "that God was reconciling the world to himself in Christ, not counting men's sins against them" (2 Corinthians 5:19).

The heart of the gospel is not God's wrath and judgment of sinners. Rather, it is the amazing fact that while God's wrath "is being revealed from heaven against all the godlessness and wickedness" (Rom. 1:18), God is still favorably inclined toward the sinner! Prior to the coming of

Christ, God **in his forbearance . . . left the sins committed beforehand unpunished** (3:25). To settle all the accounts of the law would have required the destruction of both sin and sinner. But, in the sacrifice of His Son, God dealt a deathblow to sin (**so as to be just**), but at the same time demonstrated His grace and love toward sinners (as **the one who justifies** [v. 26]).

Yes, you reply. But all this sounds too simple. Surely there is something the sinner must do to make things right with God. But if God has dealt with sin and has declared the sinner to be reconciled, *there is nothing left to do* except receive the gift. A right relationship with God is possible to all **those who have faith in Jesus** (v. 26). The demands of the law have been met by the atoning sacrifice; salvation is quite apart from the law.

2. JUSTIFICATION COMES THROUGH FAITH 3:27-31

Once again, Paul returns to his critics who depend on their status, or their strictness, to claim a right relationship with God. If God holds all humans accountable for their sins, and yet He has already reconciled humans to himself by the offering of His Son, Jesus, then the only boast (if we could even call it that) would be that an individual believed in God enough to say a sincere "yes" to His gracious gift.

Imagine a person who, through carelessness or perhaps even daredevil stupidity, decided to paddle a canoe down the Niagara River. Suddenly, the boater senses impending disaster as the roar of the Horseshoe Falls signals what lies ahead. Too late! The boater begins paddling frantically for shore, but the current draws him closer and closer to destruction. Then overhead a voice calls down from a circling helicopter. "Do you want to be rescued?" At first the boater, overcome with pride, replies, "I think I can make it myself." Foolish thought. The canoeist quickly realizes that nothing he can do will prevent certain death. Again, the voice from above . . . "Do you want me to rescue you?"

The response this time is a desperate "YES!"

"Then cling to the rope I toss you," comes the instruction. The boater clutches the rope in sheer terror, unable to do anything but cling in hope and faith to the lifeline sent his way. He is suddenly lifted from the canoe and pulled into the chopper, saved at last.

Now, imagine such a person telling a news reporter a few minutes later how smart he was to have owned a brightly colored canoe that could be detected by the pilot; how skillful he was to maneuver his boat to a spot underneath the helicopter; how coordinated he was to grasp the rope; how strong he was to hold on all the way up to the helicopter. Such boasting would be ridiculous and an insult to his rescuer listening in the background.

Paul suggests that our boasting about the role we play in the salvation saga is equally ridiculous and offensive to our Savior. To claim that the pivotal aspect of a right relationship with God is one's heritage, or the observance of some of God's commandments, is foolishness. Salvation comes from above, and the human response of faith is little more than "grasping the rope" of salvation offered to us. Just as no person is exempt from the judgment that comes from falling short of God's glory, so no person is qualified to be justified on any other basis than saying yes to God's offer of grace.

Paul then concludes that since any person can respond in faith to the call of God, there can be no distinction between Jews and Gentiles when it comes to grace. God has communicated His moral standard to all persons; He has offered His Son as a sacrifice for all sin; and He offers a restored relationship to all who respond at the level of their understanding to the good news revealed in Christ and proclaimed by Paul.

Paul firmly maintains that **a man is justified by faith apart from observing the law** (v. 28). But that does not negate the function the law has in revealing the righteousness of God and making us conscious of sin. Those who live by faith discover the positive side of the law and use it to strengthen their lives. Followers of Christ **uphold the law** (v. 31), but they never depend on knowing or keeping it in order to be reconciled to God.

5

ABRAHAM:
The Father of the Faithful

Romans 4:1-25

Religious groups frequently appeal to a founder for support and validation of their views. Lutherans quote Martin Luther, Wesleyans cite the writings of John Wesley, Buddhists read the sayings of their leader; and each group assigns special authority to the spiritual father of their tradition.

The Jews of Paul's day were no exception. Although they were the descendants of Jacob (renamed Israel), they pushed back even farther in their genealogical tree to Abraham, claiming **He is the father of us all** (4:16). The appeal to Abraham as founder of the faith led to several serious distortions of God's truth among the Jews.

We already have observed how some Jews assumed that merely being biological descendants of Abraham entitled them to a right standing with God. But this logic makes about as much sense as claiming that since one of my ancestors came to North America on the Mayflower, I must be a good citizen of the United States. Paul rejects any concept that defines righteousness simply in terms of one's birthright.

A second fallacy developed when the Jews associated the ritual of circumcision with justification. Here again, they appealed directly to the actions of their founder, Abraham. The covenant was restricted to circumcised Jews. Abraham and his descendants entered a right relationship with God when they heard God's command (law) and acted appropriately. Paul rejects outward circumcision as the evidence of having a right relationship with God. If there is any validity to circumcision, it must be the inward circumcision of the heart.

Finally, there were Jews who focused on Abraham's *works* of righteousness, suggesting that circumcision was the first and most basic act of human obedience in response to God's command. In the further development of the people of God, God gave Moses a more complete law that spelled out the details of God's moral expectations. A right relationship with God required *all* of the steps we have outlined: a Jewish heritage, the ritual of circumcision, and compliance with all the Old Testament laws. The result of such a view is an enormous shift from *God's work* of redemption to *human works* of righteousness.

The issue Paul addresses in this chapter of Romans is still very much alive in the religious community today. You will find a significant number of self-proclaimed Christians who base that claim on the fact that they have been born and raised in a particular denomination or religious community. They assume that the faith of their parents or grandparents was mysteriously imparted in them from the moment of conception.

Having been born a Catholic, Baptist or Wesleyan, they assume that salvation is automatic in their lives and remains until there is a blatant rejection of the faith of their childhood heritage. And so they drift through adolescence into adulthood with a false assumption that Christianity is a social dynamic, not a spiritual commitment.

Others realize that there is an element of human accountability to salvation . . . a believer must do *something* to demonstrate good faith toward God. But they equate the response to God's call with certain ceremonial acts, not unlike circumcision in the Old Testament. The action might be baptism, joining a church, confirmation or tithing. These persons falsely assume that God is willing to credit them with righteousness for some symbolic "wanna-be" gesture on their part.

Finally there are Christians who take the idea of God's law very seriously. They are not at all casual about their spirituality. On the contrary, they impose strict disciplines on themselves and others in order to convince God that they are worthy of salvation. Like Paul before his encounter with Christ, their zeal for righteousness is commendable, but they are building upon a false understanding of salvation.

This fourth chapter of Romans is Paul's rejection of all such views. In their place, he proposes an alternative view of salvation and defends his view by appealing to Abraham, the very authority his opponents have used to make their case!

1. FAITH RATHER THAN WORKS 4:1-8

What then shall we say that Abraham, our forefather, discovered in this matter? (v. 1). Paul has already used the Jewish Scriptures and logical reasoning to build his case for justification by faith. Now he turns to another authority to support his argument—the traditions of his religious community. The Jews shaped their identity around God's call and covenant with "Father Abraham." An appeal to the words or practices of their founder would carry much weight for both Paul and his opponents in this debate. Having distanced himself from the traditional thinking of the Jews, Paul now uses the story of Abraham to illustrate his own understanding of righteousness before God.

Believers today still draw upon the words and action of their denominational founders to support their beliefs. But, any time we appeal to human figures, no matter how spiritual they may be, there is the possibility of picking up the wrong signals from their words or actions.

John Wesley has been made to advocate bizarre ideas by some of his followers, who selectively quote from his writings or interpret what he said in ways he would have totally rejected. Even during his lifetime, Wesley had to publicly repudiate claims that his disciples were making in his name! And, unfortunately, even to this day there are those who promote unscriptural truths by proclaiming, "This is what our founder said."

This appeal to a historical figure can be even more dangerous when that leader's biography becomes the standard by which a believer's actions are to be measured. Each of us has our own pilgrimage of faith. And, while God works in mysterious ways to bring about His plans for salvation, it is a dangerous step to assume that the way grace operates in one person's life can be expanded into a rule of faith for *all* believers.

Certainly, one can learn valuable lessons about God's dealings with humans by examining the lives of saints throughout history. It is dangerous, however, to assume that because grace operated in a particular way with Noah, or Francis of Assisi, or Billy Graham, that grace will function in the same way in all cases. One would hardly want to use the crude, bombastic language of Martin Luther as the model for Christian conversation. It would be foolhardy to develop a pattern for courtship and marriage for believers by looking at the unfortunate dynamics of John Wesley's relationships with the women in his life!

But, despite the warnings, we still put our founders on a pedestal and consider them to be powerful warrants for the things we want or do not want others to do. The Jews developed an understanding of righteousness based upon ethnic identity and works. They claimed support for this view by referring to Father Abraham. Now Paul must undo their misconceptions by forcing them to reexamine the Scriptures. Paul contends that a radically different understanding of justification can be found by reading the story more carefully.

Paul builds his case from the biblical text of one of Abraham's encounters with God. In Genesis 15:6 we are told, "Abram believed the LORD, and [the Lord] credited it to him as righteousness." This passage does not report God's first encounter with Abraham; God had already appeared to him in the far-off country of Chaldea, blessing him and commanding him to relocate to the land of Canaan (Gen. 12:1-4).

Abraham (or Abram, as he was called at that time) responded to God's call and moved his family to the region that is now modern-day Israel. But the divine promise that he would lead a great nation was particularly puzzling, since he and his wife, Sarah, had been childless throughout their married life together.

In this subsequent encounter with God, Abraham raised the problem of their infertility. The divine response was a promise of miraculous grace—God would make Abram the father of a great nation. Directing Abram's attention to the stars in the night sky, God declared, "So shall your offspring be" (Gen. 15:5).

Abram might well have replied with the words of Charles Wesley's great hymn, "And Can It Be?" Instead, we have the simple declaration that "Abram believed the LORD." The writer to the Hebrews states it even more powerfully—"[Abraham] considered him faithful who had made the promise" (Heb. 11:11). But no one states it better than Paul in Romans 4:20: "He staggered not at the promise of God" (KJV).

"And [God] credited it to him as righteousness" (Gen. 15:6). The **it,** in this case, is Abram's faith. The trigger point of entering into a right relationship with God is the moment of faith in His promise of miraculous grace. For Father Abraham, the faith related to the promise of a son. For us, faith relates to God's promise of salvation through His Son, Jesus Christ. Both miracles are God's doing, not ours. Both miracles originate in God's divine power, but are accessible through faith, not the work of humans.

Paul proves this point by two separate arguments—the first from the logic of the account; the second from the chronology given in the Genesis story. Logic would suggest that if Abraham was justified by his own efforts, righteousness would be a reward for what he had done, and not the free gift of God. And Abraham would rightfully be able to point with pride (even boast) that his destiny was the direct result of what he himself had done. This is Paul's point in Romans 4:2. Imagine human creatures boasting of saving themselves. What would it suggest about their inflated views of themselves? What would it suggest about their scandalous view of God?

For Paul, coming into a right relationship with God must be the result of a divine act of free grace. It must be **a gift** (v. 4; see also 6:23). No human action can establish this right relationship. So foundational is the biblical truth that salvation is totally of God, that even faith must not be defined as some effort or decision on the part of the sinner to choose God's side or to conclude after careful reasoning that it makes sense to believe in God. Faith is simply *trusting*—a throwing of oneself completely on the promises of God to accomplish for the individual what otherwise could never happen.

Paul then directs the Jews to another giant of their religious tradition—David. Even this military-hero-turned-king could not boast of his spiritual standing. Paul quotes from Psalm 32, where David speaks of a blessed individual, whose divine favor does not come through any human effort. Instead, this man is blessed because his **transgressions are forgiven,** and **the Lord will never count [his sin] against him** (Rom. 4:7-8; Psalm 32:1-2). Note the passive grammar in these verses. This happy state comes from *the other side,* not by human engineering. Read the rest of Psalm 32, and you will discover that the only human actions described in securing God's forgiveness and blessing are acknowledging one's sins (v. 5) and exercising faith in God (v. 10). "The LORD's unfailing love surrounds the man who trusts in him" (v. 10).

Abraham, David and the Apostle Paul all discovered that a right standing with God only comes by His gracious act, prompted by a willingness in one's heart to trust Him. Martin Luther rediscovered that powerful truth as well. The opening comments in his own commentary on the book of Romans expressed this truth in powerful words:

"Faith is a living, daring confidence in God's grace, so sure, so certain that a man would stake his life on it a thousand times. This confidence in God's grace and knowledge of it makes men glad, bold and happy in dealing with God and all his creatures."[1]

It was the reading of these comments of Luther that "strangely warmed" the heart of the young John Wesley and brought him to the moment of his assurance of salvation one evening on Aldersgate Street in London. That same sense of abandonment to the mercy and grace of God is still the pivot point "for the salvation of everyone who believes" even today (Rom. 1:16). Augustus Toplady, a Methodist hymn writer and contemporary of John Wesley, expresses this dynamic of grace in wonderful lines:

> Could my tears forever flow
> Could my zeal no languor know
> These for sin could not atone
> Thou must save, and thou alone.
> In my hands no price I bring.
> Simply to thy cross I cling.

2. FAITH RATHER THAN CIRCUMCISION 4:9-15

Having dismissed the logical inconsistency of justification being earned by one's works, Paul then uses the narrative account of Abraham to argue that Abraham's right standing with God had nothing to do with obedience to specific commands (the law). The biblical passage specifically states that God declared Abraham righteous *before* he had fulfilled any of the requirements that Paul's opponents claimed were necessary for salvation (i.e., circumcision).

Like a good college professor, Paul simply inquires, "What does the text say?" And clearly the text reports that God "credited it [Abram's faith] to him as righteousness" (Gen. 15:6) at least fourteen years before the covenant ritual of circumcision was established. The Scriptures simply do not support the argument that circumcision or any compliance to God's moral commands is a prerequisite to obtaining this right standing with God. God did not tell Abraham, "Circumcise yourself, your sons and your servants, and then you will be righteous." He first declared Abraham righteous on the basis of his faith, and *then* symbolized that relationship with a covenant ceremony.

The **sign of circumcision** became **a seal of . . . righteousness** (Rom. 4:11) for Abraham and his descendants. Certainly God expected obedience from Abraham when He instituted this ritual act of the covenant. But, obedience for Abraham and for believers today does not precede and produce God's declaration of forgiveness; it follows as a natural consequence of the trust relationship.

For the Jews to look to Abraham, the patriarch, as the founder and father of the faith was most fitting. Paul does not reject the authority or status of Abraham. But he does redirect the focus of Abraham's stature as "father." In Paul's new understanding, Abraham is the **father of all who believe** (v. 11) whether they be circumcised or not. Abraham's centrality comes by way of his *spiritual* role as one who demonstrated radical faith in God, and not because of his genealogical role as progenitor of the Jewish people or his ceremonial role as initiator of the Jewish rite of circumcision. As a person of faith, Abraham becomes the role model and patriarch of all believers who **walk in the footsteps of . . . faith** (v. 12; cf. 2 Corinthians 5:7).

Having rejected salvation by birthright or ceremonial practices, Paul then eliminates the final prop of the Jewish understanding of justification—adherence to the law. Abraham pre-dated the Old Testament law by centuries. The minute details of the Mosaic Law which fascinated the minds of the scribes and Pharisees meant nothing to him. His relationship with God was defined only by faith—and the gift of grace bestowed by a merciful Father.

Paul returns briefly to his earlier theme that the law was not given to the Jews to give them the privileged status of heirs to Abraham's righteousness. The law only serves to reveal human sinfulness, not to measure human righteousness. Knowledge of God's holy standard leads to guilt and condemnation, not self-confidence and pride.

And where there is no law there is no transgression (Rom. 4:15). One can only wish that Paul had elaborated more on this passing statement. It is quite consistent with his contention that the law was given to reveal our falling short of God's standard of righteousness. But, by reversing the statement to double negatives, we are left wondering what this means. Is Paul suggesting that there are those apart from the law (3:12-18) who are sinless in God's eyes? Hardly, since Paul has already made the case that every person—Jew or Gentile—has access to God's law through the creational revelation of conscience or the special revelation of Scripture.

Rather, it would appear that Paul is hinting at the less obvious benefit that comes with the *awareness* of one's sin, because such awareness points one in the direction of God's grace. Early Christian theologians sometimes referred to the concept of *felix culpa,* a Latin term (taken from an ancient hymn) meaning "blessed sin." The term specifically refers to the transgression of Adam and Eve—tragic in its consequences upon the human race, yet strangely fortunate because it resulted in God's astounding gift of redemption through the gift of His only Son. If Eve and Adam had not sinned, their descendants might never have known the riches of God's grace and the lengths to which He went in order to restore the relationship between humans and himself.

In a similar manner, Paul seems grateful for the divine law, even the rigorous demands of the Old Testament codes given to Moses. Unlike his Jewish antagonists, he does not value the law because it makes him do right or builds his self-confidence when he follows part or even all of it. (See Philippians 3:4-9, where Paul claims to have been "faultless" in keeping the law, yet considers it as worthless "rubbish" in gaining his salvation.)

Paul finds nothing to boast about in this law or one's rigid compliance to all its expectations. The law actually serves a *negative* function for the person who does not live by faith. It repeatedly reveals the moral failures of the sinner and, in doing so, brings condemnation and guilt. In that sense, the law is the bearer of bad news! Later in this letter (Rom. 7) Paul will share his own struggles with sin and the law in gripping words. Most of us have learned with Paul that the law tells us we do not, and cannot, live up to the standard of righteousness that God has established.

No law—no awareness of sin. No awareness of sin—no perceived need for forgiveness. No perceived need for forgiveness—no faith and trust in God. No faith—no salvation and new life. That is why Paul is grateful for the law. Like the Roman slave assigned to take the young master to his school lessons, "so the law was put in charge to lead us to Christ" (Galatians 3:24).

But the law can only take us so far. The law functions very well in revealing our deep spiritual need, but it cannot makes us righteous. Such an awareness of our sinfulness and need for salvation drives the sinner to despair of ever being able to measure up to the high demands of God's righteousness. And that despair, rather than leaving the sinner frustrated and discouraged, opens his heart to trusting in the promise of God.

3. FAITH RATHER THAN UNBELIEF 4:16-25

If the law, God's standard of moral perfection, reveals our sin and leads us to despair, how can we be saved? Paul pivots directly from the wrath of God that brings us condemnation (v. 15) to **the promise [that] comes by faith** (v. 16). Since the law of God results in judgment to all who "fall short of the glory of God" (3:23), the grace of God is extended to all who, like Abraham, "walk in the footsteps of . . . faith" (4:12).

Once again, Paul acknowledges the distinctions that exist between Jew and Gentile, but does not allow those distinctions to be determining factors in entering into a right relationship with God. Faith, and faith alone (the great affirmation of the Protestant Reformation), is the one criterion that makes a person a true descendant of Abraham. And all those who have such faith can claim Abraham as their father.

The issue here is not merely one of ethnic or even religious identity. The children of Abraham are heirs of God's promise. God's covenant with Abraham was to make him more than the father of a nation. God declared, "All peoples on earth will be blessed through you" (Genesis 12:3). To be a son or daughter of Abraham meant not only that one was the recipient of his blessing, but also that one was a channel of that blessing to the world.

Paul's vision for Gentile and Jewish believers was that they would mutually participate in this blessing of the world. Through faith, therefore, Abraham becomes **the father of us all** (Rom. 4:16). Just as Jesus Christ becomes the firstfruits of all believers who have died (fallen asleep) and will rise again (1 Corinthians 15:20-22), Abraham is the firstfruits and father of all who trust in God for deliverance.

Paul characterizes that deliverance which came to Abraham in terms of two supernatural events. **God . . . gives life to the dead and calls things that are not as though they were** (Rom. 4:17). Faith can bring forth life out of death, and reality out of what seems not to be. We must watch as this letter progresses to see how Paul develops these themes out of what here appears to be just a passing observation about the childless condition of Abraham and Sarah. "Calling things that are not as though they were" is the key concept surrounding Paul's understanding of justification.

God can count sinners as righteous in His eyes because of the Cross. Paul's theme of sanctification and the transformed life could well be described by the phrase "giving life to the dead." This newness of life is the direct result of "the power of his resurrection" (Philippians 3:10). Here Paul suggests the two themes that will dominate the next major section of his letter.

The theme of life from death is first developed from the story of Abraham. As the father of many nations, Abraham dared to believe that God had power to bring life from what appeared to be lifeless—the childless relationship between himself and his wife, Sarah. Abraham's *physical* problem is presented as an illustration of the *spiritual* problem that plagues the human race.

This story opens with a hopeless situation. Approaching his hundredth birthday, Abraham had lost his physical strength and virility—

his body was as good as dead (Rom. 4:19). His wife, Sarah, beyond the age of childbearing, was likewise barren. (Interesting that in an era when infertility was always attributed to women, Paul should go beyond Sarah's condition to include Abraham in this hopeless situation. *They were both as good as dead!* No doubt Paul does this in order to remove any suggestion of human instrumentality in the miracle that is to follow.)

The Genesis account Paul is highlighting (15:1-6) tells us that Abraham was fully aware of his problem and raised the issue himself in a conversation with God. Certainly this couple had experienced the normal frustration of being childless in a culture where such a condition carried a social stigma—and often the whispered suspicion that such couples were under a divine curse.

But Abraham's concern went beyond mere social opinion or personal desires for heirs. Underlying the question he posed to God was the matter of the divine promise that had accompanied his earlier call (Gen. 12:1-3). "O Sovereign LORD, what can you give me since I remain childless . . . ?" (15:2). The question itself poses the paradox of faith and doubt. Abraham uses two strong words *(Adonai* and *Yahweh)* to address the almighty Creator. He then proceeds to point out the impossibility of any fulfillment of the divine promise because of Abraham's *human* inability to bring the promise of a great ancestry to reality.

We should pause here to draw out the underlying parallel Paul suggests between Abraham and the believers to whom this letter is written. Like Abraham and Sarah, there is a death-like quality to our lives as well. In another letter, Paul reminds the Ephesians, "You were dead in your transgressions and sins" (Eph. 2:1). To such persons comes the call of God, "Be holy, because I am holy" (1 Peter 1:16). This call is accompanied by a host of promises assuring us that we can, in fact, achieve this right standing with God, that we can come alive to Him.

But, like Abraham, we are all too aware of the problem that exists with such a call and such promises of new life. In taking an honest look at ourselves, we discover that humanly there is no way that this can be accomplished. Not only do we stand under the condemnation of divine law, but we also discover that we, in ourselves, are helpless to correct the situation. This could well be the moment of despair, described earlier (Rom. 4:15) God has asked us to do and be what is impossible! However, this moment of human despair is pivotal in the path to salvation. It shatters any false idea that we, from our side, can remedy the spiritual problem.

This moment of honest assessment is what theologians term

justification. Some individuals refuse to face the fact that they are sinners, and therefore continue living under the condemnation of God's law. As Paul has already discussed, God endeavors to reach these persons by using His revelation in Scripture and in the conscience to bring them to an awareness of sin.

But there are others who, having become aware of their sinfulness, assume they can and must do something themselves to restore their relationship with God. Like Abraham, these individuals must come to the point of honest admission before God that their spiritual batteries are **as good as dead.** Then they will be prepared to hear and respond to God's good news of salvation through grace, apart from their own strivings for righteousness. The good news is God's word of promise that He will remedy the situation.

God's promise in response to Abraham's question was incredible: "A son coming from your own body will be your heir" (Gen. 15:4). Abraham faced the ultimate test. Would he reject the good news from God as absurd? Would he continue his endeavors to arrange for an heir through legal strategies? Or would he accept God's word by faith, even when there was no visible or logical evidence to support it? The Scripture describes his response in direct and simple words: "Abraham believed God, and it was credited to him as righteousness" (Rom. 4:3).

We should note that Abraham had *already* heeded God's call and moved from a pagan culture to the land to which God had directed him (Gen. 12). He had already built an altar and "*called on the name of the* Lord" (13:4, italics mine). Worship of God was a part of Abraham's life long before this dramatic step of faith. These were all things that demonstrated Abraham's serious desire to follow God. Throughout his life, Abraham would respond in obedience to God's commands. Not only would he observe the ritual of circumcision, but he would even offer up his son, Isaac, as a sacrifice in obedience to God's demands. But it is at the point when Abraham believed God would bring to pass what was humanly impossible in and through Abraham that the moment of righteousness was defined.

We, too, can take appropriate actions to further our spiritual pilgrimage. We can walk away from sinful lifestyles and become more spiritually minded by engaging in daily devotions, attending church, and praying. Numerous acts of obedience are consistent with a Christian life—baptism, discipleship, even radical actions in response to the inner call of God. But, our right relationship with God is determined in the moment He promises to do the miraculous and bring our dead souls to life. In that moment, we must, like Abraham, respond in faith if we are to have righteousness credited to us.

Abraham's moment of faith did not come as a result of his own brilliant reasoning. He did not suddenly figure it all out. If you follow the story further, you will see how Abraham incorrectly assumed that God would only do half a miracle, using Abraham's seed and another woman, Hagar, to produce an heir. When God finally set him straight and revealed that Sarah herself, although ninety years old, would bear a son, Abraham took God at His word, **being fully persuaded that God had power to do what he had promised** (v. 21).

Such faith in the promise of God was not a work—a human effort—on the part of Abraham. But neither was this faith a supernatural gift of God. There are those, as we have suggested earlier, who are so eager to protect God's sovereign power to save that they make even the act of belief a divine gift from God. Certainly God is not oblivious of how the repentant sinner struggles to grasp by faith that a right standing with Him comes as a miracle of grace, rather than as a reward for human effort. Perhaps this is why Paul includes the phrase **was strengthened in his faith** (v. 20) in the middle of a passage that commends Abraham for believing **against all hope** (v. 18).

Here is yet another suggestion of the Wesleyan concept of prevenient grace. God is at work in our lives to draw us to himself even before the moment of justification. He draws us to himself (John 6:44), He reveals to us our sinful condition, He brings us to the point of spiritual despair, and He strengthens our faith even while we are reaching out toward the impossible news of forgiveness. All that is grace! Our role is simply to *believe* the promise that what is dead can become alive, and what is not a reality can become a reality. Recognizing our simple response of faith, God declares us to be righteous in His eyes.

Paul concludes chapter 4 by making explicit what he has been suggesting through the example of Abraham. The words **it was credited to him as righteousness** (v. 22) extend far beyond Father Abraham to all those who believe—to the Roman believers in the first century and to believers today. In a final hint of the discussion to come in chapter 5, Paul brings in another reference of death changed to life—the resurrection of Christ (v. 24). Abraham's challenge was to believe God's promise that good-as-dead bodies could produce life.

Our challenge is twofold: First, we must believe that our good-as-dead spirits can come alive. Second, we must believe that this miracle is possible because God raised Jesus Christ, His Son, from death to life.

Here Paul indicates by a passing reference that the Cross has a crucial part to play in our salvation, without spelling out the details of God's plan of redemption. Jesus **was delivered over to death for our sins and was raised to life for our justification** (v. 25). Paul views the Cross as the putting to death of our old sinful nature, and the Resurrection as the source of our newness of life—themes that will recur throughout the remainder of his letter to the Romans.

Without detailed explanations of how all this is accomplished, Paul concludes this section of the letter having demonstrated that *a right standing with God comes through faith in Christ alone,* apart from ancestry, rituals, rules and regulations, or any other effort on the part of human beings. Here is the great truth of Paul, Luther, Wesley and all those who take the book of Romans seriously—*sola fide!* Salvation comes by faith alone.

ENDNOTE

[1]Martin Luther, *Luther's Works,* vol. 7, (Philadelphia: Muhlenberg press, 1932), p. 452.

Part Three

RIGHTEOUSNESS RESTORED:
The Gift of Grace

Romans 5:1–7:25

The technological orientation of Western culture has produced a certain passion for mechanics in our thinking. Often, the first question that comes to mind when we see a new gadget is, "How does it work?" British Romantic poet, William Wordsworth, scolded our scientific temptation to kill the thing of beauty before admiring it, simply to satisfy our curiosity for how it is put together. "We murder to dissect," he laments.

Having carefully developed his case for salvation by faith alone, Paul ends chapter 4 by declaring that the death and resurrection of Christ bring us into a right relationship with God. Our natural response is, "Tell us how it works, Paul. Explain the 'how' of salvation to us."

Not so fast! First, Paul wants us to pause and celebrate the blessings and benefits of this new relationship with God. In Romans 1, he used tough words like "distress," "wrath," "condemnation" and "judgment" to describe God's attitude toward those who practice wickedness. Paul then enlarged the scope of those who are at enmity with God to include not only the wicked Gentiles, but Jews who do not keep *all* the law, and all those who presume to justify themselves by anything other than faith.

Having described in detail this enmity that exists between God and unbelievers, Paul acknowledged that there are individuals who enjoy a right relationship with God because God has declared (credited) them as righteous. But again, Paul widens the circle of those who fall in this category to include all—Gentiles and Jews—who manifest faith in God's promise like Abraham did long ago.

In this section of his letter, Paul describes the contrast between the unrighteous and righteous in the strongest terms possible. In place of wrath, he speaks of love; in place of condemnation, he speaks of reconciliation; in place judgment, salvation; and in place of enmity, peace. Although he frequently refers to the death and resurrection of Christ, Paul does not offer elaborate explanations of how these events and the believer's trust in God bring about this new relationship. But no one speaks more eloquently than Paul to the Romans about the benefits of new life in Christ.

We, too, must learn to relish the joys of our salvation. There is certainly nothing wrong with our attempts to explain the "why" of the Cross or how God's sacrifice atones for sin. But at times we need to echo the hymn of Charles Wesley:

I need no other argument,
I need no other plea,
It is enough that Jesus died
And that he died for me.

In 5:1-7:25, Paul asks us to set aside our theories and arguments and celebrate the joys of a right relationship with God.

6

THE BLESSING:
Reconciliation With God

Romans 5:1-21

Forgiven! No word in the New Testament captures the heart of the good news as much as this word, which Jesus used frequently in His earthly ministry. Yes, He spoke words of truth, demonstrated a life of love, healed the sick, even raised the dead. But, He came closest to His true identity and purpose for coming into our world when He said, "Your sins are forgiven" to a paralyzed man (Mark 2:5), to a sinful woman (Luke 7:48), and to soldiers about to put Him to death (Luke 23:34). One of the Master's boldest statements was his claim "that the Son of Man has authority on earth to forgive sins" (Luke 5:24).

Like those who had heard Jesus speak the words directly to them, the Apostle Paul grasped the significance of being reconciled to God through the authority of His Son. In this fifth chapter of Romans, Paul develops three facets of that great truth. First, he spells out a new perspective on the life that comes to one who has been justified by faith. Not only does the believer experience an inner peace and joy; there can even be hope in the face of difficult situations.

Second, Paul describes a new relationship between the believer and God. God has reconciled the sinner to himself through the death of His Son. His wrath has been overcome by an even stronger love that reaches out to us while we are still undeserving of any favor. Here is forgiveness that results from nothing else except God's great mercy and our feeble faith!

Finally, Paul describes a new identity for those who experience the forgiving power of this one man, Jesus Christ. For all the abilities and potential that human beings possess, they remain less than righteous by their birthright from Adam. A right standing with God comes only as a "gift of righteousness" (Rom. 5:17)—a gift that brings eternal life. The words still echo centuries later: "Take heart, son [or daughter]; your sins are forgiven" (Matthew 9:2).

1. A NEW PERSPECTIVE 5:1-5

Using **therefore** to signal a new theme, Paul begins with a bold assertion concerning the believer's relationship with God: **Since we have been justified through faith, we have peace with God through our Lord Jesus Christ** (v. 1). Elsewhere he uses rhetorical questions to introduce new ideas (6:1; 11:1). But here he speaks with confidence. In making this assertion, Paul appears to assume several things. First, he assumes that he has silenced all critics concerning the nature of justification—it is by faith. Paul will not return again in the book of Romans to debate this issue.

Second, Paul assumes that his readers have in fact responded in faith to the good news. There is no appeal to his readers to believe on the Lord Jesus Christ and be saved (Acts 16:31). Paul has indicated that the faith of the Romans is a matter of general knowledge and praise (Rom. 1:8). While his earlier comments might suggest that there were Jewish elements within the church at Rome who sought to obscure the truth of the gospel, he still assumes that the audience he writes to is a body of faithful believers.

We, too, would do well to assume the best in those who identify themselves with Christ. Without citing all the exceptions and disclaimers, Paul views the church in Rome as those who have trusted in God for their salvation.

Finally, Paul assumes that the benefits of a right relationship with God are direct and immediate. **We have peace with God . . . we have gained access . . . we now stand** (vv. 1-2). Just as faith is the pivotal moment that leads to a right standing with God, this moment of right standing is the point at which all the benefits of God's grace are made accessible to the believer. God does not measure out His peace and grace in small doses as He sees us take positive steps to follow Him. He offers us a new relationship and a new nature simply on the basis of our faith in Him.

Elsewhere Paul can declare, "If anyone is in Christ, he is a new creation; the old has gone, the new has come!" (2 Corinthians 5:17). Paul is certainly aware that old patterns of unrighteous behavior do persist after this moment of belief. And he will have plenty to say about moving forward in one's walk with God toward a transformed life (Rom. 12). But for all the loose ends of one's conduct and attitude that accompany the believer, Paul never minimizes the significant change that accompanies God's declaration of righteousness. At the moment of our justification, there are profound consequences for our lives. What consequences of the new birth does Paul identify?

a. We have **access . . . into this grace** (Rom. 5:2). We have already pointed out that God's grace is active in the life of *every* individual—both Jew and Gentile, believer and unbeliever alike. Faith is not some human act that turns on the switches of divine grace. Instead, the divine act of grace calls a person to faith; grace makes hope against hope possible in one's life. But now, as a new creation, faith is more than an operating principle in one's life; it is the *defining* principle. The believer is both surrounded and sustained by the loving kindness of the Father. This new relationship with God opens doors of possibilities in one's life that would have been impossible apart from faith.

The Greek word for access *(prosagogen)* has two different meanings which are both appropriate to this context. First, it refers to a formal introduction, when one is ushered into the presence of others, especially those of high position. In this context, then, faith provides us with an entrance into the presence of the Heavenly Father himself. Our minds should turn instinctively to the passage in Hebrews where we are told to "approach the throne of grace with confidence, so that we may receive mercy and find grace to help us in our time of need" (Heb. 4:16).

Second, the same Greek word is often used to describe the entrance to a port or sheltered harbor. Today, few of us can appreciate the terror of the open seas, especially during severe storms like those on the Mediterranean Sea. Finding access to quiet waters and a haven of safety is a powerful image for those whose lives have been stressed by the foolishness of their own moral flounderings. The moment of self-surrender and reliance upon God for salvation is a moment of settled peace. Christ becomes, in reality, "a shelter in the time of storm."

b. We have a place **in which we now stand** (Rom. 5:2). Access to grace, whether by way of introduction to the Father or finding refuge from the storm, brings the believer a position of security, a place to stand. One of the great blessings of our life in Christ is a sense of stability. When we gain access, by faith, to God's grace, our position in Him becomes secure. We can define who we are by reference to His changeless nature and His unfailing commitment to love us to the end (John 13:1).

After his dramatic conversion, Martin Luther often felt plagued by doubts and assaults on his spiritual life. One of the ways he overcame these episodes of spiritual discouragement was to find a secluded place and there verbally address the Devil and the forces of evil with these words: "Satan, leave me. I am baptized!" Whatever your view of the sacraments, you can still sense the power and significance of what Luther was saying.

If we, like Luther, listens to all the voices of doubt that assault us, we will find ourselves standing on shaky ground. Critics will always appear to point out our spiritual flaws and question whether we really are the Christians we claim to be. Even more threatening may be our own self-doubts and questions. At times, we may be surprised and ashamed at things we do or don't do while walking with Christ. We should never minimize the subtle work of the Evil One who finds great delight in raising questions and fears about our relationship with God, even as he did with Eve and Adam from the beginning.

In moments of doubt, we need to remind ourselves of where we stand. By faith we have trusted God for our salvation, and He has credited our faith as righteousness. As we continue to trust Him, we can shift our focus away from our sometimes less-than-perfect performance levels to be reminded that salvation is *His* work, not ours. We stand in His grace.

Of course, this concept of one's position in grace can be abused. Some people place so much stress on the *position* or status we attain through God's act of justification, that day-to-day behavior becomes almost irrelevant to the relationship with God. They make God's declaration of pardon so absolute that it is impossible for one to ever leave the presence of the Father or leave the harbor of safety to enter the storm-tossed seas of sin again.

We must note, therefore, that this standing in God's grace is closely linked with the fact that we gain this access **by faith** (v. 2). In the *life* of faith, we retain this access and this standing. Luther returned to his baptism in moments of temptation, not because that ritual guaranteed his salvation, but because underlying baptism is the bold "I believe . . ." of the Apostles' Creed. The believer's ongoing faith "in God Almighty . . . and in Jesus Christ, His Son . . . and in the forgiveness of sins" gives access to divine grace and security for the believer.

c. We have peace with God through our Lord Jesus Christ (Rom. 5:1). Although listed third in this study, the first and primary benefit of justification for Paul is peace with God—the restored relationship with our Heavenly Father. In the context of this letter to the Romans, peace has much more to do with relational dynamics than with inner tranquillity. One could certainly argue that coming into a right standing with God will do much to develop an inner calmness so that one is better able to cope with the stresses of life. But here, Paul is speaking about the cessation of hostilities between adversaries—the rebellious sinner and a God who expresses His wrathful disposition toward ungodliness and wickedness (1:18).

When a sinner turns to God in faith, trusting in divine grace rather than human efforts, God credits righteousness to that sinner and the relationship is restored. Reconciliation and access into God's grace replace the former condemnation and judgment against those who deserve death. The sinner turns away from the foolish patterns of self-worship described in chapter 1, and accepts the gracious promises of the Father. More importantly, the Father sees this new believer no longer as a sinner, but rather as a righteous person. More than that, He welcomes that person as a parent welcomes a child returning home (Luke 15). All this brings peace with God!

d. We rejoice in the hope of the glory of God (Rom. 5:2). Although the peace of 5:1 pertains more to relational dynamics than emotional states, Paul does not exclude personal feelings from the benefits derived from a right standing with God. The primary response of the human soul is not unruffled calmness, but rather overflowing joy. Having entered into this new relationship of peace with God, believers can fully expect that God will direct their paths (Proverbs 3:5-6) and that He will not withhold good from their lives (Psalm 84:11).

Certainly the awareness of sins forgiven elicits joy, but Paul suggests that the believer's perspective is shaped as much by *hope* for the future as it is by past or present circumstances. Like Father Abraham, Paul takes God's promises concerning the future for fact. His confidence is "that he who began a good work in you will carry it on to completion until the day of Christ Jesus" (Philippians 1:6).

Christians often make a distinction between happiness and joy. Happiness, they point out, is an emotional state largely affected by the circumstances of the moment. Joy, on the other hand, is a more deep-seated mind-set based upon one's relationship (standing) with God and one's long-range vision of final outcomes. Even if Webster's dictionary does not support such distinctions, the idea is very biblical and very Pauline. Joy characterizes the attitude of believers because they share an overriding **hope of the glory of God** (Rom. 5:2).

Glory, a common term in the Christian's vocabulary, is easy to use, but difficult to define. The Greek word for glory *(doxa)* comes over to English in our word *doxology,* a hymn of adoration and praise to God. A doxology focuses upon who God is in His very nature, more than what He does in his powerful actions. Glory describes the splendor and brilliance of the character of God.

In the Old Testament, it was manifested by a visible radiance, a glow that filled the Jewish Tabernacle (Exodus 40:34) and Temple (1 Kings 8:11). Moses encountered this glory on Mount Sinai and had to hide his face because the reflected glory of God was blinding to the eyes of the children of Israel (Exod. 34:29-35). The prophet Isaiah spoke of a time to come when "the glory of the LORD will be revealed" and will fill all the earth (Isa. 40:5). In one of his letters to the Christians in Corinth, Paul draws from the story of Moses to speak of the glory of Christ that is unfading and that draws us into the future with joy: "And we, who with unveiled faces all reflect the Lord's glory, are being transformed into his likeness with ever-increasing glory" (2 Cor. 3:18).

Paul indicates that the glorious Kingdom to come has already broken into the realm of time and space through the coming of Jesus Christ. Believers not only experience a new *relationship* because of God's act of grace; they also participate in a new *reality*—the in-breaking of God's glory in the everyday world of Rome, Jerusalem . . . and Los Angeles!

But it is not an easy thing to speak of hope or the coming Kingdom to the saints in Rome! For the Romans, rejoicing in the glory to come was tempered with the hard reality of their present suffering. Paul does not indicate here whether the suffering was in the form of persecution, economic hardship, or physical affliction. No doubt it could apply to any or all of these situations. The Greek word Paul uses for suffering is *thlipsis,* most often translated in the King James Version by the word "tribulation." In ordinary conversation, it simply referred to pressure or stress. But, by the time of Paul, the Christian community had associated the word with the hostile opposition of Satan and the fallen world.

In Jesus' teaching to the disciples regarding the end of this age, He described periods of tribulation and suffering. He closed His earthly ministry by reminding the disciples, "In this world you will have trouble *[thlipsis].* But take heart! I have overcome the world" (John 16:33). The New Testament believers shared a strong expectation that the old age was passing away and the new Kingdom was fast approaching. This anticipation of the end coupled with the first indications of opposition from the Roman government would cause Paul and the believers in Rome to associate the stresses of their lives with end-time sufferings.

Paul's astounding attitude toward the difficulties being encountered by his readers is to list them in the column of things in which we rejoice: **We also rejoice in our sufferings** (Rom. 5:3). Most of us would put our sufferings in a column of spiritual "downers" that should be overcome by rejoicing in hope. But, having entered into right standing with a promise-keeping God, Paul dares to believe that even the stresses of life can be used by God to bring about His glory.

How different this attitude is from the "health and wealth" gospel of our present age, which claims success, happiness and ease for those who have "real" faith in God. Paul would categorically reject such simplistic understandings of the Christian life. One does not have to escape the stresses of life to experience true joy. The person of faith can discover joy because he or she stands in a right relationship with the Creator and has a long-range view of the circumstances of life.

Paul even suggests how this rejoicing in suffering might be accomplished by tracing the sequence of effects that leads from hardship to hope. He proposes that, for the person who has experienced access to grace (v. 2), **suffering produces perseverance** (v. 3). The sufferings have potential for something meaningful rather than just putting us through the wringer of life.

In his commentary on Romans, William Barclay points out that perseverance is something much stronger than patient endurance. It is not simply putting up with rough times until things get better. Instead, it is an attitude of confident persistence that sees the potential of positive outcomes, even when circumstances suggest otherwise. In a sense, it is the hope "against all hope" (4:18) which Abraham demonstrated in the stresses of his personal life.

This persevering resolve in one's heart forms **character** (5:4). The believer uses these difficult situations to build and refine the virtues of the Christian life. I recall once reading these words on a church bulletin board: "In most of our prayers, we ask God to change our circumstances, not our character." Paul proposes that God's design for glory in our life has more to do with developing character than altering circumstances just to make things easier for the believer. This character development by enduring suffering produces a mind-set of **hope** (vv. 4-5)—not just wishful thinking about the future, but a growing confidence that grace is accomplishing the divine purpose in the believer's life.

If hope were nothing but wishing for a better tomorrow, one might be easily disappointed. But the Christian's hope **does not disappoint us,** because it is founded in the confident faith that in tough situations **God**

has poured out his love into our hearts by the Holy Spirit, whom he has given us (v. 5). Only a person of faith can survey the sufferings of life and see God's love being poured out in such stressful circumstances. One can soar from suffering to the love of God, as long as that person sees with eyes of faith and hope.

In this lyrical passage, Paul has traced out for us the benefits that result from God's sovereign act of justification. God's poured-out love has provided for us access to grace, a right standing with God, reconciliation and peace with God. That is reason enough to **rejoice in the hope of the glory of God!**

2. A NEW RELATIONSHIP 5:6-11

We have noted that Paul moved from a discussion of faith in Christ at the close of the previous chapter to a description of the benefits of justification without addressing how His death and resurrection make this right standing with God possible. Now Paul begins to interweave his understanding of the person and work of Christ (theologians call this Christology) with his continued description of what new life in Christ entails for the believer. Paul's reference, in verse 5, to the love of God poured out into our hearts gives him reason to pause and connect God's love directly with the death of Jesus Christ, His Son.

At the outset of this section, Paul identifies three striking aspects of God's love in Christ—the timing, the action, and the recipients. It might be easier to look at them in the reverse order.

First, **Christ died for the ungodly** (v. 6). Here Paul uses the same term (**ungodly**) he used earlier to describe those against whom the divine wrath is being revealed (1:18). One might expect God's love to be poured out on the Jews, the chosen people. One might even allow that God's love extends to the Gentiles who struggle to obey God by the dim light of conscience. But it is astounding to remember that the primary concern of God's love is *sinners,* those who "worshiped and served created things rather than the Creator," those who "committed indecent acts," those who were "filled with every kind of wickedness" (1:25, 27, 29).

Yet these sinners are the ones to whom God reaches out. When the Pharisees, who prided themselves in their own righteousness, criticized Jesus for the disreputable company He was keeping, Jesus offered His own mission statement: "I have not come to call the righteous, but sinners" (Mark 2:17).

Secondly, the action that demonstrates God's attitude of love is *purposeful* death—twice in this paragraph Paul indicates Christ died *for us*. This is more than dying because of us, even though it is clear that "He was despised and rejected by men" (Isaiah 53:3). This is more than dying with us, although in His incarnation He made himself one with the human race. The mystery of grace is that God's only Son died for us and for our sins.

What does dying for us mean? It suggests that we as sinners were doomed to death, and that in some way His act of death gives us life. But Paul does not specify in this passage the nature of our death sentence or how Christ's death brought life. Most scholars assume that since Paul is using legal terms like condemnation, judgment and justification, the situation described here is a spiritual "death row." Because of their offenses against the law of God, human beings stand under the sentence of death.

In some way, Christ comes to the eternal tribunal and takes our place, gaining pardon and release for us at the expense of His own life. In classical theology this is known as the substitution theory of the Atonement. In its simplest form, learned by most of us as children in Sunday school, it proclaims, "Jesus died in my place."

But there might be other reasons for giving up one's life for another. Imagine a situation of great danger, such as a fire or a flood where human lives are at risk. A hero comes on the scene, willing to sacrifice his life so that others might live. This situation does not so much characterize substitution as a powerful demonstration of self-sacrifice for a greater good. The motif would be more one of rescue than of substitutionary death.

In this passage, Paul speaks of a rare occasion when a person might be willing to sacrifice his life for a righteous or a good man. Criminals under sentence of death hardly fit this category. One might therefore argue that Paul views Christ's death as a sacrificial offering—a profound expression of generosity on God's part—rather than the substitutionary death of classical Protestantism.

Yet one might still argue that Paul views Christ's death in the legal terms of criminal law. After all, he stresses the point that it is **ungodly** sinners for whom Christ died. And he has indicated in no uncertain terms that the wicked are subject to God's anger and wrath (Rom. 2:8). This passage, then, does not resolve the ongoing discussion of *why* Christ had to die and *how* His death brings life. Paul is content to say that Christ did die on our behalf, and to give His life for sinners is the most powerful demonstration of God's love that exists.

Thirdly, the timing. We note first that it was **at just the right time** (v. 6). The Greeks had two separate words for time. One was *chronos,* which referred to quantitative or clock time. The other word, used here, was *kairos,* which referred to qualitative time. It is the distinction we make between having a good time *(kairos)* at the party, and running a good time *(chronos)* in a race at a track meet. Paul is not interested in what month or year Christ died; he is struck with the qualitative nature of this event— that it came at the best possible moment in the sovereignty of God's plan. (Paul will use the same word, *kairos,* in Galatians 4:4-5 when he declares, "When the time had fully come, God sent his Son, born of a woman, born under law, to redeem those under law.")

We would do well to remember that God's timing is based more on *kairos* than *chronos.* As humans, we stare at our watches, mark our calendars, and wonder why God is not meeting our schedules. More often than not, He is waiting for **just the right time**—a time that we would least expect.

That is the point Paul is making to the Romans. In terms of their salvation, God's timing seems strange. Christ does not arrive on the scene and offer His life after we have demonstrated our righteous character. He does not even die for us when He hears our cries for help. God's saving work takes place **when we were still powerless** (Rom. 5:6). Christ died for us **while we were still sinners** (v. 8). Again Paul strips away any idea that salvation is a reward or even a divine response to some action on our part. God always takes the first step in any aspect of salvation. We are the ones called to respond to what He has already accomplished for us.

And notice finally that Paul uses two different tenses in verse 8: **God *demonstrates* his own love . . . while we *were* still sinners** (italics mine). Is this a grammatical error? No. Christ's *act* of dying on our behalf is past tense, already accomplished once and for all on Calvary. But God's *demonstration* of His love is always present tense. This love remains; it never fails (1 Corinthians 13:8). God continues to pour out His love in our hearts, extending the work of the Cross into the present and future of our lives.

Having looked at the action, recipients and timing of God's love, Paul brings us back once more to its benefits. He echoes the opening words of Romans 5 in verse 9 of that chapter: **Since we have now been justified.** But now the focus is on Christ's work (**by his blood** [v. 9]), and not the human response ("through faith") of verse 1. The benefits are described in terms of their greatness. Twice in this paragraph, Paul uses the phrase **how much more** (vv. 9-10) to describe the powerful effects of the Cross. In doing so, he is setting the stage for his comparison of Adam and Christ in the last half of the chapter.

It is one thing for an all-powerful deity to declare a truce, ending hostility that exists between a righteous God and wicked persons. But when the peace is bought at the price of blood, **how much more** can we be certain that there is no residual anger, no possibility that the peace will be broken on His part. And if our reconciliation comes through the death of God's Son, **how much more** is God committed to accomplishing His purposes for our lives.

And what is the appropriate response to this heightened awareness that the right relationship comes **by his blood** as well as by our faith? **We . . . rejoice in God through our Lord Jesus Christ** (v. 11). Like the composer of a great symphony, Paul has woven the themes of peace, hope and joy throughout this passage, reminding us of the great benefits of being reconciled to God.

3. A NEW IDENTITY 5:12-21

As a teacher, one of my favorite test questions is to ask students to compare and contrast two different things. Comparison suggests that there are similarities that tie the two elements together; contrasts indicate that there are significant differences that must be noted as well. As a Jew, Paul was very familiar with the Creation account of Genesis and the significance of the first parents, both as prototypes of the human race and as key players in the moral breakdown of the human race—what we commonly refer to as "the Fall."

After his encounter on the Damascus road, Paul was convinced that Jesus was far more than a political Messiah or a new teacher of the law. As the incarnate Son of God, Jesus stands as a second prototype for the human race.

In other places, Paul will even refer to Christ as the "Last Adam" (1 Cor. 15:45). Here in Romans, Paul is not so much interested in comparing the nature of these two prototypes as he is in describing the results of their acts—Adam's act of disobedience and Christ's act of reconciliation.

Paul's logic is complex and almost confusing in this passage. The difficulty comes as he endeavors to draw out similarities (compare), while at the same time pointing out the superiority of the work of Christ over the "work" of Adam (contrast). Rather than addressing each of the juxtapositions Paul gives in these verses, we will look at the passage as a whole.

One might question why Eve receives no mention in this passage, since she was in fact the first to disobey, and subsequently persuaded her husband to sin. Paul is not ignorant of Eve's role in the Genesis account, and in other passages he makes specific references to her actions as well. Here, for the sake of the comparison he wants to make, Paul limits his attention to the male figures of Adam and Christ. We should recall that the Hebrew word *Adam* is the generic word for "human." All the references to Adam and men in this passage, therefore, have a generic meaning that embraces females as well as males.

Christian scholars have thought and written much concerning the account of the Creation and Fall in Genesis 1 through 3. These chapters clearly indicate that God created a good world, and that the crowning event of that process, however long it might have lasted, was the human species, Adam and Eve. The creation of humans was unique: they were fashioned in a special manner, they had intimate fellowship with God, and they received specific instructions concerning their role and responsibility in the created order. And when God was finished with this creation, He noted that "it was very good" (Gen. 1:31).

But something went awry. Enticed by the serpent, Eve and Adam disobeyed the specific command of God and **sin entered the world through one man** (Rom. 5:12). No one who accepts the authority of Scripture denies that this is the first occasion for sin. The debate centers on what effects Adam's action had upon his descendants.

From the earliest days of Christianity, a small minority of scholars have proposed that every person who is born enters the world like Adam and Eve—innocent and having at least the potential to do what is right. The overwhelming majority of Christians understand the Scriptures to teach that Adam's act had a devastating effect, not only upon the created order, but also upon the moral condition of every human being. These persons join Paul in contending that the fall of Adam has produced a fallen race, and that, from birth, human beings suffer from the detrimental consequences of Adam's act. Looking at this passage, we can discover the tragedy of the Fall for our lives.

a. Sin entered the world (v. 12). Quite apart from any negative effects that later developed, the very act of disobedience by our first parents disrupted the harmony and perfection God had designed for His creation. Eve and Adam had broken the trust relationship that had existed between God and them. Their moral perfection (holiness) was gone; the possibility for transparent (naked) fellowship with God and each other turned to concealment and shame. God's love for His creation would not end, but He would have to deal with disobedient creatures from a different frame of reference now.

b. The many were made sinners (v. 19). In fact, **all sinned** (v. 12). Having broken faith with God, Adam became, in a detrimental sense, the father of us all as well. Some Christians consider the link to Adam to be genetic in nature; the very biological nature of Adam and Eve was affected by the Fall and that defect was passed on to succeeding generations by human reproduction. However, such a view suggests that sin is a physical entity rather than something moral and spiritual. Furthermore, with the advances in genetic engineering, a view of sin that is based on chromosonal characteristics is certainly problematic.

Others suggest that this sin coming from Adam (often called "original sin") results from the changes in social environment brought on by sin. Since Adam, Eve, and all their descendants now live in a less-than-perfect state, the interpersonal dynamics are stacked against goodness and love. Sin, in this view, is not so much a genetic trait as a natural consequence of living in a world of self-interested persons. The weakness of this view is that sin is understood as little more than ignornace or social mal-adjustment. If unrighteousness can be explained that simply, one would expect the moral problems of our society to fade away with social planning and government spending.

A third way to understand the manifestation of sin in the world is to acknowledge that Adam (and Eve's) disobedience led to a broken relationship between the Creator and his creation. In this interpretation, Adam stood as representative of all humanity before God and in his fall, so we all are fallen as well. Whatever the explanation, both Scripture and routine observation lead us to the conclusion that "there is no one who does good, not even one" (Psalm 14:3; Rom. 3:10). Whereas Adam and Eve lived with the possibility of not sinning, humans now enter the world with an inevitable destiny of breaking God's law. We find it impossible not to sin.

c. Judgment followed one sin and brought condemnation (v. 16). Genesis 3 reports the confrontation between God and our first parents after the Fall. Could God have ignored their disobedience? After all, it was the first time, and it was only fruit from one tree. No, God's standard of holiness and righteousness required that the offense be condemned and punished. And it is clear that the judgment administered was more than personal; the changes imposed on Eve (pain in childbirth, submission to her husband) and Adam (toilsome work, decomposition to dust) are features of human existence to this day. There are wages to be paid because of sin, both in Adam's life and in our own, and Paul identifies the nature of those wages as death (Rom. 6:23).

d. Death came to all men (v. 12). Paul never clearly specifies whether this death is physical or spiritual, but it certainly entails both. One of the weapons of the Evil One, which is described elsewhere by Paul as the "last enemy" (1 Corinthains 15:26) is physical death. But Paul carries the motif of death into the spiritual realm as well, describing sinners as those who are "dead in trespasses and sins" (Ephesians 2:1 KJV) and believers as those who "have been raised with Christ" (Colossians 3:1).

This is a sobering description of the human race. Despite all the complexities of human anatomy, the marvels of the human mind or the intricacies of human emotions, the moral plight of the children of Adam and Eve is depressing. Not that God had totally written off the human race because of sin. Paul does acknowledge that the law of Moses was given to heighten the awareness of sin. But Paul makes it clear that God's law—whether manifested in commandments or conscience—does not *create* sin; it only exposes it to the mind and heart of the sinner. Paul seems to hint here that those with limited or no access to the law might be held less accountable, but he emphasizes a point made earlier: "All have sinned and fall short of the glory of God" (3:23).

But in the world, corrupted by godless and wicked actions of sinners, God has done a new thing, "at just the right time" (5:6). A new Son of Man has appeared, and by His actions He has countered the effects of the first man's disobedience. And Paul thinks that it is important to compare and contrast the work of these two. The most obvious similarity is that both these persons, Christ and Adam, have had a monumental effect upon the spiritual condition of the human race. Both men also have an integrity to their own person; they are both, in the words of the Creed, "very man of very man."

But, beyond that, there are striking dissimilarities. Whereas the effects of Adam's action have been detrimental to the spiritual well-being of humans, the actions of the new Man, Jesus Christ, offer profound blessings to those who are of faith. Not only do these two men differ in the consequences of their actions, the Second Adam is greater than the first, and His work is more powerful than the ravages of sin. Paul resorts again to the phrase **how much more** (vv. 15-17) to describe the work of Christ.

In alternating phrases and somewhat disjointed themes, Paul presents this striking comparison to stress the miracle of God's love toward us and the joy it produces in the believer's life. We will now trace the work of this new Man as it remedies the consequences of Adam's fall.

First, **Christ died for us** (Rom. 5:8). Although these words never appear in the text we are now examining, they are the foundation for all Paul is saying. The act of Christ was one of obedience (v. 19). In the Garden, the Master set aside His own preferences and His natural desire for life, and prayed, "Yet not what I will, but what you will" (Mark 14:36). In His final hours, Jesus was very aware of the significance of His obedience to the Father's plan. And in Paul's great hymn of praise to Christ in Philippians 2, he points out that Christ Jesus "became obedient to death—even death on a cross!" (v. 8). Contrast that with Adam, who had every natural reason to follow the command of God, but chose to be disobedient, to his and everyone else's harm!

Second, **grace . . . [did] overflow to the many** (Rom. 5:15), and **the many will be made righteous** (v. 19). Like Adam, the action of one man has an effect upon others. But, unlike Adam, whose action brought sin to *all* persons, the act of obedience by Christ extends grace to *many*. There is a clear distinction between the original sin that affects all persons, and the grace of Christ which is available to all, but is realized only in those who live by faith.

Paul clearly uses universal terms to speak of the total effect of the Fall; but one cannot make Paul a universalist—that is, a person who believes God's grace ultimately will redeem all persons, so that none will experience the wrath of His judgment. Certainly the grace made available in the Cross is sufficient to forgive all sins . . . all the sins of each sinner, and the sins of all sinners who will respond in faith. Paul would utter a hearty amen to the gospel song "Where Sin Aboundeth, Grace Aboundeth More." The grace of God is not limited by any power of the Evil One, nor is it restricted by the sovereign decrees of God; it is only limited by the refusal of some to receive what is freely offered in Christ.

Third, **the gift . . . brought justification** (Rom. 5:16). Again, Paul does not delve into *how* Christ's death reconciles us to God and puts us in a right standing with the Father. But he believes it and proclaims it with all his being. Because of Adam's sin, a penalty (wages) is upon the human race. Notice the contrast with Christ's act of love—it is a gift of the grace of God! Penalties or charges can be *imposed* upon others; a gift can be only offered and received. God's gift of love is justification with all its benefits. But it can be only *offered*; faith, as Paul understands it, is the sinner reaching out to *receive* the gift.

Fourth, **those who receive God's abundant provision of grace and of the gift of righteousness reign in life** (Rom. 5:17). Again, as with death, Paul does not make sharp distinctions between physical and spiritual aspects. Certainly he is referring to **eternal life through Jesus Christ our Lord** (v. 21). But the sharp distinction between this world and the world to come is blurred for the believer. The glories of the age to come have broken in already upon our present existence.

Jesus said, "I have come that they may have life, and have it to the full" (John 10:10). Paul sees the benefits of justification countering and even surpassing the curse of the Fall: reconciliation, peace with God, hope, joy and life . . . all these through faith in him "who loved [us] and gave himself for [us]" (Galatians 2:20). Thanks be to God!

7

THE RESULT:
New Life in Christ

Romans 6:1-23

For all of his commitment to the gospel, Paul shows considerable reserve in laying out his case for Christianity. He begins his letter with several chapters on the sinful condition of humanity and the failure of the law to bring about a right standing with God. At the close of the third chapter, he announces a new righteousness that comes through faith in Christ; but he shifts his attention to a discussion of faith as the only way to be reconciled with God. Finally, in Romans 5, he shifts the spotlight to the key player of the drama, Jesus Christ, God's gift of grace. This "New Adam" has brought us back to God by His act of obedience on the cross.

But does it really make a difference in one's life to believe this good news? Or is Paul simply speaking of historical events that happened in a faraway land decades (for us, centuries) ago? What does the death and resurrection of this Jesus mean for the believer? For Paul, the saving acts of Christ are far more than stories to inspire us or even heroic actions for us to emulate. The work of Christ results in a change of one's very nature for those who believe in who He was and what He did. The descriptions of Jesus Christ, the New Adam, in Romans 5 are not theological speculations on His relationship with the Trinity, or how He could be both divine and human at the same time. Paul gives primary attention to the effects this man has upon us.

In chapter 5, the effects were described in terms of what God does *for* us. That saving action entails justification—a new relationship with God and a new standing in His grace. Now, for several chapters, Paul will focus on the transformation that occurs *in* us. Here, theologians speak in terms of regeneration—the new nature that we receive through faith in Christ. Paul refers to this change in radical terms.

Not only did Christ die for us, but in some sense we, through faith, die with Christ. But we cannot speak of "new life" when we are dead. Common sense leads Paul to the rest of the story. Having shared in His death, believers share also in His resurrection. In Christ we are born to newness of life (6:4, KJV). For the Christian, Easter is more than a once-a-year holiday to be celebrated; it is a moment-by-moment reality to be lived!

1. DEAD TO SIN 6:1-13

Like a good preacher, the Apostle Paul had an uncanny sense of guessing where his audience would go with his ideas. It takes only moderate skill to stand up and give your opinions on a topic. But it takes a gifted communicator to second-guess the listeners and answer their questions before they are even voiced. At the beginning of chapter 6, Paul realizes (or the Spirit helps him to see) that one could take his statements about grace being greater than all our sin, and run astray with them.

How would that distortion go? A devious reader might take Paul's words in chapter 5 and argue like this: "Look, Paul, you tell me that sin is inevitable in my life because of the disobedience of Adam. But God's love was so great that He sent His Son to deal with sin and restore me to God. You tell me that this grace is a free gift and that it surpasses any unrighteousness in my life. Fine! Then why not just 'go with the flow' of my sinful nature, confident that enough grace will always be available to handle any unrighteousness in my life. It sounds like I can have my cake and eat it too! I can indulge myself in the temptations of the Evil One, and be assured that God will keep on demonstrating His love for me by forgiving my sins."

By no means! is Paul's vehement reply (v. 2). His opening remarks in this letter were largely directed to Jews who viewed righteousness as a reward to be earned by human initiative and effort. To counter such a mind-set, Paul stressed the divine initiative—"while we were still sinners Christ died for us" (5:8). And Paul stressed the gracious gift of salvation apart from any human action other than faith in the promise of God.

But to build one's Christian life only upon God's unconditional love, which quickly and casually forgives all sins, is to discredit God's holy/righteous nature and distort the purpose of His love—namely, to make us transformed individuals. God does not forgive just for the sake of forgiving, or even to demonstrate His loving nature. He reconciles us to himself for the purpose of glorifying His name through our lives.

To accomplish that goal, God works both for us *and in us*. That inner work changes the very nature of who we are by identifying us with Christ. The biblical statement is strong: **We died to sin** (6:2). And that death, according to Paul, is a crucifixion (v. 6). Elsewhere He declares, "I have been crucified with Christ" (Galatians 2:20; 6:14). For Paul, this death is more than just psychological imagination of the kind we use when singing "Were You There When They Crucified My Lord?"

Dying to sin entails a spiritual participation in the Crucifixion in such a way that there is an alteration of the believer. At the moment of justification, a person experiences a transformation that affects the **old self,** which was identified with sinful Adam. According to Paul, that **body of sin [is] done away with** (Rom. 6:6) in order that a new life might be imparted by the power of the Spirit.

It is interesting to note that here and in Galatians, Paul uses passive verbs to describe this death to the "old self," the action being *received* by the believer: **we were . . . buried with him** (Rom. 6:4); **our old self was crucified** (v. 6); **I have been crucified** (Gal. 2:20). The question then arises, who is the executioner? Who puts this old self to death?

Certainly not Satan. The Evil One delights in the fact that we are bound as slaves to sin. He would not do anything to alter the power that he has over sinners. It is possible that believers perform this act themselves. But to suggest that individuals have the power to do away with the old nature is to destroy the primacy of faith and Paul's contention that faith alone is all that one needs in order to be reconciled to God.

John the Baptizer spoke of repentance (literally, a change of thinking) as a turning from past sins and wicked practices (Luke 3:2-14). And Paul himself instructs the believers in Colossae to put to death certain sinful patterns of behavior as unfitting for the life of faith. But it is one thing to reject and mortify sinful actions in one's life; it is quite another thing to put to death the sinful *self.* We are born with this fallen nature, and it is not in our human power to choose to be otherwise.

The prophet Jeremiah had already realized the impossibility of a self-initiated transformation of one's spiritual nature from within oneself. He observed, "Can the Ethiopian change his skin or the leopard its spots? Neither can you do good who are accustomed to doing evil" (Jer. 13:23). No, the best that we can do is turn from our sins toward God and, after God himself has done this gracious work of salvation, **count [ourselves]**

dead to sin (Rom. 6:11).

We must conclude, therefore, that it is God himself who puts to death this sinful nature within us. It is God who frees us from sin (v. 7); it is God who brings eternal life (5:21). We will have to wrestle with Paul over why sin continues to be a reality in the life of a believer. But, one of the certain benefits of our reconciliation with God is that our old way of thinking, doing, and being is done away with as we become one with Christ.

Paul highlights that act of dying by reminding the Romans of their baptism. This is not the place to debate whether the early church practiced infant baptism or not. It is clear, however, that the members of the church in Rome to whom Paul is writing were first-generation believers, who came to know Christ as adults. It also seems clear from this passage that these believers were baptized by immersion in water. Paul uses that event in their lives to reinforce his claim that we have died with Christ to sin.

There are several levels to Paul's discussion of baptism, and the issues are complicated by differing views, even within Protestantism, regarding the meaning of this New Testament ritual. How is baptism an act of dying?

One could start with the simple symbolism of the act itself. The actions of baptism—disappearing below the surface, being covered, and then bursting forth once again—all remind us of what Christ experienced in His own burial and resurrection. Whether John had such ideas when he began baptizing in the Jordan River is immaterial; the early Christians certainly associated this act of initiation with the death, burial and resurrection of Christ.

But there is much more than just reenactment of the Easter story in this rite of baptism. For the believers in the New Testament, it was a visible witness to the world of their determination to follow Christ. In our Christianized Western culture, being baptized is rather routine, and often bland. It is almost a social expectation that one who attends church would be baptized. When new converts are baptized, the church rejoices and the unchurched could care less.

Not so for the Romans! Their decision to follow Christ entailed risk and threat to their lives. A commitment to Christ placed one's job, social standing, and even one's life, in jeopardy. Although the widespread persecution of Christians in the Roman arenas had not yet begun, the memories of what a Roman governor and a group of soldiers had done to Christ was a very vivid memory, as well as a real possibility for the one who entered the waters. Baptism was a witness, and the Greek word for witness—*martyr*—still has powerful connotations in the English language!

But Paul would take us to a deeper meaning than just becoming a disciple of Jesus, even when discipleship might mean following him to a cross. Paul understands faith as a complete trust in who Christ is and what he has done for sinners. The Greek word for faith (*pistis*) has the root meaning of "to throw at." A believer is one who makes a desperate, but life-saving leap, throwing themselves into the arms of the Father. That commitment is so complete that it requires an abandonment of everything associated with the former self and a willingness to allow God to make a person new in whatever way He chooses. The person who truly believes must sense this total surrender of one's claim to be in charge. For Paul, it is not too strong a statement to suggest that baptism, the witness of one's faith, is an act of dying to one's self, in order to discover a new identity in Christ

Finally, we come to what even Paul calls a mystery (Ephesians 5:32). The union of the believer with Christ finally defies our categories of discussion. Baptism, as the outward witness of an inward grace, represents for Paul a sharing in Christ's very death and resurrection . . . not in any physical sense, but in a spiritual sense that is no less real. In our modern scientific and logical way of viewing things, we want to be able to explain thoroughly in terms of behavior or psychology what this "dying with Christ" entails. Paul is willing to understand baptism as resulting in persons who are changed in their spiritual natures. That inner death and resurrection leads to changes that can be felt by the believer and observed by others, even when they cannot explain the mystery which has occurred.

Now we have moved far beyond the faith of Abraham (Rom. 4) which claimed God's promise for a medical miracle. We have even moved beyond the faith that brings a new standing through reconciliation to God. We have come to an actual identification and transformation of the individual that can only be described by Paul's repeated phrases, **with Christ** and **into Christ** (6:3, 8, 11). Our death to sin and resurrection to new life are the immediate benefits of reconciliation to God. They become reality when we live by faith.

But it is one thing to have this spiritual transformation occur in our lives; it is quite another to be consciously aware of it and live out of that awareness. One might imagine a terminally ill patient, who through treatment or a divine touch of healing experiences a total remission of the disease. One can be cured or healed even without being aware of the fact. But, *knowing* that fact would make a remarkable difference in the attitudes and actions of the patient.

Even so, Paul recognizes that there are those believers who testify to reconciliation and peace with God, but who live without an awareness of the power for life-transformation that now lies within them. They know their standing in the eyes of God, but presume that they must struggle on as before with the same debilitating **body of sin** (v. 6) disrupting their thought life and actions. Paul has told the Romans what they are in Christ—justified freely by His grace. Now He calls them to become even more than they are!

Count yourselves dead to sin but alive to God in Christ Jesus (v. 11). Paul used the same word for "count" *(logizomai)* in chapter 4 to describe God's action of crediting righteousness to Abraham and to us on the basis of faith. Just as God declares us to be what we could never make of ourselves, we must consider ourselves to have ended with sin, even when such a drastic action seems impossible to our human imagination. We must remind ourselves that it is "God who gives life to the dead and calls things that are not as though they were" (4:17).

In our human assessment, it is often difficult to grasp the reality of our new nature in Christ. But, the same faith which believes that God is the one who justifies, is the faith which must be exercised in believing that God is the one who transforms our natures into conformity with His Son. We can, by this faith, become even more than we first were in Christ—more than we even perceive we can be. That is why Paul can boldly proclaim, "Now to him who is able to do immeasurably more than all we ask or imagine . . ." (Ephesians 3:20). We often refer to this promise in terms of the needs and frustrations of daily life. We would do well to put the verse in its context, where Paul is describing the enlightening and empowering work of God in the *character* of the believer. Paul specifically identifies this divine action as an inward work, "according to his power that is at work within us" (Eph. 3:20). We are able, by His grace and through our faith, to become much more than we already are! "To him be glory in the church and in Christ Jesus throughout all generations, for ever and ever! Amen" (v. 21).

2. SLAVES TO RIGHTEOUSNESS 6:14-23

Paul's final conclusion about the new life that comes from dying with Christ is really a transition into his next major topic of discussion: How does a believer deal with the carry-over of the old way of living once he or she has entered into a new relationship with God.? He answers this question by turning to one of the social institutions of his day—slavery. Again, we do not take these passages to mean that the Scriptures condone human enslavement. Paul is dealing within the historical and social context of the first century world. We can benefit from the illustration without approving at all the inhuman and unchristian assumptions that underlie such a practice.

Paul returns again to the same misunderstanding of grace posed in the beginning of Romans 6: If God's grace is so plenteous and so free, what prevents a believer from continuing to sin, confident that God's unconditional love will forgive the offense over and over again? "Impossible," Paul would reply, "because slavery involves an obligation, even a bondage, to one's Master." **You are slaves to the one whom you obey** (6:16). Paul then echoes the words of Jesus, "No servant can serve two masters. Either he will hate the one and love the other, or he will be devoted to the one and despise the other. You cannot serve both God and Money" (Luke 16:13).

Jesus spoke specifically to the issue of material possessions; Paul takes the concept back to its root source, enslavement to sin. And, like his discussion of Adam and Christ, Paul details the comparisons and contrasts with the two masters, sin and righteousness.

Slavery to sin for the person who is not of faith is a basic assumption of Paul. He does not describe where this slavery comes from, although we might assume it is the consequence of Adam's disobedience. He makes no mention of Satan or demonic powers in this passage, although Paul certainly believed in the reality and activity of the Evil One. It suffices to declare that human beings apart from God's grace have no ability to resist the subtle but devastating activity of sin in the soul.

That enslavement to sin resulted in deliberate acts of disobedience to God's standard of morality. **You used to offer the parts of your body in slavery to impurity** (v. 19). Again the thread of immoral conduct that Paul describes in chapter one and weaves into 6:13 surfaces again. As we have seen, these sinful behaviors are progressive leading **to ever-increasing wickedness.**

Why, you might inquire, don't sinners put the brakes on their behavior? First, there is the problem of enslavement. Which one of us cannot recall some pattern of sinful behavior that we told ourselves we should stop, but in our own strength found we were unable to do so? If sin were as simple as a rational decision to behave or misbehave, many persons would know when to stop . . . and would do so. But the downward spiral described in Romans 1 is totally consistent with the concept of enslavement.

Beyond the binding element of sin is the absence of the abiding presence of God's Spirit and the new nature to assist one in overcoming evil. Not only is an evil principle operating in the sinner's life, but sinners are "free" from the control of righteousness (v. 20). Again, how many of us in our former life of sin longed to have some force or power to constrain us from what we were unable to control in ourselves. But as Paul has already told us, when a person's life is governed by unbelief, God does not make us be good. Rather, He gives us over (1:24) to what the enslaving powers of our life demand—ever hoping that the grace that condemns the sin and calls us to righteousness will lead us to repentance and faith.

And the outcome of such enslavement? Nothing of any benefit, Paul declares (v. 21). Like the Old Testament philosopher who went searching for happiness among the lives of the rich and famous, we discover that pursuing sinful indulgences is "vanity of vanities" (Ecclesiastes 1:2 KJV). Ultimately, all sons and daughters of Adam must face the final outcome of sin—death. Again, Paul is reaching beyond biological inevitability to describe a deeper and far-longer death extending into the world to come.

But God's grace gives us the freedom and power to chose a Master other than sin. Just as the life-giving Christ counters the death-giving Adam, so righteousness rather than sin can be the controlling Master of the one who is **in Christ.**

How does one become a slave to righteousness? Paul's response would be obvious. **This righteousness from God comes through faith in Jesus Christ** (3:22). The believers in Rome did not one day decide to walk away from their former master. They did not even escape by their own cunning and action. Paul reminds them, **You have been set free from sin and have become slaves to righteousness** (v. 18). And so we see yet another benefit of justification. More than peace with God, more than new life in Christ, more than death to sin, salvation puts us under new ownership. We are God's both by creation and by redemption.

Paul does not use the term "slaves of Christ" in this passage, although you recall that he describes himself in those terms in his introduction to the Romans (1:1). We are instead described as **slaves to righteousness—** God's character and standard of purity (6:18). In this passage, Paul also indicates we are slaves to obedience (v. 16). In saying this, he is not suggesting that we will always do the right thing—that we will always obey God's commands. Just as a slave to sin can on occasion do moral and righteous deeds, people who are **slaves . . . to obedience** have the freedom to act in disobedience to God's command and will. The issue, however, is control. The unbeliever who sometimes acts righteously still realizes that sin is in control. Conversely, the believer who may on occasion act contrary to God's will must realize that righteousness is the controlling element of his or her life.

And so Paul could urge the Christians in Rome to **offer the parts of your body . . . in slavery to righteousness** (v. 19), confident that there was grace and power operating in their lives to make this a real possibility. And what are the consequences of being enslaved to righteousness? This loyalty to God's standard leads again to a character transformation: **righteousness leading to holiness** (v.19).

Here Paul introduces for the first time in this letter that powerful word describing the very essence of God's nature and character—holiness. Holiness means moral purity without defect or flaw. And Paul declares that this divine quality is the outcome of those who are living by faith! He does not suggest that this holiness comes immediately upon one's justification; however, in that moment when grace renews our inner nature, crucial changes occur which change the "dip switches" of one's life. As the believer responds to those inward changes of God's grace, holiness becomes a word that is increasingly appropriate to characterize his or her life.

In this chapter, Paul has proposed three responses for the believer—responses that are corollaries to the basic act of trust in God's gift of His Son. First, **count yourselves dead to sin but alive to God** (v. 11). Second, **offer yourselves to God** (v. 13). And finally, **offer the parts of your body in slavery . . . to righteousness leading to holiness** (v. 19). The first is a new direction in one's thinking. The second is a change in one's will. The last is a change in one's conduct. Together these elements produce a holy life that reflects the very holy character of God.

The final outcome of these actions is **eternal life in Christ Jesus our Lord** (v. 23). And, just as death is more than physical, extending into the age to come, the life that comes as a result of faith is more than spiritual. It has already broken into our earthly existence and enables us "to participate in the divine nature" (2 Peter 1:4) even while we still live in Rome, Toronto or Atlanta.

This chapter closes with another of Paul's summary statements. He contrasts the **wages of sin (death)** with the free **gift of God (eternal life).**

One earns wages; they are the end result of what one deserves. Paul has made it clear that death is not an arbitrary punishment administered by a capricious god. Death is the consequence suffered by sinners as compensation for their disobedience and lack of faith.

We cannot however, apply that same thinking to the other side of the equation and assume that life is the "wages" of obedience and human efforts at being righteous. Paul is emphatic in his insistence that salvation is a gift, not an entitlement; that righteousness is a product of grace, not works, and that eternal life is a benefit of being justified by faith, not a reward for good living. All the blessings are rooted in God's ultimate gift, **Christ Jesus our Lord** (v. 23). By identifying with His death and resurrection, believers clothe themselves with Christ's nature (13:14) and assume the very qualities of His life (Colossians 3:12-13). In such a close relationship, it seems only natural that "He who has the Son has life" (1 John 5:12).

Before moving on to Romans 7, we should pause to summarize Paul's views of the relation of sin to our lives. In his discussion of salvation by grace (Romans 4–6), Paul has used several different images to describe the nature and power of sin in human life. The first image, and the one most Protestants are familiar with, was sin as a criminal act. The Scriptures clearly support such a concept stating that "everyone who sins breaks the law" (1 John 3:4). The word *justification* has this legal (we sometimes call it "forensic") view of the human predicament in mind. In such a view, we are the offenders, and Christ is the one who offers pardon for our wrongful actions. The benefits of such a divine act are reconciliation and peace with God.

In the opening verses of chapter 6, Paul shifted to the biological image of death and life to describe the condition of the human heart. Sin from this perspective is viewed as a condition of the soul. Elsewhere, Paul will tell believers "you were dead in your transgressions and sins" (Ephesians 2:1). Notice that such a view of sin calls for a different understanding of a Savior. A terminally ill person does not need a lawyer to come to the hospital bed and say, "You are pardoned for being sick." That person needs a great physician to come and restore wholeness and health. In outlining the benefits of a right relationship with God, Paul informed the Romans that in addition to forgiveness, God's grace also creates a new inner nature of life and well being.

In this final section, Paul offered us yet another perspective—sin viewed as slavery. Apart from grace humans find themselves bound to a host of masters. The cause of this slavery is the old nature that we possess as sons and daughters of Adam. Beyond that enslavement of the spirit, some persons are bound by detrimental conditioning or traumatic experiences from their past. In themselves they are unable to break the debilitating patterns that have been etched into their minds and souls. Still others have developed addictive patterns through substance abuse or immoral living that appear to be almost unbreakable.

Here again, it is not always helpful to tell enslaved persons that all they need is God's forgiveness. In many cases they do need God's pardon for actions they have committed. However, a judge telling a kleptomaniac—one pathologically bound to stealing— that he or she is pardoned for shoplifting does not guarantee that person will never steal again. Telling a converted homosexual that God forgives the homosexual acts of the past does not necessarily resolve all the psychological and spiritual dynamics that have become imbedded in that person's psyche.

One fault of the Wesleyan tradition is that we have overemphasized the legal concept of salvation to such a degree that we assume any new convert can simply choose to stop sinful behavior overnight and live the new life. Such a transformation will take more than forgiveness; it will necessitate breaking what C. S. Lewis describes in his fictional *Chronicles of Narnia* as "the deep powers of darkness."[1]

Nor does one always resolve the struggles of maintaining a Christian lifestyle by simply reminding a person that, once dead, they are now alive in Christ. Again there is a danger in expecting that this new life will give automatic victory over all the enslaving patterns of thought and behavior that characterized the former life of unbelief. Certainly, being a new creature in Christ is a powerful incentive to living a transformed life. And by faith we can **count [ourselves] dead to sin but alive to God** (Rom. 6:11). But Paul recognizes that beyond needing a Judge to pardon us, and a Physician to heal us, we need a Liberator to free us from the slavery of sin, law, the world and self. Righteousness is the combination of all of these gracious acts—forgiveness, healing and freedom—lived out in the life of an individual who not only turns to God in faith, but also opens his or her inner life to the transforming work of the Spirit.

ENDNOTE

[1]C. S. Lewis, *The Lion, the Witch and the Wardrobe, (New York: MacMillan Publishing, 1970).*

8

THE ANTAGONISTS:
Sin and the Law

Romans 7:1-25

In the opening chapters of his letter to the Romans, Paul dealt directly with those persons who claimed a right standing with God on the basis of their Jewish heritage, particularly their faithfulness to the law. While maintaining his respect for the law as God's revelation of His righteous character, Paul insisted "no one will be declared righteous in [God's] sight by observing the law" (3:20). A right standing with God comes only through faith. Paul then shares with the Romans the benefits of justification by faith, describing a life that is characterized by reconciliation, new life and righteousness. As one reads Romans 5 and 6, one could easily come to the conclusion that all the obstacles to holy living have been eliminated by one's inward faith and outward confession of Christ.

Such is not the case. Paul must now turn to address persistent antagonists to the believer's joy and happiness. Paul must speak further about the downsides of sin and the law. Here however, he speaks from the other side of justification, looking back over the fence to his pre-conversion experience. He describes how these two forces operate in the life of a person who is moving *toward* faith, but has not yet experienced the "no condemnation" of Romans 8. From his perspective of faith, Paul can look back and see how these two conspired to make him a miserable person, bound by duty and guilt. The joyous truth finally surfaces in the closing verses when Paul discovers that this wretched state was God's means to drive him to grace. Deliverance from both sin and law (as well as all the benefits of justification) comes "through Jesus Christ our Lord" (7:25).

1. SIN BRINGS BONDAGE TO THE LAW 7:1-6

In chapter 6, Paul used two illustrations to reinforce his bold claim that those who are **in Christ** are radically transformed individuals. He spoke first in biological imagery regarding the contrast between being dead to sin and alive to righteousness. In one sense, Paul calls us as believers to be resurrected corpses. We must take our death to sin, symbolized in baptism, very seriously. And we are to become more than we perceive ourselves presently to be, as we live out the new life we have received as persons risen with Christ.

The second illustration centered on the cultural practice of slavery, a thriving reality in Paul's time. He pointed out how believers are freed from the bondage of sin and its control over their lives. Paul then calls us to be liberated slaves—bound in loyalty and obligation to righteousness, which produces a godly character in us.

Now, in chapter 7, Paul calls us to be remarried widows! He uses a legal illustration dealing with marriage laws to stress that we are now related intimately to Christ and dare not share that relationship with the former suitors of our lives—sin and law.

Biblical scholars consider these first few verses of chapter 7 to be among the most difficult passages by Paul to understand. He appears to be headed in the right direction with his illustration, pointing out that an old relationship has been severed by death in order that a new relationship might be created and developed. The new relationship is obvious—it is our union with Christ which Paul elsewhere clearly parallels with the marriage relationship (see Ephesians 5:22-33).

But who is the former spouse? It would appear that it is the law, in which case Paul is addressing these verses to Jewish converts (**men who know the law** [v. 1]),who are still feeling obligated, if not wedded, to all the restrictions of their previous understanding of salvation. Yet as Paul moves through this passage the law becomes both the spouse and the legal restrictions that hold the marriage together. This gets confusing.

And, even more perplexing, who has died? Again, one might expect Paul to say that the sin has died, or that salvation by obeying the law has died. But Paul identifies the deceased as the persons he is addressing! **You also died to the law . . . that you might belong to another** (7:4). Wait a minute. Who died? Who is still living? Has the the deceased partner also become the one who remarries? This is confusing indeed!

Before sorting out this passage, we need to comment briefly on the benefits and dangers of illustrating spiritual truths with examples from everyday life. To do this is certainly appropriate. The Biblical writers offered many images from common life to help explain and enrich their understanding of God: "We are . . . the sheep of his pasture" (Psalm 100:3); "The Lord is my rock, my fortress" (Psalm 18:2). Jesus himself was the master of illustration and parable telling.

Paul also finds examples in Old Testament characters and illustrations from the culture of his day to drive home his points. Illustrations help us to see concepts more clearly by giving us concrete images from which to draw. But, we must remember that illustrations simply focus on a particular point the speaker or author wishes to make. Yes, the Lord is *like* a shepherd to us (Psalm 23). But we would not want to make every aspect of shepherding a divine attribute! The danger is to give these "word pictures" in Scripture more power than they deserve.

So, here in this passage Paul wants to emphasis further the fact that the new standing with God through Christ leads to a radical change in one's nature and relationship with past realities. Paul points to laws familiar to the Jews living in Rome which indicate that monogamy is the appropriate relationship for marriage partners. Just as a slave cannot serve two masters, a woman cannot be committed to two husbands simultaneously. But, when death ends the marriage relationship, the woman is free to bind herself to a new love relationship.

The point Paul is illustrating seems obvious. In their old lives, believers were bound to their sinful natures, unable to commit themselves to a free act of devotion to Christ. But, death to sin, described in 6:1-10, has broken that former relationship **that you might belong to another, to him who was raised from the dead, in order that we might bear fruit to God** (Rom. 7:4).

Simple enough—until Paul weaves into this illustration the motif of the law. The result is a double bondage: on the one hand, these Jewish converts had been bound *to* sin; but they were also bound *by* law. Having clearly established our freedom from the sin nature by our identification with Christ, Paul now turns to an earlier topic—the nature and function of the law. Although it is sin that corrupts us and brings the wages of death, the law is also present in a "good news/bad news" sort of way. The good news is that we become conscious of sin through the law. But the bad news is that we can easily assume that by keeping the laws we gain access to the grace of God. Paul has returned to his deep concern that Jewish Christians are still committed to **the old way of the written code** (v. 6), rather than finding joyous freedom in their newfound relationship with Christ. In this sense, they have experienced a bad marriage—one that faith in Christ has nullified because death has ended the old relationship. In one sense the law has died. Not that the law has no place in the believer's life; rather, it has lost its hold of obligation and condemnation upon the person who now is "in Christ Jesus."

But in another sense, the believer is the partner who has died . . . and risen again to new life and a new partnership with Christ. Without trying to make all the points of this illustration fit, we accept the underlying point of Paul's discussion; the person who lives by faith is no longer under the oppression of the law but is free to love and serve Jesus Christ. **By dying to what once bound us** [both sin and the law]**, we have been released from the law so that we serve in the new way of the Spirit** (v. 6).

2. THE LAW BRINGS AWARENESS OF SIN 7:7-13

In this letter, we have observed Paul as a theologian. We have been impressed with his knowledge of the Scriptures; we have seen his skill in rhetoric and debate. He has displayed creativity in the images he has used to illustrate his points. But, here in chapter 7, Paul steps off the platform for a few minutes. He maintains the logical flow of his case for salvation by faith, but the style makes an abrupt shift. Paul becomes personal.

We notice first the introduction of the personal pronoun in verse 9. Now it is not the story of Everyman; Paul wants to explain his point by telling *his own* story. And what a powerful story it is! Almost everyone who has read Romans 7 winces at the anguish Paul expresses as he describes his struggles with sin in his life. But, while we all identify with the issues Paul describes, we must remember that the gospel is strangely unique to each of us. Paul could not say, "Once I was a homosexual," as described in chapter 1. He admits elsewhere that he was "faultless" in keeping the legalistic requirements of the law (Phil. 3:6).

As a devout Jew, he probably never once thought of substituting worship of created things for worship of the Creator. But, despite his outwardly righteous life, Paul had experienced his own inner struggle with sin. In his case, it was the sin of "Pharisaism"—the futile attempt to use the law to gain a right standing with God. Now, that may not seem nearly as despicable as some of the immoralities and blasphemies found in his culture and ours today. But God stands opposed to all unrighteousness and, however sin manifests itself in our lives, it must be acknowledged and cleansed by the grace of God.

We are building to Paul's shouts of victory in Romans 8. But pause and listen to his moving testimony: **Once I was. . . .** Then pause for a moment and remember your own story of sin and redemption, and you will join millions of saints who one day will echo the refrain of the old gospel song: "I was once a sinner, but I came, pardon to receive from my Lord." In Paul's story and in ours, we discover the riches of God's grace toward us, who were once sinners.

Paul has declared that the believer through death with Christ has broken company with the partners of the past life—sin and the law. But in making this declaration he raises significant questions that beg to be resolved. If we are freed from sin by this act of reconciliation, why does temptation, and at times unrighteous behavior, continue in the believer's life? Paul has addressed this issue briefly in his appeal to the Romans to count themselves dead to sin and become alive to Christ. Paul will return to that matter again in chapter 12 when he calls the believers in Rome to a transformed life by a dramatic act of self sacrifice.

Here in chapter 7, Paul must address another question regarding the law. The issue simply stated is this: How can the law, which was given by God and is the focal point of the Jewish religion, be considered as something detrimental to the believer? Why would a person of faith have to die to the law? One could easily understand why we should die to sin and be freed from its control over our lives. After all, sin is of the Devil; it is contrary to all the righteousness of God. But, when Paul describes the law in similar terms of bondage, death and freedom, it would seem that he is close to suggesting that the law is evil. Paul's response to this assumption is immediate and emphatic: **Certainly not!** (v. 7).

Once again, Paul finds it necessary to make fine distinctions in order to clarify the priority of God's grace and the individual's faith in justification. Paul's deep conviction, both from his Jewish heritage and his own understanding of the gospel, is that **the law is holy, and the commandment is holy, righteous and good** (v. 12). Certainly the law, God's absolute moral standard given to His people, revealing His righteous character and calling them to be holy as He is holy (Leviticus 19:2) could not be evil.

True. But when the law encounters fallen human beings, it does strange things. On the positive side, it exposes unrighteousness for what it really is—a violation of God's will for our lives: **I would not have known what sin was except through the law** (v. 7). Paul is not suggesting that sin does not exist before law reveals it; sin is sin even when committed in ignorance. But accountability for one's actions changes drastically with knowledge. All of us know the difference between driving too fast through a speed zone without being aware of the speed limit, as opposed to driving through that zone with a full awareness of how fast we are going and how fast we *should* be going.

And God, "who knows the heart" (Acts 15:8) makes that distinction as well. That is why Paul suggests that **apart from law, sin is dead** (v. 8). He previously has told the Romans that God will deal on a different basis with those who live apart from the law (2:12-16). Paul can even recall instances in his own life when ignorance of God's moral requirements afforded him an opportunity to live without condemnation. (Whether Paul is speaking of childhood innocence or gaps in his moral understanding during his mature years, the text does not indicate.) Whatever the circumstances were that provided this measure of "life," **when the commandment came . . . I died** (v. 9). The innocence that is bliss—if, in fact, that is a true statement—is replaced by the knowledge that brings alienation from God. God's commands, designed to produce holiness and happiness, bring anything but happiness into the life of a sinner. Knowledge of broken laws brings misery.

But that is only half of the problem with the law. The problem would be much simpler if awareness of right or wrong produced an immediate response of "I'm sorry. Now I see what I should do, and from now on I will do what is right." But that is not the case. The law of God, whether conscience or written commandments, becomes a powerful tool of the Evil One to lead us deeper into sin.

Paul describes Satan's devious strategy, without mentioning him specifically, by saying that **sin, seizing the opportunity afforded by the commandment, deceived me, and . . . put me to death** (v. 11). One has only to recall the serpent in the Garden discussing God's law with Eve in deceptive phrases like, "Did God really say . . . ?" and, "You will not surely die" (Genesis 3:1, 4). Paul uses a strong word to describe this deception; we might just as well translate Paul's words as "sin seduced me."

Explaining how this seduction works is difficult. Perhaps we are drawn to sin because its evil nature heightens the sense of risk and danger in our minds, making the action, in some diabolical sense, exciting. Perhaps it is the appeal to nonconformity. Since everyone is expected to act morally, some individuals choose to take a different path and break with convention, thus drawing attention to themselves. Perhaps the self-centeredness of human nature pushes persons to defy the boundaries that others, including God, impose on them. Likely, it is all of the above!

The story of St. Augustine's adolescent life comes to mind. As students in Carthage, Augustine and his friends observed a pear tree growing near the school. One night, just before the pears would have been harvested, these rogues climbed a wall, entered the garden where the tree was located, stripped off the pears and ran away, smashing the pears in the street as they escaped. In reflecting on the event, Augustine was puzzled and ashamed by his behavior. He wondered why he did not eat the pears or sell them for profit. Why did he steal the pears simply for the purpose of discarding them? His conclusion was that he did it for the sheer joy of sinning itself.[1] What a classic illustration of the seductive power of sin that uses the commandment "Thou shalt not steal" (Exod. 20:15 KJV) to seduce people into committing unrighteous acts.

And so Paul untangles the problematic nature of the law by taking us back into his own story. His exposure to the law, in the context of his Jewish heritage, caused the sins he had committed in ignorance to take on new life and power. And the wages of this awakened sin nature (the old self of Romans 6) was death. He was dead to God and was under the sentence of eternal death for his sins. The righteous law of God had been used by Satan to seduce Paul into a relationship with sin that alienated him from the One who gave the law in the first place.

But, just when the law seems to have lost its halo and become a tool of unrighteousness, Paul recognizes that God's sovereign love uses the law to bring Paul to his senses. In God's prevenient grace, He allows the law to bring sin to its fullest expression so that it can be identified, destroyed, and replaced with righteousness. It is like the weed killer I put on my lawn each spring which forces the dandelions to thrive and grow like crazy until they destroy themselves from within. The law makes sin visible and potent for the very purpose that it might be put to death by the power of the Cross.

3. SIN AND LAW BRING INNER CONFLICT 7:14-25

Having described his struggle with law-awakened sin in historical terms, Paul now becomes even more personal and intense. He continues the discussion by speaking of the inner dynamics of his soul and emotions as he deals with this matter.

We must make note, however, of the shift of tenses in this paragraph. Paul has just finished a section written in the past tense—**once I was. . . .** Now he moves to the present tense and describes a situation as if he were currently experiencing it. This shift in tenses (and other theological considerations) has led to several different interpretations of when the struggle between sin and good occurs in an individual's life. (These interpretations are built on the assumption that what Paul describes here is a universal experience—a risky enterprise that we have already discussed.)

For the sake of our discussion, we will also assume that this inner struggle is common to most, if not all, believers at some point in their spiritual struggle. But at what point?

Some take the present tense quite literally and say this is the turmoil that believers experience even during their new life in Christ. Although the sin nature has been declared dead in God's eyes, the reality of sin is still very much present in the life of the believer, so long as he or she is in this present life as a child of Adam. Those who take this view cite verse 25 as Paul's affirmation that *by faith* one is able to overcome this struggle and trust in God rather than self for righteousness. But, in their opinion, the struggle Paul describes here is the spiritual warfare of believers mentioned in other passages (e.g. Ephesians 6:12).

The theology of Martin Luther and many of the reformers would follow this line of interpretation. Wanting to avoid any suggestion that salvation depended on works, Luther declared that all goodness that was the product of human effort, or even choice, was like filthy rags in the eyes of God. Faith alone reconciles one to God, and God chooses to declare us *what we are not*—righteous. But, in the eyes of the world (and ourselves), we remain the same "struggler in the storm-tossed sea" that we were before salvation, with the one monumental difference that we dare to believe what does not seem to be so.

Thus Luther could summarize his view of salvation by declaring that we are "at the same time, sinner and saint, always repenting." Sinner in our own eyes and daily experiences; saint in the eyes of God because of our radical faith in the Cross. While this view is a powerful corrective for those who think that their actions earn God's favor, even when they are believers, it has serious flaws as well. It seems to negate the present reality of salvation in the life of the believer. Paul hints at some of these ideas in Romans as he suggests that we are declared righteous by faith in God's promise to do what seems impossible. Paul also affirms that sin is dead—even while he concedes that the Romans do not act in accordance with their new nature.

But one has to take seriously Paul's statements about the benefits of justification that produce a new person and a transformed life. To suggest that this struggle with sin is the best life that Christianity offers negates the power of the Cross. These verses clearly suggest a time in Paul's life when sin was master, and righteousness did not control. If that is the case, Paul is contradicting what he has just declared in chapter 6!

Some from the Wesleyan tradition have used their understanding of salvation gleaned from other passages to suggest another option. They suggest that this passage describes Paul as a new convert, who has experienced forgiveness from sin, but still has not experienced *entire* sanctification—that deeper work of the Spirit that destroys the power of sin. They argue that Paul's **desire to do what is good** (7:18) and his **delight in God's law** (v. 22) are characteristic of a believer who has not yet given himself totally to God as a living sacrifice (12:1). They say that this describes the turmoil of a person not yet completely made holy (sanctified) by the Spirit of God. This passage, then, describes the carnal and divided believer, "unstable in all he does" (James 1:8).

While such feelings and struggles may characterize a person who is new in the faith, it does not conform with Paul's line of argument and the order of salvation he is outlining in these chapters of Romans. Again, Paul has declared that when believers die with Christ in the baptismal witness to their newfound faith, the control of sin and the law are broken. Whatever struggles with temptation and past patterns of sin the convert deals with, it would not be consistent to align this passage with a post-conversion Paul. How could he close chapter 7 with such a guilt-ridden description of himself, and open chapter 8 with "There is now no condemnation for those who are in Christ Jesus" (v. 1)?

We choose, then, the option followed by most scholars—that Paul is continuing his discussion regarding his pre-conversion struggle with the goodness of the law and the seduction of sin in his daily experience. He describes a time in his life when he was **unspiritual** (7:14). More literally, he describes himself as "fleshly" *(sarkinos)*. Here he does not mean his physical constitution, as in flesh and blood. Rather, he alludes to his connection with the first Adam—the old self—which predetermined him to be inclined toward disobedience and death.

But, in this state of spiritual lifelessness, Paul was already experiencing God's prevenient grace by means of the law. Yes, a recognition of God's law had entered Paul's life in childhood or adolescence, and was used by sin to seduce him away from God. But God used that same law to call Paul to righteousness. You can well imagine the tug-of-war that the law created. And Paul describes that tension in powerful language: **I do what I do not want to do** (v. 16); **I have the desire to do what is good, but I cannot carry it out** (v. 18).

Here is a struggle between two masters, both vying for Paul's loyalty. But sin is the master and wins. The old nature is not yet dead; and while there is an awareness of the law of God—even a desire to obey it—there is no reference to the new life or the gift of grace that breaks the power of the old nature.

One can almost see Paul, the young Pharisee in Jerusalem struggling to establish his righteousness through zeal for the law and the traditions of the Jews. One can imagine his almost daily vows to be blameless before God, only to see patterns of thought and behavior that suggest he is guilty of violating the standard of perfection and holiness the law demands. What a strange contradiction. A person passionate for the very law that plagues his conscience. A person eager to do God's will, but inwardly incapable of doing it in his own strength. **What a wretched man . . . !** (v. 24).

But Paul is not the last sinner to wallow in the no-man's-land of conviction, caught between the indulgence of moral rebellion and the joy of peace with God. In such a state, the holiness of God's law eliminates the pleasure and delight of sin. But the persistent nature of the old self, not yet renewed by grace, makes obedience to the law an impossibility. A slave of two masters: one, the Spirit-awakened mind; and the other, the sin-controlled human nature. How does one make it to the winning side, or, as Paul expresses it, **Who will rescue me from this body of death?** (v. 24).

The answer simply explodes from the text. God must be the Liberator from this bondage to sin. **Through Jesus Christ** (v. 25) the sinner is freed from the power of sin, the condemnation of the law, and the helplessness of the old self to make things right. And this Jesus is more than friend to sinners, more than giver of life; He is **Christ our Lord** (v. 25). And, in Christ's lordship, Paul discovers the sovereign power to break from the past and live in newness of life.

ENDNOTE

[1]Augustine, ed., *The Confessions of St. Augustine,* John Ryan, ed., (New York: Doubleday and Co., 1960), p. 70.

Part Four

RIGHTEOUSNESS RENEWED:
Life in the Spirit
Romans 8:1-39

T he Apostle Paul has presented his case for the gospel—justification by faith. By careful reasoning, scriptural quotations, appropriate illustrations, and finally a personal testimony, he has declared that a right standing with God comes not through any human endeavor to do good and thus measure up to God's holy standard, but rather through faith in His gracious gift. Paul has pointed out the immediate benefits of God's reconciling act for the believer: peace, joy, and a transformed identity.

But where does all this take someone after the fireworks of conversion fade away? What difference will this new relationship with God make in the daily routines of living for the Christians in Rome? Building on the distinctions between the old and new self that have dominated the past few chapters of Romans, Paul now takes the discussion in a new direction that focuses on the life of salvation. He moves from the initial experience of dying and rising with Christ to describe the dynamics of life in Christ.

Theologians identify this ongoing dimension of the Christian life by the term "sanctification." The word itself is derived from the Latin word *sanctus,* which means "holy." We have already read in 6:22 that being set free from sin "leads to holiness."

Certainly the joyous experience of being justified by faith produces immediate benefits and alterations in our lives. But justification by itself is not the whole story of salvation; God's work extends beyond that moment into a new dimension of grace and Christian living.

John Wesley used the image of a building to describe the work of redemption in our lives. He identified justification as the *door* of salvation—the entrance point where we step across the threshold into a new realm of existence. If justification is the door, Wesley proposes, then repentance is the *porch*. There is a moving toward God that precedes our reconciliation, an episode of existing as the "almost Christian," which Paul described in Romans 7. Sanctification, according to Wesley, is the *house*, the dwelling place of salvation.

Entering a room or a building can be a rather momentous occasion. Newlyweds often dramatize this event by the carrying of the bride over the threshold. But standing in the doorway for hours to relish the moment is foolish—and tiresome. And repeating the entrance over and over again is ridiculous. Having entered the new dwelling place, the bride and groom settle down to the tasks of life together.

Our spiritual life is similar to this. The moment we enter into a new standing with God by faith is significant. Without this event, one never can enjoy life in the Spirit. But to suggest that justification is all there is, or even stress it to the neglect of the holy life that comes later, is to distort the gospel. So it is that Wesley and his followers give particular attention to the *life*, as well as the *event* of salvation.

This twofold nature of salvation—justification and sanctification—can be clarified in another way. Here again we draw on Wesley's thoughts when he contrasts the two works of God's one great gift of grace. Justification, he suggests, is a *relative* (we would say "relational") change between the believer and God. Through reconciliation, we who were once "far away" have been brought near to Christ (Ephesians 2:13). This relationship is so strong that "to all who received him, to those who believed in his name, he gave the right to become children of God" (John 1:12). In Romans 8, Paul uses the legal act of adoption to bring out the same point. This relational benefit brings peace and access to the Father.

Sanctification, on the other hand, is a *real* change in the believer. Beyond having a new relationship with God, the Christian has a *new nature* and experiences a transformation of the self through God's grace. That transforming work of sanctification begins at the very moment of justification as the person experiences a new life in Christ. In Jesus' conversation with Nicodemus (John 3), He used the analogy of birth to describe this change. For this reason, Wesleyans teach that *regeneration*, the theological term for being born again, is the initial work of sanctification. Paul does not use the image of birth in Romans; rather he ties this spiritual change to dying and rising with Christ. In faith, the

Christian dies to sin and rises with Christ to a new life.

The point of both images, however, is the same. God does more than just perceive the person of faith in a new way; He also enters the believer's life and brings that person into closer conformity with the New Adam, Jesus Christ. The results of such a work of grace are real—that is, discernible to believers and to those around them.

But, in making these helpful distinctions between justification and sanctification, Wesleyans sometimes make serious blunders that distort the message of Scripture, and especially the teaching of Paul. One error is to so emphasize the differences between these dimensions of salvation that they become separated from each other and lose their essential unity in the grace of God. It is totally appropriate to speak of two works of grace, but we must never forget there is "one Lord, one faith, one baptism" (Eph. 4:5). Furthermore, when followers of the holiness movement describe their spiritual pilgrimage only in terms of "getting saved" and "getting sanctified," they have reduced the gospel to little more than a two-stage spiritual rocket . . . rather than the eternal plan of redemption working itself out in the lives of believers. We will observe how Paul unites these two experiences and holds them together as the great gift of salvation in Christ.

Another danger of the holiness movement is to give so much attention to sanctification as to lose the significance and value of one's relational standing with God through Christ. The Protestant reformers were overwhelmed with new insights regarding justification by faith. Followers of Luther (and, to a lesser degree, Calvin) have at times neglected sanctification in their passion for a gospel that is the result of divine grace, not human endeavors.

John Wesley sensed the imbalance in their teachings that gave no attention to sanctification and the life of holiness. He described this message of heart holiness as the "grand deposit" of the Wesleyan movement. But he never forgot his own experience with justifying grace and the power he sensed in his life when, at Aldersgate Street, he trusted "in Christ, Christ alone for salvation."[1] While Wesley has earned a place of honor in the history of Christianity for his views on holiness, he devoted much of his time to preaching sermons on justification by faith to unchurched miners and laborers in England.

Some of his followers, however, have out-Wesleyed Wesley in their passion for sanctification. And they have done so to the neglect of justification by faith. In stressing the transformed life and the call to holiness, there is always the subtle danger of slipping back into a salvation by works of the law. In this case, it is not the law of Moses, but the religious expectations of the group of holy people who have defined the word in behavioral terms, and who judge others by *their* standards of holiness (see Romans 2 for Paul's assessment of such endeavors). Again, we shall see in chapter 8 how Paul balances the "no condemnation" of justification with the "life . . . through his Spirit" of sanctification (8:1, 11).

A final danger comes from endeavoring to make the parts of the twofold work of salvation a left- and right-hand glove, corresponding to each other at every point. In explaining the work of God in sanctification, some Wesleyans endeavor to make the components and mechanics of both experiences identical. Wesley himself was fascinated with the parallels between justification and sanctification. In several sermons,[2] he points out that both involve an awareness of sin, both require repentance, both are accomplished through faith and not by works, and both have an instantaneous dimension to them.

But, to push the parallels too far is to miss the striking differences in the nature of these two aspects of salvation and the different effects they produce upon the believer's life. The result of this line of thinking is to suggest that justification is only a half-salvation, and that one has to go through the steps of conversion a second time in order to get entirely saved. Another variation of this heresy is to suggest that when one is justified, he "receives Jesus"; when he gets sanctified, he "gets the Spirit." We will see how Paul shatters all such simplistic charts, and presents a far richer understanding of how the believer moves from the relational change of justification to the transforming change of sanctification.

And, to complete the picture, Paul will lead us in this passage to the culminating aspect of one's salvation—glorification. There is a confident hope for Christians that God's ultimate plan for His creation will be accomplished through the work of His grace. Paul's letter to the Romans leads us from alienation from God, to reconciliation with God, to transformation by God, to eternal life in God.

ENDNOTE

[1]Wesley, *Works,* vol. 1, p. 103.

[2]Wesley, "Repentance of Believers," *Works,* vol. 5, pp. 156-170; "The Scripture Way of Salvation," *Works,* vol. 6, pp. 43ff.

9

THE BELIEVER'S NEW IDENTITY

Romans 8:1-17

Few passages in the Bible, or in all literature, describe the despair of self-condemnation as graphically as the closing verses of chapter 7.

In the midst of his discussion of reconciliation with God and the benefits which that restored relationship offers one who believes, Paul reminds his readers of the anguish that was his (and no doubt theirs, as well) at a time when sin and law conspired to rob life of all its joy and sense of accomplishment. He closes his account of the struggle of the will to follow both sin and the law of God with a shout of gratitude to God for the deliverance he has found "through Jesus Christ our Lord!" (7:25). But that word of praise is still drowned out by the echoing cries of "wretched man" and the haunting question, "Who will rescue me from this body of death ?" (v. 24).

The answer to that question is provided in chapter 8. Deliverance from the struggle with sin and the guilty verdict of the law comes to those **who are in Christ Jesus** (v. 1). Jesus has both condemned sin and fulfilled the law; those who remain in him through faith are free! This freedom is not only a "freedom *from*"; it is also a freedom *to* operate in a new dimension, which Paul describes as living **according to the Spirit** (v. 4). Justificaction releases one from the condemnation of the past, while sanctification—a life controlled by God's Spirit—releases one from the power of unrightouesness. Here again, as in his discussion of justification in Romans 5, Paul counterbalances the work that God has done in Christ, with the responsibility of believers to utilize the gift and **have their minds set on what the Spirit desires** (v. 5). Prevenient grace applies equally to this advanced stage of our spiritual piligrimage as it did at the very beginning. The divine initiative has provided the Spirit to control and energize the life of the believer. The means of attaining this life is always the same: "The righteous will live by faith" (1:17).

1. FREED FROM CONDEMNATION 8:1-4

Having used the literary motif of a flashback to describe his struggle with sin and the righteousness of the law, Paul brings his readers back to the **now** (8:1) and to his description of the benefits of reconciliation. His opening words of chapter 8 echo the themes of 5:1: Those who have been "justified through faith" are now **those who are in Christ Jesus;** the benefit of "peace with God" is now expressed as **no condemnation,** to reinforce the glorious liberation that comes through Jesus Christ our Lord.

Yes, many believers do struggle with remorse, even feelings of guilt, for past sins. But Paul declares that from God's side, the forgiveness is complete. In a musical setting of this verse, the great composer, J. S. Bach, repeats the "no" (German, *nicht*) an emphatic three times to remind the hearers that we are genuinely **free from the law of sin and death** (8:2).

Although Paul opens this portion of his letter by returning to the themes of sin and reconciliation through the sacrificial death of God's Son, his focus quickly shifts toward a new image and dimension of the Christian experience—life in the Spirit. If you consult a King James Version of the Bible, you will notice a phrase added to the end of the first verse that is not in other more modern translations. This additional phrase does not appear in the earliest Greek manuscripts of this letter: ". . . who walk not after the flesh, but after the Spirit." It is quite possible that some ancient copyist's marginal comment became absorbed into the text and thus was passed down to more recent times. Even if the words are not Paul's, they provide a wonderful summary statement for the discussion that follows. Before looking at another of Paul's compare-and-contrast passages, we need to understand the two key words that highlight these verses.

Paul speaks of those who live "after the flesh" (8:4-5 KJV). The translators of the New International Version, recognizing the confusion that might result from the word "flesh" *(sarx)*, substituted the term **sinful nature.** This choice of words is helpful . . . and risky.

Paul uses the word "flesh" in at least three different ways in his writings. At times, it takes the obvious meaning of the *material substance* of the human body. In Galatians, Paul refers to men as "flesh and blood" (1:16 KJV). Elsewhere in Romans, he speaks of circumcision of the flesh (2:28 KJV). In this sense, flesh is something that all humans have by virtue of having physical bodies. Since the material substance (dust) from which God created humanity was not evil, and since God declared His finished creation to be "very good" (Genesis 1:31), we can assume there is nothing sinful in this understanding of the term "flesh." One can certainly commit unrighteous deeds with the flesh, but that does not make flesh evil, any more than hitting one's thumb with a hammer makes the hammer evil.

Scripture also uses the word in a more general sense as the *human nature* we were given at Creation. The Apostle John declares that "the Word became flesh" (John 1:14) to describe the entrance of the divine Son into our world of human existence. Paul describes his own human existence by saying, "The life which I now live in the flesh I live by . . . faith" (Gal. 2:20 KJV). Such expressions go beyond the biological meaning of body tissue; they suggest the social, moral and spiritual dimensions of a person, as well.

Here again, we return to the Creation account and observe that God's creating Adam and Eve with a human nature (a fleshly existence) did not suggest at all that this nature was evil. But the stakes in the game were raised considerably by adding a moral quality to their human nature. As creatures of reason, will, and moral choice, Adam and Eve were now capable of making moral choices that could lead to blessing or condemnation.

The beguiling aspect of sin led to Adam's fall and an alteration of basic human nature. This alteration of the moral and spiritual character of humans finally brings us to the meaning of "flesh" used to describe unbelievers in Romans 8. Here, flesh assumes a negative quality because the disobedience of Adam has affected the moral neutrality of human nature. In Paul's understanding, the entire human race is now tainted by the "bent to sinning." And this downward pull has a controlling aspect to it, so that "those controlled by the sinful nature *[sarx]* cannot please God" (8:8).

The NIV's substitution of "sinful nature" for the more literal word "flesh" reinforces Paul's focus upon the unrighteous character of the human individual apart from God's grace. But, such a translation takes the risk of suggesting that human nature is now irretrievably sinful. One of the strong emphases of the Wesleyan tradition is that while humanity is fallen, it is redeemable in its moral and spiritual capacities by the work of the Cross. We have already pointed out that the ancient gnostic heresy equated matter (including human flesh) with evil. The New Testament writers vigorously opposed this idea, since it would undermine the doctrine of Incarnation—that a holy God became fully human, *yet without sin* (Hebrews 2:14, 17; 4:15).

Paul makes the same point by stressing that believers who used to yield the parts of their bodies to sin are now able to yield them as instruments of righteousness (6:13). If Paul intends to contrast the freedom of life in the Spirit (8:1-4) with the pre-conversion struggle he experienced with the law of sin (7:23), then it would be appropriate to consider the "flesh" as *sinful human nature*. But the good news is that the sinful nature can be put to death in Christ, and that a new nature, equally human and fashioned after the New Adam, can emerge.

Paul describes this new nature by using another rich biblical term—**Spirit** (vv. 2, 4). The spiritual significance of this word extends all the way back to the beginning when "the Spirit of God was hovering over the waters" (Gen. 1:2). Both the Hebrew word for "spirit" *(ruach)* and its Greek equivalent *(pneuma)* associate the spirit with breath or wind.

To explore all the nuances of that image as it relates to the third person of the Trinity and the dimension of the human person we call spirit is impossible. But we quickly form thoughts of breath, life, power, invisibility and freedom when thinking of this word. The intimate tie between the divine Spirit and the human spirit occurs in the account of Adam where God "breathed into his nostrils the breath of life, and the man became a living being" (Gen. 2:7).

Elsewhere in the Old Testament, the coming of the Spirit is associated with energy and power, whether it be the strong man, Samson (Judges 14:6); the warrior-king, David (1 Samuel 16:13); or the dry bones of Ezekiel's vision (Ezekiel 37). It is, no doubt, these images that Paul draws upon to describe the life of the person of faith as **according to the Spirit** (8:4).

As Paul begins to lay out the contrast between living according to the sinful nature and living according to the Spirit, he boldly declares that the pivot point between these two ways of existing is redemption **through Christ Jesus** (8:2). In the span of a few words, Paul refers to three different laws: **the law of the Spirit, the law of sin and death, and the [revealed] law** (vv. 2, 4). Paul already described the paradox of the Jewish law and introduced the concept of a law of sin at the close of chapter 7. Now he speaks of yet another law that is spiritual in nature.

In his writings, Paul usually avoids associating the law with Christ, no doubt because Jewish converts still had distorted views of the role of law as it related to salvation. And here, Paul is not speaking of law in the sense of codes of conduct or even moral standards; he uses the term in the sense of power and control. Ungodly persons who disregard the Creator find themselves bound under the law of sin. The rules under which sinners operate appear to be few and easy, but in reality the sinful nature is a tyrant, and soon the apparent freedom of the world becomes a bondage to death. The law of God reveals His moral code and condemns the sinners for their disobedience. But, as Paul observes, the sin-weakened self does not have the power to switch allegiance from the laws of sin to the law of God.

What a wretched situation! One thinks of the African-American slaves of a century ago who, hearing the Constitution of the country in which they lived, wanted to be free and governed by its laws. But, they were reminded that they were under another law—the law of their masters. Although they yearned for the freedom of the laws described in the Bill of Rights, they remained powerless to change that situation in themselves. And then, into the situation stepped a liberator, a chief executive who proclaimed that they were freed from the law of the slave owners. What the slaves could not do for themselves, and what the Constitution itself was incapable of accomplishing, Abraham Lincoln did with a proclamation of emancipation.

Their freedom came at great cost; the price was blood. But when a slave asked, "What do I have to do to be free," the response was, "Nothing! The new law of Mr. Lincoln makes you free."

Paul's reasoning follows a somewhat similar pattern. God's righteous law declares what we as humans ought to be. But sin, the slavemaster, held us under its rule. Yet, **what the law [of God] was powerless to do . . . God did** (8:3). And He accomplished this **by sending his own Son in the likeness of sinful man** (the literal translation is *flesh of sin*). In His radical identification with humanity—not as a sinner, but as one born under the condemnation of the first Adam—this Second Adam assumed "the very nature of a servant, being made in human likeness" (Philippians 2:7). And, by His death, He struck down the law of sin, superseding it with the law of the Spirit of life.

Here Paul suggests a new understanding of Christ's dying for sinners. We spoke earlier of ideas of legal substitution (dying for the condemned criminal) and sacrificial love (giving oneself for helpless victims). Now Paul uses language from the Greek Old Testament that hints of the Old Testament sacrificial system where the life of an animal was given as a **sin offering** (Rom. 8:3).

Just as God required the death of an animal as a prerequisite for the forgiveness of sins, Jesus fulfills those requirements as "the Lamb of God, who takes away the sin of the world" (John 1:29). Once again, Paul does not give a full analysis of how Christ's death deals with sin. He simply declares the fact of that deliverance and accepts by faith that no condemnation and *no bondage* remains for those who have died and risen with Christ.

2. CONTROLLED BY THE SPIRIT 8:5-11

This freedom from sin accomplished by the Son results in a new way of living. Paul introduces the contrast in the closing phrase of verse 4: ". . . who do not live according to the sinful nature [or flesh], but according to the Spirit." Note first the lifestyle of the sinful nature. Here Paul reviews characteristics he has already spelled out in earlier chapters. These persons are controlled by the sinful nature, and in such a state they are alienated from God, even **hostile** to Him (8:7). They do not submit to God's law, either by choice (hence they are accountable) or by inner compulsion (hence they are fallen). Their mind-set is oriented on their own desires (v. 5).

Here one wishes that the translators had used the more literal "flesh" in its multi-layered meanings. There is a sense in which the flesh (i.e., sinful nature) draws us to the desires of the flesh (i.e., human appetites). Elsewhere, Paul describes such individuals as those whose "god is their stomach" (Phil. 3:19). Martin Luther observed that sinful persons are "curved in on themselves."[1]

Whatever strivings for greatness they have, whether good or corrupt, their efforts always end up being self-centered and designed for personal aggrandizement. Such a mind-set leads to self-destruction and death (8:6). One needs only to look at the folk heroes of our modern culture— Marilyn Monroe, Elvis Presley, Magic Johnson—to find supporting evidence for Paul's description of those whose mind-set and behavior **cannot please God** (v. 8).

By contrast, Paul describes one who lives according to the Spirit. First, such a life is possible only because the Spirit dwells (literally, "to take up residence") in the believer. Living **in accordance with the Spirit** is more than occasionally thinking spiritual thoughts; it is even more than a supernatural influence affecting our behavior. It is the presence of the divine nature *in us,* enabling us to be **controlled** by (Greek, *in*) the Spirit. Perhaps Paul is thinking of the air we breathe when he plays on the image of the Spirit (air) being in the believer while the believer is in the Spirit (air). It is certainly consistent with Paul's observation on Mars Hill concerning a God in whom "we live and move and have our being"(Acts 17:28). At the same time, this God, through His eternal Spirit, is in us!

The abiding presence of this Spirit motivates the believer to develop a mind-set oriented toward spiritual desires (v. 5). Paul does not negate the natural desires; instead he urges believers to bring them under the control of the Spirit. Such a mind-set leads to **life and peace** (v. 6). In extolling the glories of the Spirit-life, Paul does not overstate the realities we still must face. Our mortal bodies are still with us; we are not exempt from the aches, pains and frustrations of human existence. But, even when conceding the inevitability of death, Paul leaps into the future dimension where God, **who raised Christ from the dead will also give life to your mortal bodies through his Spirit, who lives in you** (v. 11).

The presence of the Spirit, transforming our sinful nature into the image of Christ, gives us reason to think that the life of glory has in some mysterious way already broken through into our present realm of existence. We live with both feet still in this age, but with a breakthrough point already established in the age to come.

3. ADOPTED BY THE FATHER 8:12-17

After spelling out the distinctive features of new life in the Spirit, Paul once again calls upon the believers in Rome to become more than they already are by actively participating in the work of salvation. Having urged them previously to "count [themselves] dead to sin" (6:11), and to "offer [themselves] to God . . . and offer the parts of [their] body to . . . righteousness" (v. 13), Paul now instructs believers to **put to death the misdeeds of the body,** and in doing so to be **led by the Spirit** (8:13-14).

The Greek word for **misdeeds** is *praxis,* which we have brought across to the English language to describe the actions and practices of our beliefs. It is the root for our English word "practical" and sooner or later someone will ask the tough question "How can you make all these big ideas of yours practical?" Despite all the benefits of sorting out and explaining the doctrine of sanctification, the real test for the believer is the willingness to respond to the directions of the Spirit that dwells within, particularly when the Spirit directs attention to specific behavioral patterns that are best described as **misdeeds of the body.**

Although Paul will get to practical instructions later on in his letter, he simply leaves the misdeeds to the convicting work of the Spirit at this point. And we would do well to follow his pattern in our initial encounters with new believers. We would be tempted to identify all the misdeeds, and more often than not they are defined by as much cultural ethics and religious traditions as clear scriptural commandments. One can only imagine a body of believers where each person was keenly sensitive to the Spirit's leading in terms of that individual's own sins and character flaws, while everyone remained gracious and forbearing in terms of judging flaws in others.

Too often, holiness becomes regimented by the group rather than revealed by the Spirit. The resulting danger is twofold. On the one hand, the church becomes legalistic as it defines the misdeeds for every person by the standard of the group. But the church can just as easily become lax and worldly as the behavioral patterns of the majority become the norm by which everyone judges his own spirituality, rather than letting the Spirit do a "custom job" on the identity of each believer.

The **obligation** (v. 12) that lies on each believer is directly tied to the new identity, which Paul now associates with belonging to a family as **sons [or daughters] of God** (v. 14). Our behavior ought to reflect both who we are and *whose* we are. I remember when as a teenager I left the house to go out with the guys, or, on less frequent occasions, a girl, my mother's parting comment to me was often, "Remember, Bud, your mother is a Lytle and your father is a Bence."

She had developed an expectation that I ought to live up to the name and reputation of the family to which I belonged. In the same way, Paul reminds the Christians in Rome of the obligation to make their lives conform to the name and reputation of their Heavenly Father.

But Paul dwells only briefly on the expectations of children of God. Paul does not choose to motivate by guilt or duty. Instead he shifts to the wonderful benefits that are entailed in this relationship, using the legal customs of adoption in his day to illustrate his point. Here again, we must remember that illustrations clarify concepts; they are not substitutes for the ideas themselves. The Apostles John and Peter describe a person's entrance into the household of God by references to natural birth. Such allusions stress our creational ties to the Father and the radically new starting point of life in Christ.

Paul, on the other hand, makes our sonship a matter of divine choice, and stresses the sharp difference between the sinful nature and the divine nature of righteousness and love. The adopted child enters the family as a stranger, declared to be a son or daughter even when outward appearances suggest otherwise. It mattered not in a Roman court whether an individual looked, thought or acted like his or her adoptive father. The law of adoption determined whose child they were; conformity to that new identify came later and over time.

William Barclay offers a detailed explanation of Roman practices of adoption and their applications to this text. He identifies several key elements of this procedure: First, the adopted son lost all rights to his previous family and assumed the standing of a fully legitimate child of his new family. In this legal standing, he then became a full heir to the father's estate (**Then we are . . . heirs of God** [8:17]). Finally, all the obligations, debts, legal charges and other aspects of the son's former life were canceled. The adopted son entered his new family relationship as a new person with his former identity blotted out. One could understand why Paul might use adoption to illustrate the themes of justification as God's gift![2]

The effect of entering this new relationship as a child of God is that the believer can approach God without fear and in a direct manner. The hostility that God might have demonstrated toward the sinner is overcome by love, so much so that we, like Jesus, can call the infinite Creator our Father. Note that Paul uses both the Aramaic and Greek terms, no doubt to relate to both the Jewish and Gentile converts he is addressing. (In the centuries preceding the New Testament, Greece had been a world power and had imposed its language upon the peoples it conquered in order to facilitate politics, business and international communication. That is why the New Testament was written in Greek rather than the languages of Palestine. One could understand Paul's use of the Greek *pater* [father] to communicate this close relationship to Gentile believers who had no understanding of the terms of endearment in another language. But for the Jewish believers, Paul pauses and inserts the Aramaic word *abba* as well. Aramaic was a language related closely to the ancient Hebrew.)

It is one thing for us to speak to God in terms of a parent/child relationship. But even more amazing is the fact that He communicates that same intimate relationship to us. And He calls individuals "child" by means of the Spirit that dwells within every believer. This passage provides the inspiration and foundation for what Wesleyan theologians term "the doctrine of assurance."

The doctrine of assurance attempts to resolve a persistent question among Christians: "How can one know for sure that he or she is a child of God?" In traditions like Roman Catholicism, where great emphasis is placed upon the sacramental rituals as a means of grace, one could answer the question quickly with, "I have been baptized." Legalists who erroneously substitute keeping the law for salvation through faith would look to certain behavioral patterns to convince themselves that a person is a true disciple of God.

But, for evangelical Protestants, external rituals or behavior cannot provide the evidence of a work of God's grace which is *inward* and *spiritual*. The world is filled with the misguided or the hypocritical who give outward appearances of this transformation, while on the inside they "are like whitewashed tombs" (Matthew 23:27).

Other Christians draw upon scriptural texts, largely from the Old Testament, which indicate that God blesses the righteous and brings hardship, even calamity, upon the wicked. Psalm 1 would be a good example. In speaking of the righteous man, the Psalmist informs us that "whatever he does prospers" (1:3). A few verses later, the contrast between the righteous and wicked is stated explicitly: "For the LORD watches over the way of the righteous, but the way of the wicked will perish" (v. 6).

No indication is given here of what God's blessing or disapproval entails. But, from other passages and biblical examples, one can argue that the blessings and cursings relate to success, happiness and material possessions. Hence a subtle but dangerous theology has persisted since Old Testament times: you can know that you are God's child if He treats you well in terms of this world's definitions of success and prosperity.

And there is a margin of truth in these words. God is the giver of all blessings in our lives. We are acting most appropriately as believers when we acknowledge His undeserved acts of mercy upon us which are "new every morning" (Lamentations 3:23). Furthermore, those whose lives are led by the Spirit are quite likely to find their life situations improved as they become more honest, diligent, and disciplined in patterns of work, leisure, and handling of finances. John Wesley himself once observed that his new converts to Methodism often rose from impoverishment to middle-class respectability by the power of the transformed life.

But, we must never use our external experiences as the yardstick of our salvation or our relationship with God. Jesus reminds us that the Father in heaven sends "rain on the righteous and the unrighteous" (Matthew 5:45). The book of Hebrews reminds us that discipline and hardship are sometimes the maturing forces that God uses to make us more conformed to His family identity (Hebrews 12:6-7). Just as human parents show deep love for their children in ways other than indulging them, the Father does what is best for our well-being, and not what we think will make life easier. No, the assumption that one's social or economic status gives proof of his righteousness is one of the saddest and most dangerous distortions of the doctrine of assurance.

Let us assume, then, that the awareness of one's right standing with God is an inward assurance that might not be evidenced by any outward act or condition. We are left with two final alternatives. One is the argument that assurance is a matter of faith alone. A believer must exercise the same "blind trust" for assurance that was exercised in coming to Christ for salvation. Like Abraham, the Christian must accept the reality that perhaps is not seen or even felt. To depend upon visible acts or even psychological (or emotional) feelings leads to self-deception. In this religious tradition, it would not be unusual to see a person directed to a salvation text like "If we confess our sins, he is faithful and just and will forgive us our sins" (1 John 1:9), and then close the matter with the observation, "God's word says it. I believe it. That settles it." Assurance is simply a mental commitment—counting oneself to be a child of God.

Now, there is much to say for this understanding of assurance in a world that is so dependent upon feelings to define one's condition. At the very time when our society, including the church, is inclined to judge the significance of an experience by the hype it produces, we have also become experts in psychological manipulation of the very feelings that are becoming the accepted standard of what is "real." We can describe this with a paraphrase of Jesus' words from Matthew 15:14 as "the blind manipulators leading the blind gullible thrill-seekers."

A call to base one's spiritual relationship with God on something deeper than feelings and psychological states is welcome. But the danger of such a view is to ignore the indwelling Spirit that is in the process of transforming the believer into a new creature. And one aspect of that transformation is an open line of communication with God that not only allows us to address Him as "Father," but enables Him to call us "son" or "daughter."

In most cases, this communication is not audible, nor is it necessarily accompanied by warm, fuzzy feelings. But, in the supernatural dimension, which Christians assert is more than a psychological state, a clear awareness comes to those of us who believe, and the indwelling **Spirit himself testifies with our spirit that we are God's children** (Rom. 8:16).

Paul declares that this assurance is one of the benefits available to those who are born of God. But the fact is that not every Christian lives with this knowledge. And even saints have at times experienced a "dark night of the soul" when the sense of assurance fades or is drowned out by the stresses of life. Here it would be well to remember again the distinction between justification as a relational act and sanctification as a transformational experience of one's life. If a believer lives by faith, the justification is established whether there is awareness of all the ramifications of that reality or not. The Scriptures simply declare that "there is now no condemnation for those who are in Christ Jesus" (8:1).

However, in the transformation dimensions of sanctification, the reality is accessible to us by grace; but, it must be appropriated by a conscious act of the believer. Those who live by the Spirit count themselves alive to God in Christ (6:11) and **put to death the misdeeds of the body** (8:13). In these actions of response, the reality which is there comes to the surface and manifests itself in a life leading to holiness. So it is with the inner witness, which assures our salvation. God waits to give us the whisper, but we must open our spiritual ears to hear. This is something more than blind faith in the authority of the Bible; it is more than positive thinking. It is living **according to the Spirit** (v. 4), the theme of Romans 8.

The logical consequence of becoming a child of God is that we now share in the Father's estate. Like the earthly father in Jesus' well-known parable of the prodigal son, the Heavenly Father now assures us, "You are always with me, and everything I have is yours" (Luke 15:31). As brothers and sisters of Jesus Christ, we share what is His. And Paul once again brings his Roman readers into the reality of what being one with Christ entails. It is sharing in both His suffering and His glory (Rom. 8:17).

Here Paul gives the first hint of a thought that will be expressed most powerfully in his future letter to the Philippians: "I want to know Christ and the power of his resurrection and the fellowship of sharing in his sufferings, becoming like him in his death, and so, somehow, to attain to the resurrection from the dead" (3:10-11). The paradox of present suffering and future glory becomes the topic of the passage that follows.

ENDNOTE

[1]John Loeschen, *Wrestling With Luther,* (St. Louis: Concordian Publishing House, 1976), pp. 43-58.

[2]William Barclay, *The Letter to the Romans,* (Philadelphia: Westminster Press, 1957), pp. 109ff.

10

THE
BELIEVER'S HOPE

Romans 8:18-39

A person does not need a deep understanding of God or of human existence to conclude that life should be miserable for those who are under the wrath of God for their ungodly behavior. And it would seem equally sensible that daily existence for those who, by faith, are children of God should be qualitatively better than that of the ungodly. But, as we have already observed, the facts do not always line up with this simplistic equation of good and evil.

Long ago, the psalmist struggled with the question, "Why do the wicked prosper?" (Psalm 73). And equally perplexing for the Christians in Rome was the question of why bad things happen to good people. Paul has been almost lyrical in describing the benefits of those who have entered a right standing with God through faith in Christ. But he dare not forget that he is writing to believers who are confronted with "present sufferings" (Rom. 8:18).

He could follow the example of Christian Scientists, who argue that evil does not really exist and that the believer triumphs by refusing to view what others would consider to be pain and suffering in negative terms. But looking at life through such rose-colored glasses, even if they be spiritual spectacles, is both unrealistic and unscriptural.

Paul might have turned the problem of suffering back on the Christians in Rome, suggesting that their sinful conduct, spiritual laziness, or lack of faith had stirred up God's wrath once again. As a result, they were being punished by hard times. But, such a view creates false guilt, does not always concur with the realities of the situation, and undermines Paul's entire declaration that "no condemnation" remains for those who are in Christ.

No, Paul takes the stresses of the Christian life seriously, whether they be physical, relational or spiritual in nature. He candidly discusses his personal struggles with a "thorn in the flesh" (2 Corinthians 12:7). He addresses the personal and political squabbles that exist in the churches he has planted (Philippians 4:2; 1 Corinthians 1:10-13). He describes the life of the believer as warfare with Satan and the forces of evil (Ephesians 6:10-17). He offers no deep philosophical analysis for why suffering persists after Jesus' death and resurrection, particularly for those who are in Christ.

But, Paul is unshakable in his confidence that God is sovereign and that all aspects of existence, including the dark side, are in God's control. Scholars wrestle with a precise translation of Romans 8:28. Do "all things work together for good" (KJV), or does God work for good **in all things**? The wording here doesn't matter that much if one believes in "one God and Father of all, who is over all and through all and in all" (Eph. 4:6).

Paul's strategy for handling the present suffering is to keep the long view of the future in mind. Such a perspective builds a genuine hope for the **glorious freedom** which lies ahead when **creation itself will be liberated** (Rom. 8:21). This hope also keeps us focused on the divine process of redemption that reaches back from the glorious freedom in the future to God's first awareness of the human predicament and His designs to rescue us from sin (vv. 29-30). This hope convinces us that no one can condemn us for what lies in the past (v. 34), and that nothing that lies in the future **will be able to separate us from the love of God that is in Christ Jesus** (v. 39).

Romans 8:28 is much more than a spiritual Band-Aid for hard times. It is one of the foundational assumptions of Paul's gospel. As a foundation, it applies to the pleasant episodes of the Christian's life, as well as difficult experiences. It extends beyond the personal experiences of one saint to embrace the church, society and all the kingdoms of this world, which are becoming "the kingdom of our Lord and of his Christ" (Revelation 11:15). It stretches through history from the creation of the first Adam to the return of the Second Adam to claim His bride.

To those "who love him, who have been called according to **his** purpose," the present, even with its suffering, is the entrance point to an unimaginable future which God has prepared for those who love Him (8:28).

1. THE CREATION'S EXPECTATION 8:18-27

Paul himself acknowledges his penchant for comparison—in this case he compares the present state of the believer with what lies in the future. In doing so, he does not want to minimize at all what the person of faith already has attained. There is "no condemnation" (v. 1), but there is death to sin, a new life in Christ, and the indwelling presence of the Spirit for those who are justified and regenerated.

But, when one moves outside the inner realm of self to outward circumstances, it is not unusual to encounter **present sufferings** (v. 18). The matter can be explained in part because of the believer's continued existence in a created order that has not yet been redeemed. The Christian still lives in what the New Testament writers often called *the world*. Jesus himself recognized the paradox facing His followers when He told the Father that they were not "of the world," while at the same time indicating that He did not yet want them to be removed "from the world" (John 17:14-16).

The task of being *in but not of* the world is still the greatest challenge for the person walking according to the Spirit. Too much *of,* and we lose the identity we are called to demonstrate as children of God. Not enough *in,* and we lose touch with those to whom we are indebted to display and proclaim the gospel. We stay in this fallen world because it is not yet redeemed, and God intends for us to be His instruments of righteousness. For Paul, the risks of living with present sufferings are worth it when compared **with the glory that will be revealed in us** (v. 18).

That glory will be revealed in part by our transformation into the likeness of God's Son here on earth. But, Paul also looks ahead to the future glory when the fallen world will be transformed into the new earth (Rev. 21:1). Paul reminds us that the disobedience of Adam and Eve had far-ranging effects, extending beyond human morality to the very interconnectedness of the created order.

Speculating on the perfection of the original creation seems a futile task. Were there mosquitoes in the Garden? Did lions and lambs play together? What is very obvious is that the world we live in today has become "damaged goods." In the internal structures of the natural order, there are destructive forces that bring calamity and destruction. Beyond that, the world is corrupted by the selfish acts of human beings who have been poor stewards of the earth entrusted to them. Not that created matter itself is evil; that would be the ancient gnostic heresy again. Rather, God, who works all things for good, has allowed creation to experience the effects of the Fall so that even the natural order might participate in His glorious plan of redemption.

Paul even has an environmental theology! Like John the Revelator, Paul envisions a new earth that is restored to its original goodness by the same Spirit operating in the lives of humans to undo the effects of Adam's disobedience on them. Paul uses the anguish of childbirth to describe the intense yearning of all creation for deliverance—an image that Jesus himself used to describe the approaching end of this age and the breaking through of the age to come (Matthew 24:8).

But before the prophets of doom can raise their signs declaring "the end is near," Paul introduces one of his most revolutionary ideas: the coming age has already broken in upon the old. Believers, having died and risen with Christ, are those "who enjoy the Spirit as a foretaste of the future" (Rom. 8:23 Williams). The "in, but not of the world" paradox of space is matched by a paradox of time, described by a recent theologian as the *already/not yet* of the kingdom of God.[1]

By His incarnation and resurrection, Christ has already ushered in the eternal kingdom. That is why John the Baptist could declare, "The kingdom of heaven is near" (Matt. 3:2) two thousand years ago, and Jesus could report that "the kingdom of God is within you" (Luke 17:21). Not only did Jesus break the law of sin and death, but He also sent His Spirit to dwell in us. Our lives already manifest aspects of this future glory.

However, we too sense the incomplete nature of our redemption; and we sense it particularly in the areas of our physical (fleshly) existence. While the sinful nature of flesh has been nullified, we are still limited in any number of ways by our bodies. It is interesting that Paul refers to the future glory of a resurrected body as our adoption—just after using the same image to describe our justification. Rather than a contradiction, we can view this double meaning as yet another instance of the *already/not yet* motif.

Paul closes this glimpse toward the future glory with a surprising statement: **In this hope we were saved** (Rom. 8:24). But isn't salvation by *faith?* For Paul, the two terms are almost interchangeable. The Christian hope is more than wishful thinking about the future. It is even more than tentative expectancy. It is an overwhelming confidence that God will perform what He promises.

One recalls the earlier discussion of Abraham, who "in hope believed" that God could perform the inconceivable (4:18). Like Abraham, we must extend our faith beyond what God already has done (our justification) to what He now is doing (our sanctification) and what He yet intends to "carry . . . on to completion [our glorification] until the day of Christ Jesus" (Philippians 1:6).

Paul completes the progression of his thought by spiraling back to the Spirit who lives within us. The groanings of creation as it waits redemption are echoed by the inward groanings of believers who wait in hope for the redemption of their mortal bodies. And now the Spirit adds another voice to the heavenward prayer. The Spirit, whom Paul closely associates with Christ ("The Lord is the Spirit" [2 Corinthians 3:17]) assumes the role of mediator between the Father and His children.

Not only does the Spirit of Christ communicate the Father's love (Rom. 8:16) and desires (v. 14) to the believer; this same Spirit communicates our desires to the Father (v. 27). And so sensitive is the Spirit that the communication goes beyond what we conceive or can express in words.

There are those who interpret the **groans that words cannot express** (v. 26) as a reference to "glossolalia," the gift of speaking in tongues that Paul refers to in 1 Corinthians 12 and 14. Such a view lessens the impact of this passage, for it is the Spirit and not the Spirit-empowered believer who intercedes to the Father. Furthermore, the groans refer to the longing of the believer caught in the *already/not yet* of human existence, and not to the joyous ecstasies of devotion or worship.

Here, then, is a neglected aspect of our transformation toward holiness. Sanctification is not only what *we* are doing to conform to God's will; it is *the Spirit* interceding to the Father **for the saints** (Rom. 8:27; Greek, *holy ones*) in accordance with God's will. Whatever we choose to say about offering ourselves to God (12:1), we must also remember that the Spirit offers us to the Father in prayer. That is why Paul can speak of the twofold dimension of our transformation, incorporating both God's initiative and our response.

Throughout this chapter, Paul has reminded the believers in Rome that the Spirit is acting on their behalf in transforming them into heirs of God and co-heirs with Jesus Christ (v. 17). The Spirit frees them from the law of sin (v. 2), controls their minds (v. 6), lives within them (v. 9), gives life to their mortal bodies (v. 11), leads them (v. 14), testifies to the spirit (v. 16) and finally, intercedes on their behalf (v. 26). Here is God himself, through his Spirit intimately involved with the daily life of the believer. Here is the Spirit creating the life of holiness in those of us who have been reconciled to God by faith.

To the believers in Philippi, Paul gives the following admonition. "Continue to work out your salvation with fear and trembling" (Phil. 2:12). Paul does not suggest there are certain behaviors or works that must be done in order to be saved. This verse follows immediately upon Paul's great tribute to Christ for self-emptying love that led him to death on a cross. Instead Paul is urging the believers to *live* out the salvation they have received as a gift by acting in conformity to the will of the Spirit that dwells in them. Christians are called to demonstrate in outward actions the new reality that is within them. But such an endeavor is only possible because of the divine work that precedes it: "For it is God who works in you to will and to act according to his good purpose" (v. 13). The Spirit intercedes, the Father acts, the believer continues to work out salvation . . . and all this leads to holiness and eternal life.

2. THE FATHER'S PURPOSE 8:28-30

Paul could handle present sufferings because he had a confident hope in God's plan for the future redemption of all creation. It is no wonder, then, that he can accept that all things are working for the good of those who have united themselves in love to the Father.

But, once again, Paul wants to dispel any hint that a human action, even one as noble as our love, is what causes God to act on our behalf. Immediately conjoined to **those who love him** is the divine initiative that makes such love possible—being **called according to his purpose** (v. 28). And that sequence is essential to a Christian understanding of the gospel. Paul's colleague in the faith, the Apostle John, states it most clearly: "We love because he first loved us" (1 John 4:19).

The pattern of divine call and human response is the key to the gospel, but the plan of redemption is actually more complex than that. Paul lays out a five-step sequence (Rom. 8:29-30) that takes us from the eternal dimension to another. The sequence is given chronologically—that is, Paul moves through "clock time" in spelling out the order of salvation. The sequence is as follows: divine foreknowledge, predestination, calling, justification and glorification.

From a casual reading of these verses, it would appear that once an individual gets in line at foreknowledge, that person will come out the other end as a glorified saint. But there are two different understandings of that sequence, depending on which end the interpreter highlights. In his insightful analysis of John Wesley's thought, Harald Lindström defines these two approaches.[2] There is first a *causal* theology, which starts with the eternal past and moves toward the future.

Such a theology places great emphasis on how events which have already occurred produce results in the present or the future. Hence the term "causal theology." It might help to understand this view if you could imagine the opening shot of a billiard game. Once the player pushes the cue, the sequence takes over: cue hits cue ball, cue ball hits center cluster, balls scatter across the table. Each step in that process is determined by a previous action, and the sequence can be traced back to the initial action of the player.

Is that what Paul is describing here? Did God, at some time long ago, set into motion a sequence of cause-and-effect events that inevitably resulted in the salvation of Paul's readers? When God acts, do individuals really have any freedom to respond, or is it all programmed ahead of time? Lindström suggests that the theology of the sixteenth-century Reformers, particularly Calvin, is based on this causal pattern. Calvinists emphasize the powerful action of God in the past (predestination, election, redemption) that all but eliminates human participation or freedom in the saving act.

John Wesley, argues Lindström, viewed salvation in a different way than other Protestant theologians. His theology was a *teleological* approach—a technical term that, for our purposes, could be called a *goal-oriented* approach. (The Greek word *telos* means "goal.") Wesleyan theology does not start at the beginning, but rather at the *end* of the story. God, who exists outside of human categories of clock time (*chronos),* envisions an eternal kingdom where human beings, created in His image, will experience eternal life and fellowship with Him.

In Paul's understanding, this glorified existence includes not the age to come, but the "foretaste of glory" that a transformed believer attains (or experiences) in sanctification. But, in order to be glorified, one must enter into a right relationship with God—one must be justified. And, for one to be justified, that individual must hear the call of God, which includes both a condemnation of sin and the good news of salvation. But, in order for one to hear the call, God must determine out of His grace and goodness to redeem the lost by the free gift of His Son.

In a teleological pattern, one must work back from the goal and create the *means* to achieve that goal. Our illustration of a billiard game might be helpful again. A player in a difficult situation might choose to make a combination shot. Wanting to get a particular ball in the side pocket, she might see another ball that, if hit just right, could make that happen. She must decide carefully how to position the cue so that each other ball in sequence will go where it needs to go in order to achieve the final goal. That is goal-oriented thinking.

The sequence of events, whether in billiards or Romans 8:29-30, is the same if one thinks in causal or goal-oriented terms. But the understanding of the sequence is altered considerably. Viewing Paul's sequence from past decrees of a sovereign, all-knowing God borders on *determinism*—a chain of events that works itself out in salvation for those whom God has already chosen to be saved.

The goal-oriented approach appears to allow more freedom. God has made ample provision for our future glory, but leaves human beings free to accept or refuse those provisions at each step of the sequence. Having "so loved the world [God] gave his one and only Son, that whoever believes in him shall not perish but have eternal life" (John 3:16). Here is the ultimate statement regarding a goal-oriented God! His saving work predestined all to salvation and provided a means powerful enough to save the entire race. He leaves to humans, however, the free choice to accept the gift and share in His glory.

It would seem to be totally inconsistent with Paul's reasoning in these chapters on salvation to conclude that believers have no part in this path to the future. Paul has endeavored to destroy any thought that what individuals do causes them to be right with God. He even rejects the view that hints at cooperation, where God does part of the job and we must do the rest. But Paul does declare that there are appropriate *responses* we can make to God's great provisions for salvation. We can believe in His promise; we can die and rise with Christ; we can be led by the Spirit. All of these responses of the believing follower of Christ are enriched by the full awareness that God is working all things for our good as we open our lives to Him.

3. THE BELIEVER'S CONFIDENCE 8:31-39

In the first eight chapters of his letter to the Romans, Paul has presented his understanding of God's righteousness and how one can attain it. He has traced the downward spiral of sin, the futile attempts of humans to justify themselves, and finally the great gift of grace that both reconciles and transforms an individual in anticipation of the glory that is to come. Looking back on the entire panorama of salvation, Paul inquires, **What, then, shall we say in response to this?** (v. 31). His response here will be expressed in praise to God. As he opens chapter 12, Paul will be addressing another underlying question that is equally important: "What then shall we *do* in response to this?"

But for now, Paul's verbal reply is to conclude that **in all these things we are more than conquerors** (8:37). If the Father's final goal is to conform us **to the likeness of his Son** (v. 29), and He **did not spare his own Son, but gave him up for us all—how will he not also, along with him, graciously give us all things** (v. 32), including victory over all those forces that threaten to undo us?

It is interesting that again Paul makes no specific mention of Satan, the archenemy of Christ and the believer. Instead Paul alludes to lesser principalities and powers that were commonly associated with the spiritual realm in his time. And, rather than itemizing all the potential forces that might come against the believer, he addresses the two major fronts on which the assault might be made: condemnation and separation.

The Scriptures begin with the account of a creative God who fashioned humans in His likeness and established intimate fellowship with them. Adam and Eve enjoyed evening walks with the Creator (Gen. 3:8). But their disobedience resulted in alienation—alienation characterized by guilt ("they realized they were naked" [Gen. 3:7, 10]) and separation ("the Lord God banished him from the garden" [Gen. 3:23]). Now, having described God's wonderful provision for reconciling the descendants of Adam to himself, Paul returns to the same two issues: Can the believer who has found peace be once again declared guilty, and if so, who is able to do this? Can the believer who has God's Spirit dwelling within once again be separated from God? If so, who or what can do this?

And Paul's answer is crystal clear: *no one* can condemn, and *nothing* can separate us from God's love. No doubt Paul is thinking of the future day of wrath, "when [God's] righteous judgment will be revealed" (Rom. 2:5). One can almost envision the individual standing in the presence of God to give an account of the deeds done in the flesh (14:12). The charges against this person of faith are to be read aloud . . . but no one steps forward to declare them.

Satan can't—his law of sin and death has been nullified by "the law of the Spirit of life" (8:2). Other humans can't—they have all fallen "short of the glory of God" (3:23) and stand equally condemned before the righteous Judge. Christ as perfect human could, but He won't—He has died for us and is now our Advocate and Mediator (8:34; 1 John 2:1-2). And God himself? Hardly—**It is God who justifies** (Rom. 8:33) out of His mercy and love for us. Hearing no accusation, the case is dismissed.

There is now no condemnation for those who are in Christ Jesus (v. 1).

No poet has described this truth more powerfully than John Wesley's brother, Charles, who opens his hymn text with the call, "Arise, my soul, arise; shake off thy guilty fears," and closes that hymn with the joyous response, "With confidence I now draw nigh, and 'Father, Abba, Father' cry."

No condemnation flows logically to the further conclusion—no separation. Paul first suggests that the stressful circumstances of this life—**trouble, hardship, danger, famine** (8:35)—are not powerful enough to distract the person who has the proper assessment of "present sufferings" (8:18; cf. 5:3). Included in those circumstances are even greater threats that represent an assault upon one's faith—**persecution, sword** (8:35). The witness (*martyrs*) of the early Roman Christians in the arenas gives ample proof of Paul's assertion that believers can be "more than conquerors" (8:37) against such assaults. Even ancient tradition reports that the Roman Emperor Julian, who bitterly opposed Christianity during his reign (361-363 A.D.), exclaimed on his deathbed, "You have conquered, O Galilean!" Even the combined forces of the Roman Empire could not defeat the followers of the King of the Jews.

Victorious over the foes of this world, yes. But what about the cosmic forces? Here (Rom. 8:38-39) Paul combines spiritual powers (**angels, demons, powers**) with temporal categories (**present** and **future**), spatial dimensions (**height** and **depth**), and the dynamics of human existence (**life** and **death**). However, these terms are to be understood in first- and twentieth-century thinking, they represent a range of forces beyond the human plane that create interference, if not alienation, between the believer and God. And Paul rejects any suggestion that these facets of creation can be of greater power that the One who created them in the first place.

In listing what cannot separate us from the love of God, Paul omits one significant reference, and theologians have been arguing from his silence for centuries. Paul does not mention humans themselves. If there is not **anything else in all creation** that can separate us from God's love (v. 39), would it not seem logical that the believer, who is certainly part of the creation, would be included?

Those who accept this logic argue for the doctrine of "eternal security." They assert that once God has justified the repentant sinner and has imparted new life, nothing—not even the individual—is able to reverse God's purposes. That believer may live below God's moral standard of holiness or even break fellowship with the Father.

Nevertheless, they claim, one's justification is secure. God's unconditional love will see beyond the disobedient thoughts and actions to the Cross, where salvation was determined for eternity. The believer can live with the full confidence that God will not permit sin to condemn, nor unbelief to separate a child of God from his Heavenly Father.

Without attempting to unravel all the theological arguments and scriptural texts used to debate the issue of eternal security, it is sufficient to point out that the context of Romans 8 does not support such a view. The focus of Paul's letter has been upon the damaging effects of sin (Adam's and ours) and the freedom from bondage that is offered in Christ. Paul wants the believers in Rome to become aware of both God's grace and His power to accomplish His purposes in their lives, without any works of self-righteousness on their part . . . or any interference on the part of the dark forces of sin and evil.

But, the book of Romans does not suggest a determinism that removes the freedom of the believer to "trust and obey." Our faith and our obedience to the Spirit do not save us; salvation is the free gift of God. But our *response* of faith and our willingness to be led by the Spirit are essential actions to open up the possibilities of this goal-oriented path to glory.

Wesleyans would contend that the very freedom we have in Christ is the freedom of Adam and Eve to live the righteous life, or to move away from fellowship with God by unbelief and false worship. We are free to choose the downward spiral, but the sinful nature that makes us incapable of attaining righteousness has been put to death through the Cross. We are free to love and serve God, and nothing *else* can seperate us from that love because our faith and His love are both rooted **in Christ Jesus our Lord** (v. 39).

ENDNOTE

[1]Oscar Cullmann, *Salvation in History*, (New York: Harper and Row, 1967), p. 172.

[2]Harald Lindström, *Wesley and Sanctification*, (Wilmore, KY: Francis Asbury Publishing Co., n.d.), pp. 184-197.

Part Five

ISRAEL REDEEMED:
The Drama of Righteousness
Romans 9:1–11:36

I f the book of Romans were a sermon, one might well expect that the soaring testimony at the close of chapter 8 would be followed immediately by a closing hymn and benediction. But Romans is not a sermon, and Paul's agenda with the recipients of this letter does not end with declaring the benefits of justification by faith.

While outlining the great plan of redemption that extends to all the sons and daughters of Adam, Paul has spent considerable time criticizing one particular religious tradition—his own, Judaism. The children of Israel, Paul argues, have been given so much, yet have handled poorly the revelation they received by substituting a "works" righteousness for the provisions of God's gracious promise.

One could expect Jewish believers in Rome to bristle at Paul's criticisms. At least they would be wondering whether Paul is suggesting that their "chosen" status with God should now be viewed as a liability. Perhaps Paul is saying that being heirs of the promise has excluded them from God's blessing. Paul now pauses in his letter to affirm his deep appreciation for his own spiritual heritage, and his desire that the inclusive scope of the gospel would reach out and encircle his own people, as well as the newly-established Gentile community of faith. Paul offers words of assurance not only to the Jewish believers in Rome, but to all future generations of his people as well.

Paul's understanding of salvation, processed by his logical mind and guided by the inspiration of the Holy Spirit, remains consistent, even in this discourse. He cannot develop one view of God's dealing with humans that applies to Jews, and another that applies to Gentiles. Yet a puzzling question persists for Paul and for us: How can we reconcile God's purposes for redemption under the old covenant with the provisions of grace under the new covenant?

In these three chapters, Paul wrestles with the questions of the old and new covenants. His particular focus is his own race, the people of the covenant. But his underlying assumptions about God's dealings remain the same as his earlier discussion of salvation for the Gentiles in Rome. God desires the salvation of all persons, and makes salvation available to those who accept His promises by trusting his grace, rather than by striving to earn a right standing with God.

Paul examines the history of the Jews from the perspective of God's provision for their salvation, their failure to accept the promise by faith, and God's persistent grace that will use those considered to be "non-people," the Gentiles, to draw His people, the Jews, back to a right relationship with God.

Commentators have long debated how to approach this section of the book of Romans. Because of its ethnic focus, readers have sometimes been advised to move directly from the close of chapter 8 to the beginning of chapter 12, where Paul again picks up the theme of salvation for individual believers. Other scholars with strong interests in prophetic events scrutinize chapters 9 through 11 to discover how the Jewish people and the modern state of Israel fit into God's plan for the final redemption of the world.

A few scholars have argued that these chapters form the interpretive key to the entire book of Romans. They contend that Paul's primary objective in writing to the Romans was to resolve the tensions existing between Jewish and Gentile believers. Paul's deep aspirations for the salvation of his own people form the heart of his message, with the discussions on sin, faith and justification addressed as secondary issues.

We will approach these chapters by trying to understand them in the context of Paul's own time. A remarkable transition was taking place in the New Testament church at this time. A spiritual reality had sprung up through the life and ministry of a Jewish rabbi who was also the Messiah and divine Son of God. Jesus devoted much of His teaching and healing ministry to His own people, the Jews. But His message was good news for all people. Difficult circumstances in Jerusalem after His resurrection and ascension had forced the core of Jewish believers to scatter outward from the geographic and cultural boundaries of Israel.

As the first Gentiles received the gospel and turned to Christ, they were accepted, albeit somewhat reluctantly, into what were formerly strictly Jewish congregations. But now, by the time of the writing of this letter, Paul and his cohorts had begun an aggressive outreach ministry to Gentiles with great success. We enter the scene as the balance is shifting away from the ethnic focus of messianic Judaism to a new perspective where "there is neither Jew nor Greek, slave nor free, male nor female, for . . . all [are] one in Christ Jesus" (Galatians 3:28).

The first-century issue of how Jews and Gentiles fit into the body of Christ is no longer a matter of great debate in our modern world. Paul's vision of "one body . . . one faith, one baptism; one God and Father of all" (Ephesians 4:4-6), incorporating the twin traditions of Jewish and non-Jewish Christianity, has not materialized in the past two thousand years. For the most part, the Jewish community has not accepted Jesus as Messiah and continues to search for and claim a right relationship with God through patterns established before His gospel was proclaimed.

Gentile believers, for their part, have not shared Paul's deep compassion for Jews, and have often taken deliberate steps to emphasize the differences rather than the commonalties of traditions that worship the same God. (For example, the long-standing tradition of eating ham on Easter originated as a deliberate statement against Jewish dietary laws.) As a result, we do not yet experience the remarkable "grafting" of the Jewish branch into the tree of faith in our world today.

So, we must examine this passage looking for clues to help us understand how God deals with humans of all ethnic backgrounds. In this discussion of one particular group's search for God, we may discover timeless truths that apply to our walk with God and our relationship to those around us who manifest a zeal for God and search for relationships that are not based on knowledge (Rom. 10:2). But, at a deeper level, we listen to God's promise to His chosen people through His "prophet," the Apostle Paul. In Romans 9 through 11 we read of God's persistent call to the Jews, their failure to heed that call, and the gracious mercy and sovereign love of God that yearns, in His grace and perfect timing, to bring His people to righteousness and a right standing with God.

ISRAEL'S FAILURE

Romans 9:1–10:21

P aul's discussion of the future salvation of the Jewish people is difficult to interpret from any perspective. In his letter to the Romans, he is obviously plowing new ground in his views on what it means to be a Jew and how the new covenant in Christ relates to the old covenant with Abraham. The religious assumptions of the Jews in Paul's day were centered in ethnic identity. They believed they enjoyed "most-favored status" with God on the basis of their genetic and cultural ties to Abraham.

In chapter 4, Paul argued that those who share the *faith,* not the genes, of Abraham are his true descendants. God's favor depends far more on one's heart attitude rather than one's ancestry or religious affiliation. Paul now returns to that earlier understanding, but views it from the divine perspective of God's *initiative* in choosing Abraham and others for salvation, rather than giving attention to the human response of faith. In this passage, the contrast is not between human endeavor or faith, but rather human endeavor and divine election—**not by works but by him who calls** (9:12).

Throughout the biblical narrative, one encounters the obvious fact that God has chosen particular individuals and groups to receive special revelations of His truth. Furthermore, God has involved himself directly in the events related to these persons and groups in order to accomplish His divine purposes for them. The aspect of being chosen leads one to the logical conclusion that others have *not* been chosen.

In raising this concept of divine election as it relates to the people of Israel, Paul draws us into the age-old question of divine sovereignty and human freedom. His earlier responses (chap. 2) were that since all have a knowledge of God's law, all persons are accountable and responsible. In chapter 9, Paul offers a much more perplexing response: **Shall what** is formed say to him who formed it, **"Why did you make me like this?" Does not the potter have the right to make out of the same lump of clay some pottery for noble purposes and some for common use?** (vv. 20-21).

Without satisfying the gnawing issues of God's fairness, Paul declares the sovereign right of God to call a special people and to shape the circumstances of their destiny. By offering this bold statement about the sovereignty of God, Paul provides a corollary to his earlier affirmation that "in all things God works for the good of those . . . who have been called according to his purpose" (8:28).

1. GOD'S CALL TO ISRAEL 9:1-29

One looks in vain in the closing verses of chapter 8 for some clue to explain Paul's sudden shift of focus to the Jews in chapter 9. Paul moves from the ecstasy of confident joy to **great sorrow and unceasing anguish** (9:2) without providing any logical bridge to his new topic. We can only assume that Paul thought questions raised concerning the place of the law and the significance of the Jewish people needed to be addressed further in this letter. Having outlined God's design for all believers (predestination, calling, justification and glorification) in 8:30, Paul now looks at the more focused picture of God's design for His chosen people, the Jews.

In his attitude toward the unbelieving Jews, Paul demonstrates for us the appropriate Christian perspective toward those who live apart from faith. In his various writings, Paul expresses considerable agitation, even anger, at the distortions and abuses of Jewish teaching as it relates to his understanding of the gospel. In his letter to the Galatians, Paul even wishes that those who stress circumcision would go one step *beyond* the standard procedure in their surgical practice (Gal. 5:12).

But Paul's vehement statements about the thinking or practice of those who oppose him is never directed toward them *as persons*. When thinking of his own race, Paul feels **great sorrow and unceasing anguish** (Rom. 9:2). So deep is Paul's compassion for his people that he would sacrifice his most valued treasure—eternal life in Christ—for the sake of their salvation (v. 3). Is this not a reflection of the character of God, who "so loved the world that he gave his one and only Son" (John 3:16)? Is this not the mind of Christ, who "made himself nothing. . . . and became obedient to death" (Philippians 2:7-8)?

In an age when Christians confront so much that is offensive to the gospel, we must learn like Paul to be outspoken in our condemnation of sin, but always retain a broken heart and a compassionate spirit for those who are sinners—those who are the potential recipients of the same grace that has come to us.

Paul's anguish is all the more intense because he is grieving for those who have already been the benefactors of God's grace. These are not pagan Gentiles, living out the depravity of moral darkness; these are the people of Israel. Paul checks off all the blessings God has bestowed upon them: **adoption as sons, divine glory, the covenants, the receiving of the law, the temple worship, the promises, the patriarchs,** and **the human ancestry of Christ** (Rom. 9:4-5).

The question for Paul, and for all who read the Old Testament from the perspective of the Christian faith, is simply, "What went wrong?" How could those who had received so much special favor and so many spiritual resources end up so far from a right standing with God?

Paul begins his response by ruling out one option as simply unthinkable. The problem is not with God, he says. God's choice of a particular group to be the recipients of His favor is justified.

To set the record straight, Paul points to an error that has persisted down to the present time, namely that every person who can trace his or her genealogy to Abraham is a son or daughter of promise. Here Paul begins to dismantle the concept of ethnic salvation. Even among the offspring of Abraham, God reserved His freedom to determine the recipients of grace. Abraham had *two* sons; both were his natural children, but only the descendants of Isaac were **the children of the promise** (v. 8). Similarly, Isaac had two sons, but only the children of Jacob (Israel) were chosen.

The point is clear—God is free to choose whom He pleases for His blessing, and the reasons for His choices are not always clearly understood from a human perspective. Too often we expect the choices all to be clear-cut and according to the rules. The rules, of course, are the way *we* think the game should be played. And when God doesn't act according to our assessment, we are tempted to ask, **Is God unjust?** (v. 14).

"No," Paul replies. We must remember who it is that writes the rules. Paul is not trying to find a way to allow God to act in irrational and arbitrary ways. Paul is defending the sovereignty of the Father Almighty, who introduced himself to Moses by the unspeakable name "I AM WHO I AM" (Exodus 3:14)—or, as some scholars suggest, "I will be What I will be." Such a sovereign God has the right to show mercy to whom He wishes. God's highest virtue is not to be fair even in every situation; it is to demonstrate compassion and mercy, when such an attitude is unwarranted on the part of the recipient. In doing so, God is still just.

Paul could very easily be pushed into a corner at this point. One might ask, "If God does *not* choose to show mercy, or if He does *not* select some for salvation, isn't He by His non-action writing them off from His divine plan?" Isn't Paul moving toward a divine determinism when he makes this argument and supports it with the Old Testament quotation, **Jacob I loved, but Esau I hated** (Rom. 9:13; cf. Malachi 1:2-3)?

Paul appears to be caught on the horns of a dilemma. Whichever way he moves, he creates an unacceptable view of salvation. If God saves human beings on the basis of who they are, what they do, or any other standard consistent with *our* game plans, He loses His sovereign power and His divine initiative as the author of salvation. On the other hand, if God elects persons for salvation completely on the basis of His own preferences, apart from any human involvement or response, then humans lose all sense of accountability and become mere game pieces in a game of cosmic fatalism.

In Paul's letter to the Romans, he is addressing primarily a Jewish audience whose tendency has been to assume they have earned the right of salvation. Hence he will counterbalance that false conception of salvation by defending God's sovereign choices.

But there is ample evidence elsewhere in Paul's writings and in the whole of Scripture to suggest that God's choice for salvation is more inclusive than it is exclusive. God's decision to **have compassion on whom [He will] have compassion** (Rom. 9:15) has resulted in an enlarging, rather than a shrinking, of His circle of mercy and love. Without slipping into a false universalism where everyone is caught up in the open arms of salvation, Paul describes the gracious love of the Father which embraces all the children of Abraham through both *promise* (the divine initiative) and *faith* (the human response).

The concept of election—God's sovereign right to choose—works well when kept in the abstract and general terms of theology. The specific outworking of this doctrine in individual lives, however, is more difficult to explain. Will Pharaoh be excused because God hardened his heart in order to deliver Israel from Egypt (Exodus 7:3, 13)? Will Joseph's brothers be off the hook because "God intended [their evil] for good . . . the saving of many lives" (Genesis 50:20)? Will Judas argue that he was simply a pawn in God's bigger plan of redemption, and not "the one doomed to destruction" according to Jesus' own words (John 17:12)?

168

Paul's observations in Romans 9 leave us reeling with questions. For all of his ability to anticipate objections and offer detailed responses, Paul silences our calls for clarification with two strong assertions.

First, there are some matters that must be left to God's sovereign and mysterious will. Clay does not have the right to question the potter's designs (v. 21). Paul is no doubt alluding to Jeremiah's visit to the house of a potter, and the lesson he learned there about God's ability to shape the destiny of nations by His sovereign power (Jer. 18:6-11). Again, we must remember that Paul's purpose in proclaiming God's sovereignty is not to make Him out to be capricious or vindictive; rather, Paul is refuting the assertions of those who presume to determine, on the basis of their own rules and regulations, who is in a right relationship with God.

We will all encounter situations where we feel the obligation, in the words of the poet John Milton, to "justify the ways of God to man" *(Paradise Lost)*. Or, failing in our attempts to accomplish this task, we face the more serious inclination to complain directly to God about His dealings. A clear assessment of who we are in relation to God, whose "ways [are] higher than [our] ways and . . . thoughts than [our] thoughts" (Isaiah 55:9), would be wise in such circumstances.

God does not despise our honest questions, but neither does He feel constrained to resolve all of our confusion by reason, Scripture or divine insight. One important aspect of faith is to be willing to remain pliable in His hands as He conforms us to the likeness He has designed—the likeness of His Son.

Although submission to the inscrutable will of God is one expression of faith, Paul does not leave believers groping in the dark with "blind faith." The silencing of the questioning soul is based upon a deeper conviction—that God's actions in history are designed **to make the riches of his glory known to the objects of his mercy, whom he prepared in advance for glory** (Rom. 9:23). And who are these objects of His mercy? **Even us, whom he also called, not only from the Jews but also from the Gentiles** (v. 24).

Paul brings us back to God's goal-oriented redemption. If we are to understand the mysteries of life, we can do it only by standing back and gazing at the whole of God's plan. Throughout the span of history, there always has been a remnant—a persistent thread of God's redemptive plan that moves toward future glory.

One could think of several times in history when the light of redemption flickered and almost disappeared. For the Jews, those dark hours included the captivity in Babylon, the destruction of Jerusalem at the close of the New Testament era, and the Holocaust of our own century. But, these people of promise have survived under incredible adversity. Paul would argue that the final chapter has not yet been written for the Jews, and God's sovereign choice can be traced in the background of every puzzling event in their history.

So also with the church, the body of Christ, a similar scanning of history will reveal moments when the survival of vital faith was in question. But God fully intends that there will always be a remnant known as **my people** (v. 25). God intends to maintain the family line of **sons of the living God** (v. 26). Paul would echo the words of one of his best interpreters—the great reformer, Martin Luther—who concluded his famous hymn, *A Mighty Fortress*, with the words, "God's truth abideth still, His kingdom is forever."

In this ninth chapter of Romans, Paul offers two wonderful strategies for believers who are attempting to plumb the mysteries of how God is working in the world. First, we must have a humility which leaves the ultimate answers to an all-wise God. Second, we must have a confidence which dares to believe that the promises God has made on our behalf never will be nullified. Paul has not sorted out all the answers regarding his own race, the Jews. But he is confident that God will be faithful to His people and to His nature of steadfast love. We would do well to exemplify Paul's confidence in a sovereign God.

2. ISRAEL'S LACK OF FAITH 9:30-10:13

We applaud Paul's bold assertion that a sovereign God may choose whom He will, and act as He wishes to accomplish His plans. But Paul's earlier discussion of God's chosen people, the Jews, clearly suggests that something has gone drastically awry with God's designs for these people.

Now, at the close of chapter 9, Paul states the problem in very pointed words: **Gentiles, who did not pursue righteousness, have obtained it . . . by faith; but Israel, who pursued a law of righteousness, has not attained it** (vv. 30-31). In other words, those whom God elected for a right relationship with Him are more distant than ever from that relationship, while those to whom God has given no special revelation (the Gentiles) are now the recipients of His mercy and favor.

Paul, of course, attempts to explain this puzzle. He begins by alluding to an Old Testament theme that carries particular significance to several New Testament writers: the rejected stone. The concept of God as the "Rock of Israel" first appears in Genesis (49:24), and surfaces again in the literature of the Psalms. Isaiah goes beyond the imagery of the rock as place of refuge and strength to suggest that this divine stone will also cause some to stumble and fall (8:14-15).

In the later prophets, the image is expanded further by suggestions that a new stone, "a precious cornerstone," will be "cut out of a mountain" by a supernatural agency (Isaiah 28:16; Daniel 2:45). This stone will be more than a fortress stronghold for the people of God; it will destroy their enemies and become a "rock of offense" (Isa. 8:14 KJV) for those who oppose the Righteous One.

Jesus connects these images with himself by quoting another passage from the Psalms as being fulfilled in Him: "The stone the builders rejected has become the capstone; the LORD has done this, and it is marvelous in our eyes" (Psalm 118:22; Matthew 21:42). Finally, Peter and Paul both use this motif to describe the person and work of Christ (Acts 4:11; Ephesians 2:20; 1 Peter 2:4-6).

Here in Romans, Paul blends the two Isaiah passages together to give prophetic significance to the fact that, for the people of promise, the Messiah has become a **stumbling stone** because of their persistence in seeking righteousness by their own works (9:32-33; see also 1 Corinthians 1:23). Paul cannot escape noting the inclusive nature of the Jewish Scriptures as he observes that **the one who trusts in [Christ] will never be put to shame** (Rom. 9:33). Implicit in Paul's reference to "the one" are those Gentile Christians who have accepted the promise by faith.

However, the failure of the Jews to respond to God's call was more than fulfillment of Old Testament prophecy; it was misguided zeal as well. Having received a special revelation of God's law, they chose to use their *own* attempts to measure up to that righteousness as a means of attaining a right standing with God. Such attempts were futile.

In this passage of Romans, Paul echoes the downward spiral he had described in detail in chapter 1. Israel's ignorance of God's righteousness led to foolish attempts at self-righteousness, which eventually resulted in unrighteousness. By substituting their own works in place of faith in the righteousness that comes from God, they became both disobedient and unbelieving, and in such a state **they did not submit to God's righteousness** (10:3). Note how quickly Paul has shifted from the divine act of election to human responsibility for faith and submission to God!

This self-righteousness (which was, in fact, unrighteousness) was based upon the Jews' strict adherence to the law. Paul boldly asserts that **Christ is the end of the law** (v. 4). The Greek and English wording of this statement allows for two separate meanings, both supported in other places by the statements of Paul and Jesus.

One possible meaning would be that Paul is indicating that the law was terminated by the advent of the Messiah. In this view, the law cannot function as the instrument of salvation, because the law only produces condemnation. Its function is to bring us to an awareness of sin, and our need of the gospel is completed at the moment we respond in faith. The believer, then, is no longer bound to the law, but rather to Christ. In this understanding, the law ceases to be relevant to the person who believes.

The dangers of such a view are obvious. Apart from any function of the law, the believer is apt to slip into a moral freedom that is, in fact, a return to unrighteousness. Paul will warn the Galatians, "Do not use your freedom [from the law] to indulge the sinful nature" (5:13). This antinomian (literally *against the law*) approach to Christianity has caused moral and spiritual disaster repeatedly throughout the history of the church.

It is better to understand the phrase in Romans 10:4 in terms of fulfillment or completion. The Greek word for "end" *(telos)* that Paul uses can equally mean "goal" as it does "terminus." In this latter sense, Christ is the culmination and *fulfillment* of all the law was intended to be and to do. Jesus himself told the crowds, "Do not think that I have come to abolish the Law or the Prophets; I have not come to abolish them but to fulfill them" (Matt. 5:17).

Through His death and resurrection, Jesus offers the gift of forgiveness and life—the remedy for the condemnation that comes from the law. The law can reveal the righteousness of God, but only the grace of Christ can bring one to a right standing with God. In such a view, the law may still function in the life of the believer to reveal righteousness and, at times, *unrighteousness*, and the person who is sensitive to the Holy Spirit will be drawn to Christ **so that there may be righteousness for everyone who believes** (Rom. 10:4).

For Paul, the response of faith is not another *work* of human effort. Faith is simply the acceptance of the gift offered to us. The gift is a promise to be accepted in one's heart, and an affirmation to be expressed with one's mouth. Furthermore, one does not have to search high and low for this faith, or conjure it up.

This **word** of promise and affirmation **is near you; it is in your mouth and in your heart** (v. 8). Paul is repeating a quote from Moses recorded in the Jewish Scriptures (Deuteronomy 30:12-14), lest the Jews reply, "That is only what you say, Paul." One could hardly accuse Paul of prooftexting or twisting Scripture to his own purposes, after looking at the passage surrounding this text. Moses appeals to the Israelites "to love the LORD your God, to walk in his ways, and to keep his commands" (Deut. 30:16). The sequence is worth noting: love, walk, keep (obey). Relationship leads to fellowship, which leads to conduct. Paul has stressed the same sequence in his Romans "road to salvation."

The mistake of the Jews—and of many self-proclaimed followers of Christ—is that they *begin* the sequence with obedience, presuming to restore the relationship to God through their own efforts, thus earning the right of fellowship with God. Not so! Salvation begins in the inward person and manifests itself in outward works.

Paul does move beyond the Old Testament text to describe what that response of mouth and heart should be. The affirmation of the mouth was simple and all too familiar to the Romans. They had, no doubt, attended public gatherings where the ancient pledge of allegiance to Rome was uttered. Just three words: *Caesar is Lord.* In that simple statement, the relationship of the citizen to Caesar was described, and the authority of Caesar over that individual was acknowledged.

Similarly, Christians simply bring their acknowledgment of who is sovereign and who merits their allegiance when they testify that *Jesus is Lord.* Individuals coming to Christ need not bring long grocery lists of moral accomplishments. Nor do they need to recite lengthy creeds or give detailed explanations of theological doctrines. Underlying the affirmation that Jesus is Lord is a heart confidence (belief) that God has accomplished in Christ what He promised to do—namely, put to death what is old, and create new life. Believing and affirming that simple fact is what justifies a person before God and saves that person from condemnation.

How inclusive is this offer of salvation? Should we think of it as restricted to those whom God has elected? Is salvation only for the Jews? In statements that appear almost contradictory to Romans 9, Paul now removes all restrictions from this gift of grace. The only conditions are these: **If you confess . . . and believe . . . you will be saved** (10:9). Lest the readers confuse who is included in the "you," Paul repeats the earlier quotation from Isaiah: *Anyone* **who trusts in him** (v. 11, italics mine). And, just in case it still isn't clear, Paul offers one of his boldest statements on the recipients of grace: **There is no difference between Jew and Gentile—the same Lord is Lord of all and richly blesses all who call on him** (v. 12).

We must take this latter statement as the focal point for Paul's understanding of salvation. It is hard to reconcile these words with his

173

statements concerning God's election of the remnant in chapter 9. We must again assume that Paul begins with the sovereign initiative of God to redeem His creation by an act of deliberate choice.

There have been moments in history when God's choosing has resulted in the calling of specific individuals and groups. At times, His choosing has led to His intervention in the course of historical events. But, in His supreme act of redemption—the gift of His Son—God has declared His purpose that all should be saved. The gift is available to all—that is, all who will respond to the call of God with a call of their own; **everyone who** [in faith] **calls on the name of the Lord!** (10:13).

We must be honest and confess that there is a pattern similar to Israel's in the salvation story of many of us, particularly those who have been raised within the traditions of Christianity. Like the Jews of old, we have been chosen for salvation by a loving God. Like them, we have been given special insight into the mysteries of the gospel through exposure to biblical truths at home and church. Like the Jews, we have watched our personal lives be shaped by acts of divine providence. And what has been the result of all these blessings?

All too often we have pursued a righteousness of our own making. Many of us have convinced ourselves that "church-ianity" would make things right with God. And, like the Jews, we have at times become offended and scandalized when "outsiders" to our denominational biases grasped the gospel by sheer faith in God's goodness, without buying into all our procedures and rules.

We must listen to Paul's gospel once again. God has chosen us and directed our lives for the purpose of *redemption,* not privilege. We are blessed to have been born in areas more civilized than others. But that does not make us superior in God's eyes. We have had the benefits of education, technology and culture. But we are not holier persons because of these things. Many of us are fortunate enough to have been raised in Christian homes with close ties to the church. These are gestures of God's mercy to us, not proofs of His favor.

In the final analysis, we stand on level ground with all who call upon the name of the Lord. And we are members of the family of God only because "while we were still sinners, Christ died for us" (5:8), and because we have *by faith* accepted His gift of salvation and have confessed Him as "Lord."

3. ISRAEL'S REJECTION OF GOD 10:14-21

Let us try to summarize the key points in Paul's understanding of how God deals with his own race, the Jews:

a. God, who wills the salvation of all humanity, has revealed himself to His creatures through conscience, the law and His incarnate Son.

b. In His mercy, God has chosen to deal in unique ways with a select group of Abraham's descendants—the remnant of Israel.

c. Sensitized to the righteousness of God, the Jews misdirected their zeal toward acts of obedience and self-righteousness, rather than faith in the promise of God.

d. God, whose mercy extends to all humans, has redeemed everyone who has called on Him and accepted His gift of grace by faith alone.

e. The recipients of God's grace include both Jews and Gentiles; God is Lord of all.

At this point, Paul interjects a brief rationale for his own ministry of evangelization, and by doing so issues an urgent call for fellow workers in the task. He lays out another goal-oriented process to match this heavenly sequence of predestination leading to calling, justification and, ultimately, glorification (8:29-30). Here Paul offers a sequence of human activities illustrating the appropriate means necessary to secure the desired results—salvation for everyone. Calling on the name of the Lord necessitates belief, belief necessitates information (hearing), information necessitates a messenger, and a messenger necessitates a commission (10:14-15).

At the risk of being redundant, we need to "fast forward" the sequence to catch the vision Paul has for spreading the good news. A divine *call* draws forth a *messenger,* who shares the good news to *listeners,* who may respond in *faith* and *call on the name of the Lord* to be saved. Along with Paul's earnest desire to visit Rome to "impart . . . some spiritual gift" (1:11), his great passion includes the desire to proclaim the gospel to all who will receive it—whether they are Jew or Gentile.

That this appeal for missionaries—messengers of the good news—appears in the middle of Paul's discussion regarding the salvation of the Jews is both strange and striking. Was not Paul "the apostle to the Gentiles" (11:13), specifically commissioned for the task of spreading good news to those outside of his tradition? Furthermore, had not the Jews been "entrusted with the very words of God" (3:2)? Why then this deep concern for a message to be preached so that the listeners would call upon God?

These words can certainly be applied to the broader audience of Gentile believers. We do no injustice to apply this text to world evangelism. But Paul's anguish for his Jewish brothers (9:3) surfaces here again. Evangelism must always be two-fold—it is a word for the uninformed and a word for the *misinformed*. Paul sensed the need for a witness among those who had a "zeal . . . not based on knowledge" (10:2).

In our deep concern for the lost, we must never allow ourselves to think that the *only* task is to reach those places where the Word of God has never reached. We must also be aware of those who have heard a false or misleading word. Like Paul, we must bring good news to those on the mountain whose understanding prevents them from truly believing. Paul would have been delighted if the solution to the question of why the Jews had not accepted Jesus as Messiah could be traced simply to a lack of hearing the message. Unfortunately, the problem goes much deeper. Despite all the efforts of Paul and the other apostles to proclaim Christ, **not all the Israelites accepted the good news** (10:16). Paul must acknowledge that, among those who had heard the message, many remained a **disobedient and obstinate people** (v. 21).

Once again, Paul turns to his own Bible, the Old Testament, to find passages which suggest that God is not therefore bound to any exclusive agreement with His chosen people. He reserves the right to reach beyond those who reject His grace and offer it to others whose relationship to God might be suspect in the eyes of human judgment.

Paul's thinking parallels closely the theme of Jesus' parable of the great banquet, recorded in Luke 14. Out of overflowing generosity, a certain master invited "many guests" to a banquet. But, despite some initial interest, they reneged on their commitment at the last minute. When their refusal to join his celebration was reported, the master turned to persons who were not likely candidates for his generosity—"the poor, the crippled, the blind and the lame" (v. 21). But even these late arrivals did not satisfy the master's great hospitality. His invitation extended to all the passersby on "the roads and country lanes . . . so that my house will be full" (v. 23).

The obvious application of this parable is the point of Paul's discussion in Romans 10. The Jews, recipients of the Master's special invitation, declined His grace. In His overflowing mercy, the Master has turned to the spiritually challenged—Gentiles and pagans. And, from this story and from history as well, we learn several great truths:

- The sovereign God has extended a widespread invitation to come to Him.
- Humans are given the freedom to refuse the invitation.
- There is a wideness in God's mercy that reaches out to others who would not seem to be appropriate recipients of His love.
- His ultimate purposes cannot be thwarted by human obstinacy.

Thus, in the words of the old gospel song, the invitation is extended to all: "'Come and dine,' the Master calleth; 'Come and dine.'"

12

ISRAEL'S DESTINY

Romans 11:1-36

The parable of the great feast in Luke 14 closes with sobering words of judgment regarding those who refused to accept the generosity of the master: "I tell you, not one of those men who were invited will get a taste of my banquet" (v. 24; see Matthew 22:13 for a more violent ending to this parable). The point of Jesus' teaching was the serious consequence of rejecting God's grace. Most commentators agree that Jesus was speaking to both individuals and groups, like the people of Israel, who do not respond to God's offer of salvation. Paul wrestles with this same issue in the context of his own people, the Jews. To this point in his letter, Paul has dealt with God's wrath upon all unrighteousness— whether committed by Jews or Gentiles (1:18). Furthermore, he has described the special relationship God established with Israel, pointing out that the covenant relationship in itself does not bring a right relationship; one must follow Abraham's faith to become a person of promise (4:16). In Paul's understanding, even Gentiles who believe can consider themselves part of God's family (4:11-12).

Now, Paul has shifted from discussing the *spiritual* Israel to a discussing of the *ethnic* Israel—those whose identity with Abraham is by birthright, not by faith. What has been God's response to the repeated backsliding of those He chose as His special people? With the advent and rejection of His Son, the Messiah, will God continue to be gracious? What lies ahead for the Jews?

Here Paul introduces his readers to the mystery of divine grace. For all the obstinacy of the children of Israel (9:20f.), there is a persistent quality to God's compassion for His creation, described by one songwriter as "God's stubborn love." However, before developing a complete theology from the parable of the great banquet, one must read and reflect on the parable of the prodigal son and his gracious father who

179

waits expectantly for his son's return. Based upon his understanding of a God of steadfast love, Paul outlines a scenario for the future of his own race in the larger picture of divine redemption.

1. THE CHOSEN REMNANT 11:1-10

In developing this scenario of redemption, Paul does not take his readers to the teachings of Jesus; instead, he draws them back to the Old Testament account of Elijah in the book of 1 Kings. When the prophet concluded that the light of divine favor had all but flickered out in Israel, God encountered him and revealed that things were not nearly as dark as they appeared to be. To Elijah's **I am the only one left** (Rom. 11:3), God countered with **I have reserved for myself seven thousand who have not bowed the knee to Baal** (v. 4). In other words, the seven thousand were those who remained faithful to God.

Faith is the key to a proper assessment of God's relationship with humans. Were one to look for other factors (prosperity, political power, zeal for the law, adherence to rituals) to describe those in right standing with God, all such measuring sticks would be **works,** which would mean that **grace would no longer be grace** (v. 6). Instead, the starting point for assessing our spiritual life and health must be the grace offered by God and received in simple trust.

This group of seven thousand faithful—much larger than Elijah had imagined—was nonetheless a small fraction of those who had received the covenant promises in Elijah's day. How do we reconcile the election of a nation with the faith of a few? Here Paul reverts to an Old Testament theme of **a remnant chosen by grace** (v. 5), a subset of the Jewish people who, in faith, preserved the promise and relationship with God, even while the majority refused to submit to His righteousness.

At a first reading, one would wonder if Paul is not once again vacillating between human accountability and divine sovereignty. The Jews, by their obstinacy and self-righteousness, have forfeited their exclusive claim on God's blessing. This sounds like human accountability. Yet, God has **chosen by grace** a remnant. This sounds like divine sovereignty!

A Wesleyan perspective again reads these verses as God's *provision* for the salvation of the remnant, and not a determinism that *causes* their salvation. Similarly, the fact that **others were hardened** (v. 7) or their **eyes [were] darkened** (v. 10) does not mean God was preventing some Jews from calling on the Lord, but rather that He was permitting sin to work out its full consequences of death, in order for the glories of salvation by grace to be experienced to the fullest.

2. THE GRAFTED BRANCH 11:11-24

The history of the Jews up to the time of Paul could be described as long periods of spiritual rebellion and political struggle interspersed with episodes of God's deliverance and a return of the people to the covenant relationship. In the first century, there was little evidence to suggest that the Jews were anywhere near to entering a golden age. Despite the completion of Herod's great Temple in Jerusalem within the lifetime of Paul, it was still Paul's assessment that these were dismal days for the Jews. Politically, they were dominated by Rome; religiously, they were divided by various factions (Pharisees, Sadducees, Zealots, Hellenists). Spiritually, they were persons bound by law, rather than living by faith.

Now, in these dark hours, the good news of God's righteousness was spreading to the Gentiles. God's "non-people" were now becoming children of the Kingdom. Granted, a small remnant of believing (we would say "completed") Jews could be found scattered throughout Paul's newly established congregations. But, for the most part, the people of God seemed spiritually abandoned, so much so that Paul raises the unthinkable possibility: **Did [the Jews] stumble so as to fall beyond recovery?** (v. 11). Would the remnant itself dwindle away to nothingness and be replaced by a Gentile community of faith? Paul cannot allow himself to think of such a possibility. His devotion to his people and his confidence in the unfailing love of Yahweh leads Paul to propose other explanations for this remnant of faith.

His first explanation for the spiritual failure of the Jewish people is that it has opened the door of salvation to the Gentiles. Here is another example of the "blessed sin" *(felix culpa)* that was described earlier in Romans 4:15. The disobedience of the Jews has allowed grace to abound to persons of faith, no matter what their religious or ethnic heritage might be.

But the spread of the gospel to the Gentiles is not without its fringe benefits to the Jews. Gentiles have been offered the gift of eternal life, not only because God is not willing that they should perish, but also **to make Israel envious** (11:11). It is God's way of provoking unresponsive Jews to jealousy, and thus to Christ. In God's good timing, the riches of grace will be fulfilled in the response of the Jews to the gospel.

Searching for some visual aid to describe this future development,

Paul turns to agriculture and the grafting of a new branch into a mature plant with a developed system of roots. Again Paul echoes an image suggested by the Master teacher. Jesus once described a farmer who planted a fig tree which failed to produce fruit. In time, the farmer was faced with the choice of writing off the attempt and destroying the plant, or exercising stubborn love to restore fruitfulness to the vine. He chose the latter (Luke 13:6-9).

In Paul's parable, the vine is replaced by an olive tree, noted for its ability to send up new sprouts from its roots, even when the trunk is damaged or severed. Israel, a tree of God's own planting (Isaiah 61:3) has proven to be unfruitful. In an act of judgment for her apostasy, her spiritually withered branches **were broken off** (v. 20). However, rather than a spontaneous regeneration of sprouts appearing from the existing Jewish stock, **a wild olive shoot [has] been grafted in among the others** (v. 17).

This new reality—the Gentile community of faith—has no reason to boast in its new life. Its vitality depends upon the gracious act of the One who grafted it, and its nourishment is drawn from Jewish roots which are not its own. Furthermore, its continued existence depends upon "remaining in the vine" (John 15:1-17); any return to self-righteousness will result in the same removal from the tree that occurred in God's judgment upon the natural branches—the chosen, but unbelieving Jews (Rom. 11:21).

Paul's image is still powerful and helps us as we wrestle with the relationship between the old and new covenants. Jesus himself declared that He was offering a counter-proposal to what was said to the people long ago (Matthew 5:21-22). The writer of the book of Hebrews proposes that in these last days a covenant "superior to the old one" has appeared (Hebrews 8:6). Certainly the tensions between Jewish and Gentile Christians which Paul addresses in this letter give evidence of the difficulty of merging these two traditions. How, then, do we affirm the Jewish roots of our faith, while holding to the clear teachings of the New Testament? For even today, the intermingling of these two traditions makes for unique challenges in both worship and doctrine.

We begin to resolve this puzzle by acknowledging the existence of the roots we share with the children of Israel. We worship the same God, who has chosen us for fellowship with Him, has revealed His righteousness through creation and His Word, and has made provision for our reconciliation through faith in His promise. As believers in Jesus the Messiah, we have an obligation to study the Old Testament, and even to

182

explore the traditions of Judaism, in order to better understand the common heritage we share.

The danger exists, however, that in drawing nourishment from our Jewish roots, we will fall into the same self-deception that substitutes a zeal for commandments, religious practices, and traditions of the past, for the life of the Spirit maintained by faith in Christ. We are in equal peril whether we ignore the old covenant or worship it. The heart of Christianity is not to be found in roots, but in the "growing edge" of our present life in Christ.

3. THE REDEEMED NATION 11:25-32

Despite his earlier condemnation of the Jews for rejecting the revelation and promise of God, Paul now makes one of his boldest statements: **so all Israel will be saved** (v. 26). What Paul means by this statement, and who he considers Israel to be, have been the subject of considerable debate by his interpreters. It is clear that Paul has moved far beyond the "remnant theology" of verse 5 to envision a universal return of *Israel*—however that term is defined—to Jehovah. We pause, before proceeding further, to look at three differing opinions on the future of Israel, the people chosen of God.

Some biblical scholars take very literally the promises made to Israel in the Old Testament. While there is little evidence to indicate that there has been a spiritual conversion of the Jewish nation, and nothing in the political system of modern-day Israel to suggest a return to the Davidic kingdom, these Christians hold that God will remain faithful to all the promises He has made. And He will fulfill these promises to the people who define themselves ethnically and religiously as Jews.

This view has been popularized in the past century by Christians who term themselves "dispensationalists." A "dispensation" is a period of history or a particular stage in which God unfolds a portion of His plan for the world. While there are several varieties of this tradition, all dispensationalists hold in common a belief that the relationship that God established with the Jews during the first covenant (the dispensation of the law) will be restored and will flourish alongside God's later covenant with the Gentiles (the dispensation of grace).

Some of the more strident advocates of this position even suggest that the Temple must be rebuilt and the Old Testament system of sacrifices restored in order for God to bring to pass all His promises to His people, the Jews. More moderate advocates of dispensationalism do not require that the entire ceremonial law of the Old Testament be restored; but they still see a glorious future for a specific group of individuals, which we identify today with the Jewish people and state.

Dispensationalists believe that before the end of history there will be a large-scale conversion of Jews to faith in Jesus the Messiah. They point to the 144,000 witnesses taken from the twelve tribes of Israel (Revelation 7) as support for this view. Naturally, they keep their eyes focused on the events of the Middle East, and Israel in particular, in order to detect early signs of this literal fulfillment of God's promises to His people in the Old Testament prophecies.

A second and opposing view is taken by those who see God's covenant with the Jews of the Old Testament as conditional and dependent upon their response of faith. These Christians are often associated with the theological tradition known as "amillennialism" (meaning there will be no literal earthly reign of Christ during the 1000-year period known as the millennium in Revelation 20:4ff.). They consider the Jews' rejection of both the covenant and the messianic claims of Jesus as reason for the nullification of the Old Testament prophecies directed specifically to the Jewish nation. Amillennialists would cite Jesus' own indictment, "the kingdom of God will be taken away from you and given to a people who will produce its fruit" (Matt. 21:43) as proof that the promises of the Old Testament no longer apply to the Jews as a race or religious tradition.

Should we just ignore all those promises of a future kingdom and blessing to the Jews? Certainly not, these amillennialists would reply. God has transferred those promises of the children of Abraham to His new chosen people—the members of the church, the body of Christ. Citing Romans 11, they suggest that out of the cut-off stump of Judaism God has created a new tree of righteousness.

As sons and daughters of God, those who believe in Christ are citizens of this new Kingdom, which has replaced the former nation of Israel. Turning to the book of Revelation, they point to 1:6, where the Apostle John gives praise to God who "has made us [as believers] to be a kingdom and priests to serve his God and Father." Peter refers to similar themes in his letters to the early Christians as well (see 1 Peter 2:5, 9-10).

This position is often accused of "liberalism" for denying (or at least ignoring) many verses which give specific promises to the descendants of Abraham and the covenant community of the law. Amillennialists quickly retort that because they take the New Testament *seriously,* they cannot advocate any divine salvation that circumvents the cross and the empty tomb, even if the recipients of that grace are the Jews.

This group reminds us that "salvation is found in no one else, for there is no other name under heaven given to men by which we must be saved" (Acts 4:12). In short, they would rather reinterpret the passages of the Old Testament, and Paul's comments in this passage of Romans, to see Christians as the new Jewish nation, rather than maintain a literalism that suggests a return to the very law which, Paul argues, cannot save.

A third view endeavors to strike some balance between the two previous views. Those who hold this view agree that the new covenant of Christ has done away with the former covenant of circumcision and ceremonial law. Many of the promises given to the people of Israel were accompanied by the condition that the Jews must be faithful to Yahweh. Furthermore, Christ himself is the fulfillment of the old covenant, so that salvation must be centered in His gracious death and powerful resurrection.

The whole point of Paul's discussion in Romans 2 through 4 is that justification comes through faith and not through ethnic identity or moral codes of conduct. If Paul envisions a time when **all Israel will be saved** (11:26), that salvation can be only through faith in the work of Christ, rather than a return to Old Testament law.

But, this moderating position cannot ignore the drama of history as it has unfolded in the scriptural revelation. God did choose *a specific race*—the descendants of Jacob—to reveal His saving acts. At just the right moment in history *(kairos)*, Jesus of Nazareth was "born under law" (Galatians 4:4) as the divine Son of God *and* as the promised Messiah.

While there are solid theological reasons for viewing many Old Testament prophecies as having a figurative rather than a literal fulfillment, one cannot spiritualize away the concrete, "in the flesh" nature of God's revelation and dealings with humanity. If Christianity is divorced from its specific ties to historical times, places and people, it becomes just another myth. "Christ is the end of the law" (Rom. 10:4), but He is also the Lord of history. Such a belief requires us to take seriously His special relationship with the children of the covenant, and Paul's inspired prophecy that those who are true children of Abraham have not been cast aside by a God of steadfast love.

If we accept this moderate position and Paul's statements in this passage, it appears to leave us no other option—we are still left to explain the meaning of Israel as Paul uses it here. One could argue that it applies to the modern political state of Israel. Yet these Jews, for the most part, not only have rejected the Messiah, but have abandoned their faith in

Yahweh as well. These modern Jews function much as unbelievers do in other modern cultures. Their claim to be Jewish is based on ethnic, not spiritual, characteristics.

Even if one did choose to equate Israel with the biological descendants of Abraham, the problem persists. The racial identity of the modern Jew has been lost. No one can trace his or her "begats" back to the twelve tribes; most modern Jews are descendants of European or Asian Gentiles who converted to Judaism centuries ago. It would require a miracle of enormous significance for the bloodlines of the twelve tribes of Israel to reappear, in order to constitute a literal 144,000.

The best interpretation of this difficult passage is to view Israel as all those persons who worship the God of Abraham, Isaac and Jacob, and who take seriously His commandments to "love the Lord your God with all your heart and with all your soul and with all your mind" (Matthew 22:37; cf. Deuteronomy 6:5). These persons of the covenant no doubt share a religious tie to the religion of the Old Testament; it would be a matter of considerable debate as to how much of the ceremonial law they must follow in order to be "the people of God."

Paul does proclaim that a distinct group, which he ties closely to the Jewish community of his own day, will, after a period of disobedience, once more experience the promise and gift of God's mercy. They will be grafted back into the tree of God's redemption, there to flourish with the "wild olive shoot" of the church which sprouted and began to grow at the time of the Apostle Paul.

We should return briefly to the motif of the grafted tree discussed above. Dispensationalists imagine a tree with two branches—one of Jews and one of Gentiles—following parallel, but very distinct, patterns of redemption. Amillennialists see a tree with Jewish roots, but a trunk and branches made up solely of New Testament Christianity. If Jews are grafted into the tree, it is only on the basis of accepting Christian truths; their ethnic identity is no more relevant than it would be for Chinese, African, or American believers.

The moderating view attempts to give some credence to Paul's vision of a tree with Jewish roots and a trunk of New Testament Christianity, with both Gentile and Jewish branches. The branches of this restored Israel draw their sustenance from the gospel, not from the law and traditions of the former covenant. Their status in the tree, however, is significant because they give powerful witness to the unfailing love of God, who never forgets His promises and who is not willing to give up on the people of his choosing (Hosea 11:8).

Now, to the text itself. The closing verses of Romans 11 are difficult verses to explain, particularly from the Wesleyan perspective which takes seriously the role of human response in the plan of salvation. A fast reading of these verses suggests that God deliberately predestined the disobedience of His chosen people in order to give the Gentiles an opportunity for salvation as well.

However, the God who hardened Israel will remain faithful to His promises, and at some future point will have mercy upon them and bring them to salvation, **for God's gifts and his call are irrevocable** (v. 29). If one holds to a strong Calvinist position, these verses are theologically easy to swallow, despite the fact that no great spiritual revival has occurred among the Jews in the past two thousand years.

A Wesleyan reading of these verses stresses the long-suffering nature of God's love. God's inclusive view of redemption has drawn and embraced the Gentiles. Having come to His own and experienced rejection from them (John 1:11), the divine Word empowered all who believe (Gentiles and Jews) "to become children of God" (John 1:12).

God's wrath upon all ungodliness (Rom. 1:18) does not necessitate dooming His people, as a corporate entity, to destruction. Despising the sin, God still loves the sinner. It is His *promise of salvation* to everyone who calls upon Him that is irrevocable; all the detailed prophecies of the Old Testament must be filtered through this greater vision of God's redemptive plan for humanity.

Thus, while the unbelieving Jews remain **enemies** (11:28), from the perspective of Christian Gentiles, they still are the objects of God's compassion and mercy. Paul's conclusion that **God has bound all men over to disobedience so that he may have mercy on them all** (v. 32) is a refrain of his earlier statement that "all have sinned and fall short of the glory of God, *and* are justified freely by his grace" (3:23-24, italics mine).

4. THE UNSEARCHABLE WISDOM 11:33-36

However one attempts to wrestle with Paul's views in the previous passage, all believers can join together in unison as Paul offers a stirring doxology at the close of this section of his letter. Rather than feeling frustrated over Paul's complex views on the future of Israel, the value of the law, or the nature of the new life in Christ, we can join Paul in awesome praise for **the depth of the riches of the wisdom and knowledge of God!** (v. 33).

Like Job, we finally reach a point in our speculation concerning the outworkings of history where we "let God be God." Paul does not bury his head in the sand, nor mumble some philosophical platitude like, "What will be will be." Instead, he affirms out of his faith commitment that God's **paths [are] beyond tracing out!** (v. 33). Whether the issue is as cosmic as the final destiny of Israel, or as personal as the spiritual transformation that enables us to put to death our old nature and live by the Spirit, God knows how to do it! Paul concludes with an all-embracing affirmation concerning the sovereignty of God (v. 36):

From him . . . are all things. God is the *Source* of all being and all grace. He is the First Cause. If there are energies and forces in the past that have spun out the reality we now see and experience, those forces are divine. Here, Paul lays the foundation for the modern-day doxology we sing in our worship: "Praise God, *from whom all blessings flow.*"

Through him . . . are all things. It is not enough to affirm that God is the Creator and Source of all things. He also must be acknowledged as the *Sustainer* of all things. The glue of the universe is His Word. Elsewhere, Paul extends this vision of God to the second person of the Trinity, and declares, "In him all things hold together" (Colossians 1:17).

This sustaining power of God is also both cosmic and personal. Beyond His ability to hold the created order together, God has power to sustain and nurture the life of each believer as well. Thus, Paul can declare that "Christ lives in me. The life I live in the body, I live by faith in the Son of God" (Gal. 2:20).

To him are all things. If "from him" is Paul's backward glance into the past, and "through him" is Paul's present experience of grace, then "to him" is Paul's confident vision of the future. The God who is Creator and Sustainer is also the Consummator of all things. Ultimately, every event in history moves toward the goal of His kingdom. The revelation of the law, the incarnation of the Son, and the redemption of Gentiles and Jews all point toward God's sovereign plan to bring all things under the headship of Christ (Ephesians 1:10).

To him be the glory forever! Amen. The great medieval theologian, Thomas Aquinas, spent several years of his adult life writing *Summa Theologica*, his great masterpiece of Catholic theology. One day, while Aquinas was writing on the doctrine of the Incarnation, his servant entered the room and discovered him lying prostrate on the floor amidst his books and papers. Thinking that some illness or injury had befallen his master, the servant rushed to Aquinas's side, only to discover that he was engrossed in prayer and adoration of God. When the servant asked for an explanation from his master, Aquinas replied, "There are moments when one must cease his theological speculations and fall on his face in worship."

How fitting that in the middle of a letter where Paul endeavors to spell out some of the most profound mysteries of the Christian faith, he pauses from his deep thoughts to declare, **How unsearchable [God's] judgments** (Rom. 11:33). We would profit from that same spirit of humility and devotion in our study of these scriptures as well.

Part Six

RIGHTEOUSNESS REFLECTED:
The Ethics of Love
Romans 12:1–16:27

Paul has twice led the Roman believers into "the depth of the riches of the wisdom and knowledge of God" (Romans 11:33). The first time was when he explored the mystery of divine redemption as it is played out in the life of an individual person who lives by faith. Having described how one can experience a transforming grace that puts the sinful nature to death and raises one to life in the Spirit, Paul concluded with the powerful affirmation that no reality or power "in all creation, will be able to separate us from the love of God that is in Christ Jesus our Lord" (8:39).

Paul then addressed the mystery of redemption as it applies to the larger dimension of history and his own people of Israel. Again he affirmed that despite human disobedience, grace can and will triumph over sin for those who call upon the name of the Lord. God desires all the branches of His tree of righteousness (Isaiah 61:3) to flourish and continue in His grace. And again, Paul closes his discussion with a hymn of praise to the God around whom all reality centers.

Paul has outlined the mystery of divine grace; now he turns his attention to the response of the believer. He already has defined the one essential condition for justification: faith in God's saving work in Christ. That act of faith can occur in a moment of time. It is as simple as confessing "Jesus is Lord" and believing in one's heart "that God raised him from the dead" (Rom. 10:9).

But the instantaneous act of faith results in a life-transforming *process,* which Paul terms as being "led by the Spirit" (8:14). Already, Paul has suggested that this new relationship with God calls for a new self-perception and act of the will. He has appealed to the believers in Rome to "count [themselves] dead to sin but alive to God in Christ Jesus" (6:11). Now he concludes his letter with an extensive discussion of how that new orientation is accomplished, and what the consequences might be in the everyday situations of life.

In shifting from the more theoretical and doctrinal aspects of faith to its practical outworkings, Paul is consistent with his other letters. In a few of his letters (1 Corinthians; 1 and 2 Timothy), Paul's moral instructions are interspersed throughout the entire epistle. In Romans, as in Galatians, Colossians and Ephesians, he lays down the theological foundations of the Christian life before dealing with the specific aspects of everyday living. Scholars give the technical name of *parenaesis* (from the Greek word for "advice") to these extended passages on moral behavior. Quite often, Paul uses strong commanding statements in order to give a sense of directness and urgency to his instructions (see, for example, 12:9-13). In any case, he does not hesitate to deal with specific areas of one's personal life, such as family relationships, finances, interpersonal dynamics, and conduct within the body of Christ.

Paul's comments in the closing chapters of Romans (12–16) span a wide range of topics. After a brief introduction, in which Paul establishes the mind-set that undergirds our conduct (12:1-2), he gives specific attention to interpersonal relationships (12:3-21), societal expectations (13:1-14), and the dynamics of differing moral standards within the body of Christ (14:1–15:13). In a world where great attention is given to matters of appearance and style, Paul offers very practical words which are also God's words to us—**clothe yourselves with the Lord Jesus Christ** (13:14).

13

LOVE WITHIN THE FELLOWSHIP

Romans 12:1-21

The book of Romans offers many quotable passages and sermon texts. Probably none has been repeated from the pulpit more often than the opening verses of chapter 12, where believers are challenged to commit themselves to Christ and to a life-transforming process. Paul shifts his attention from the great doctrinal themes of justification by faith to the practical details of living out that new relationship. He builds a foundation for his pastoral instructions by once more calling the believers in Rome to become something more than they already are. Yes, they have been "justified through faith" (5:1), "set free from sin" (6:18), "released from the law" (7:6), and made "alive" in Christ (8:10). As the result of a divine act of grace, all God's blessings are theirs (and ours) as well. The only human contribution to that reality is faith in the promise of God.

Now Paul appeals to the believers in Rome to go beyond that *inner* reality to a conscious act of surrender and a "renewing of [the] mind" (12:1-2). The inner transformation now becomes an *outward* witness to others. This outward witness will set one apart from the world's way of thinking and behavior. A Christian is by nature a nonconformist. His or her conformity is defined in terms of being shaped by the pleasing and perfect will of God, not "the pattern of this world" (12:2).

How does this nonconformity express itself? In acts of humility and love. Paul will point us toward the pattern of Christ without referring even once to His earthly ministry. But here in Romans 12 we discover how the inner *presence* of Christ becomes the outer *life* of Christ for the person who lives by faith.

1. THE SACRIFICE THAT TRANSFORMS 12:1-2

Paul offers his readers the literary cue **therefore** (v. 1) to alert them of a new direction in his discourse. At times it is difficult to detect the logical significance of this transitional word; it is usually used simply to signal a transition. Here, however, it carries great significance.

Paul's great discussion of sin, faith, and divine grace that leads to salvation could stand on its own as a masterpiece of theological reasoning. But all of the great ideas Paul presented in the first eleven chapters are like a proof in geometry; they move forward in a definite sequence toward a compelling conclusion. And, like Paul's discussion, a geometric proof closes with a "therefore" (indicated in the proof by a mathematical symbol) to indicate "this is what all the steps above are seeking to demonstrate."

Paul's **therefore** in the opening sentence of chapter 12 affirms that God's plan of salvation for every person should lead to a transformed life. Justification—a right standing with God—is a glorious experience for the person who lives by faith. But the goal *(telos)* of this new relationship with God is a new creation as well.

Paul can appeal to the Romans to become more than they ever have been, not on the basis of more human effort or "cleaning up their act," but rather **in view of God's mercy** (v. 1), which He demonstrates by loving and redeeming sinners who have been condemned by His righteous law. Having closed Romans 11 with an expression of hope regarding the mercy of God that will redeem both Gentile and Jew, Paul now turns his attention back to a specific group of those recipients of mercy, and points out how their own personal history can likewise be transformed by the grace of God.

But, we must stress that a grasp of God's mercy is the appropriate starting point for this new direction in Paul's outline. Having declared that salvation is by grace alone through faith alone, Paul now appeals to the Romans to respond to that grace by specific actions. The temptation, of course, is to make the false assumption that God forgives the sins of the past, but the Christian is responsible for *present* behavior, and that God's continuing grace *depends* on one's actions.

Such an understanding of the Christian faith is abhorrent to Paul. He has already detected this flaw in the believers in Galatia and has labeled it "foolish" (Galatians 3:1). Paul suggests that they have been deceived, even "bewitched," by this false understanding, and inquires, "After beginning with the Spirit, are you now trying to attain your goal by human effort?" (v. 3).

In all the detailed instructions Paul gives in these closing chapters of Romans, we must always listen for the background choir singing **in view of God's mercy** (12:1). Centuries earlier, David discovered this secret of the life of faith, and he embedded in his most familiar psalm this testimony: "Surely . . . mercy shall follow me all the days of my life" (Ps. 23:6 KJV). God's gracious act of mercy gives us both the ability and strength to respond to His grace. This response is not so much a *saving* act as it is a **spiritual act of worship** (Rom. 12:1). It is a *loving* act.

Having experienced the great benefits of justification (peace, joy, hope, assurance), the believer is now capable of a **spiritual** (i.e., Spirit-empowered) response. Here again, Wesley's concept of prevenient grace is helpful. We already have pointed out that God takes the first steps toward the sinner and offers a "grace that comes before," enabling the helpless person to reach out toward God in faith. Now, as a believer, that same prevenient grace from God acts in another manner, enabling believers to do what would seem otherwise impossible—offer themselves as sacrifices.

Dr. Dennis Kinlaw, former president of Asbury College, would remind his students that the motivations which prompt unbelievers to turn to Christ are based largely upon self-interest and gain. People come to Christ to escape hell, gain eternal life, or put their shambled lives together. Kinlaw is not surprised nor dismayed by this "selfish" motivation of new converts. After all, as creatures of flesh (the sinful nature), they have no reason to want the grace that God offers, other than self-interest.

However, Kinlaw suggests it can be otherwise with the believer whose sinful nature has been crucified and replaced by the presence of the Spirit. This individual is capable of a truly selfless act—an act of spiritual worship. The believer offers himself or herself to God, not so much for what can be gained, but rather as an expression of pure devotion **in view of God's mercy,** which has already been experienced.

This distinction is helpful in counteracting a false impression many Christians have concerning consecrating themselves to God. And often the fault is not their own. It is sometimes the fault of overzealous preachers and others of us who try to urge Christians to a deeper walk with God for the wrong reasons. How have we turned this act of worship Paul describes into something else?

a. We have made it a requirement for salvation, rather than a freely expressed offering of oneself. Many pastors and evangelists, in their passion to move believers along in their faith walk, have suggested that failure to take this step could send a believer directly to hell (without passing "Go" or collecting $200!). Many sincere Christians have been *driven* to this experience, rather than invited to participate in an act of spiritual worship.

b. We have used guilt to coerce believers to offer themselves to God. As Paul has pointed out, it is easy to find places in one's life where the law of God has been offended. It may not be one of the "Big Ten," but in the depths of our inner selves and in the little daily actions, all of us "fall short of the glory of God" (3:23). To play on those shortcomings, and then suggest that what Paul describes in 12:1 is a form of spiritual housecleaning, is to misunderstand both Paul and the biblical doctrine of sanctification. There is an ongoing process that requires confessing our sin and experiencing the cleansing, healing reality of God's grace (1 John 1:9; James 5:16). But this action, even when it happens in the excitement and drama of a revival event, does not constitute the **spiritual act of worship.**

c. We appeal to believers' selfish instincts in order to bring them to this act. We promise them a victorious life, overcoming power for some besetting sin, perfect love, a life without sin, and, in more crass terms, health, wealth and prosperity—all if they will surrender themselves completely to God. Now some, if not all, of the things just listed may be blessings that come to those who take such an act. But, Paul wants us to make this commitment an act of *worship*—not a quarter in the candy machine that gives quick gratification to one's spiritual cravings.

When John Wesley was asked by his followers how they should preach his idea of a holy life, he responded, "Always drawing, rather than driving."[1] What powerful advice. One might go to great lengths to lead a sinner to salvation. But only the believer is capable of offering himself or herself to God in a joyous act of selfless worship.

We have walked around the edges of Romans 12:1, and now finally come to its heart: What is this spiritual act that Paul urges us to take in view of God's mercy? **Offer your bodies as living sacrifices.**

Paul takes us to the Temple in Jerusalem, and beyond to the Old Testament Tabernacle, where the people offered God a choice animal from their livestock. There were many different offerings, but Paul is no doubt referring to the burnt offering—an animal brought to God as an expression of devotion, and which was totally consumed by fire on the altar. Certainly there must have been moments when the priest and the one offering the sacrifice questioned the practical wisdom of such "waste." Think of the roasts and steaks that were burned to a crisp, rather than being eaten. Many of the other offerings did allow for beneficial uses of parts of the sacrifice. But the burnt offering was a total gift to God, **holy and pleasing** in His sight, just as our offering of ourselves to God must be (Rom. 12:1).

So, there must be a moment in our lives when we give *all* of ourselves to God. We perform this act of worship, not for the benefits that will accrue for us, but as an offering of love to the Father of all mercies.

Note that Paul urges us to offer our **bodies** to God. Here Paul resists the ancient Greek (and still modern) concept that the important element in our relationship with God deals with spirit, and not the stuff of matter. But, far too many Christians are willing to present their "spirits," not their bodies, to God. The Old Testament sacrifice was not just a spiritual offering; it required the flesh and blood of an animal. God so loved the world that before He sent His Spirit, He gave his Son, born from the womb of Mary, *in the flesh*. So our devotion finally comes down to offering more than our immortal spirits to God. He wants our bodies— all the very physical and visible realities of our day-to-day existence.

The Greek word Paul uses here is not the word *flesh (sarx)* that we saw in Romans 8. Flesh refers to a sinful nature which is inexplicably bound to the fallen "dust" we inherit as offspring of Adam. That flesh was crucified with Christ in our justification. Here in chapter 12, Paul uses the word *body (soma)* that refers to the good "earth" from which the Master Designer fashioned the human race, and which makes us His creatures. *Body* implies more than hands, feet, head and torso; it suggests all that we do with the body in daily activities. One can see why the subject of surrendering the body is crucial to this section of Romans, where Paul will describe very ordinary actions that comprise the life of the believer.

Paul urges the believers in Rome **to offer** their bodies. He uses a particular Greek verb tense *(aorist)* that has no direct parallel in the English language. The aorist tense indicates that some action has reached a point of completion; it is a finished event, rather than an ongoing process. Much is made in Wesleyan circles of the aorist tense in Romans 12:1. It would seem to give strong credence to the argument that there is a specific moment in the life of a believer when the act of consecration (offering oneself) is a finished act. And it would be consistent with the urgency Paul expresses to the Romans that this surrender of the body is not to be a slow, prolonged evolution into a more Christian lifestyle. "Do it!" Paul urges. "And do it now!"

There are Christians who resist any suggestion that there is a second aspect of the Christian life subsequent to repentance and conversion. Without defending all the strange interpretations of the concept of a decisive moment of dedication, consecration, sanctification, or whatever term is attached to it, we must acknowledge that Paul called upon believers in Rome to make a decisive act of worship that entailed offering themselves—their bodies—to God.

There is a danger of overloading this particular passage with a theology it cannot support. In the late nineteenth century, holiness preachers and scholars adopted a view that this act of human consecration was identical to the divine act of sanctification which is mentioned throughout Scripture and which is the heart of John Wesley's message. Alluding to Old Testament worship practices, they claimed that "the altar sanctifies the gift." Just as an animal became holy when offered on the altar of God, so believers become holy (entirely sanctified) the moment they present themselves to God. Paul's short phrase, **holy and pleasing to God** (12:1), is used to further support this view.

We must draw back from these assumptions. This verse is the prelude to several chapters of moral instruction, dealing with very difficult issues of everyday life. Paul does not expand upon the blessings and significance of this act in the same way that he did with justification in chapters 5, 6 and 8. Rather than giving an extensive description of the sanctified life in terms and categories familiar to theologians, Paul moves directly to living out the act of consecration in the tough decisions of daily life.

In fact, after the powerful statement, **Offer your bodies,** Paul moves directly to the equally powerful *command,* **Be transformed by the renewing of your mind.** This passage does not support the dramatic crisis of Wesleyan perfectionism as a completed work of God's grace. Rather, it suggests that consecration of oneself is the foundation for the ongoing work of sanctification in the life of the believer.

By this, we do not reject the great Wesleyan doctrine of an entire sanctification that affects all of the believer's body, soul and spirit (1 Thessalonians 5:23). We do not deny the reality of an experience that can fulfill Jesus' command and promise that we "be perfect . . . as [our] heavenly Father is perfect" (Matthew 5:48). The offering of oneself in consecration to God is an essential *step* on this "path to perfection"—it ought not be equated with the final destination. The text in Romans suggests that the *act* of consecration is what is holy (and thus pleasing) to God, and not the *object* of consecration. When we present ourselves in response to God's mercies, He gives us yet more grace to become transformed individuals in this world.

Most of us have heard the tongue-in-cheek response to Paul's urging in 12:1—"The problem with living sacrifices is that they keep crawling off the altar!" We would not detract from the force and power of Paul's great appeal to be consecrated individuals; however, most believers discover that there are opposing forces which make sustaining a consecrated life difficult. Paul acknowledges this reality, as well, by further urging the Roman Christians, **Do not conform any longer to the pattern of this world** (v. 2). Paul was writing to first-generation believers at a time when the culture had not yet been influenced by Christian values. To be a Christian in Paul's day was to be plagued continually by one's past lifestyle (Eph. 2:1-2) and assaulted by the present society (1 John 2:15). In our day, as well as in Paul's, presenting one's body as a living sacrifice necessitates our being "wise as serpents" (Matt. 10:16 KJV) as we encounter threats from the world.

This **world** (Rom. 12:2), whose pattern we are to avoid, is not identical with the world *(kosmos)* that "God so loved" (John 3:16) because it was His original creation. In 12:2 Paul uses another word *(aion),* sometimes translated "age," to describe the spiritual dimension of the forces that oppose life in the Spirit. Jewish theology of Paul's day relegated certain regions to powers and forces—both good and bad. Satan was "the ruler of the kingdom of the air" (Eph. 2:2) and "the prince of this world" (John 16:11). Paul is not suggesting an other-worldliness that rejects all of art, culture and technology. Instead, he warns believers not to allow the prevailing *world view* to shape their thoughts and behavior.

We can be grateful we live in a culture that has benefited from strong Christian influences over the past centuries. We can bemoan the immorality that exists in our American society, but we must remind ourselves that the underpinnings of our culture (and cultures in many parts of our world today) are far more Christian than they were in Paul's time. Furthermore, many of us are now third- and fourth-generation Christians who have benefited from a godly heritage.

But, despite all of these positive influences, Paul's warning is equally applicable to us today. A spirit of this age, which is very alien to the gospel of righteousness, still shapes much of our economy, politics and (God forbid!) religion. We must be very alert to those areas of our lives where we unwittingly allow a different set of values and priorities to dictate our patterns of behavior.

The solution is more than simply being defensive and wary about the world. Paul moves quickly to a proactive mode: **But be transformed by the renewing of your mind** (Rom. 12:2). The Greek word for this transformation should be easily recognized—*metamorphousthe*. The image of a butterfly emerging from its chrysalis comes to mind immediately. Here is a creation whose outward appearance may take very different shapes, but whose inner form *(morphe)* remains constant. The identity of the butterfly comes from that inner blueprint, and not from the changing expressions visible to the eye.

To emphasize this point, we should return to Paul's word for conformity—*syschematizesthe*. Buried in all those letters is the root of our English word *schema,* as in schematic drawings. Schematic drawings are those designs created by the architect to show us how something will look from the outside. They focus on appearance. But, far more important to the contractor are the blueprints and specification sheets which define the actual form *(morphe)* of the structure. The world is concerned about appearances, and would like us to follow their fashion and design for behavior. Paul calls for us to go inward to the Master plan and to govern our lives by the Master's specifications.

That plan for our lives is an ongoing process of **the renewing of [our] mind.** While we offer our *bodies,* we get our sense of direction from renewing our *minds,* which entails both the discipline of clear thinking and the discipline of opening one's thoughts to the whispers of the Holy Spirit. Here, two of John Wesley's criteria for determining what is authoritative come into play: reason and personal experience. The ability to think logically, combined with a sensitivity to God's still, small voice, will allow the believer to **test and approve what God's will is** (v. 2). That divine will, even when it clashes with the fashion of the world, will be **good, pleasing and perfect.**

2. THE BODY THAT WORKS TOGETHER 12:3-8

Paul now is prepared to take the Roman Christians into the details of his instructions on Christian living *(parenaesis).* This would be a good place to stop and review the basic features of salvation as Paul has presented them thus far in this letter:

a. All have come short of God's righteousness and are condemned by that standard.
b. Attempts to save ourselves by any human means are futile.

c. A right standing with God (justification) comes only by faith in His promise of grace offered through Jesus Christ.

d. The person who is justified by faith experiences both a relational change (peace with God) and a real change (new life in Christ).

e. Our justification has done away with the former sinful self and has enabled us to experience the reality of God's Spirit in us.

f. Believers must continually count themselves dead to sin and alive to Christ, becoming more than they presently are.

g. In an act of consecration, believers present their bodies as living sacrifices to God.

h. These consecrated individuals develop a mind-set that resists the pattern of this present age and shapes their thinking in accordance with the will of God.

What powerful truths! If Christians would only grasp the significance of each of these points and conscientiously apply them to their lives, the specifics of Christian living would, for the most part, fall into place. Certainly there have been numerous situations where no clear instructions or solutions can be found within the pages of the Bible. Yet, believers have been able to use the "renewing mind" and other great principles of the gospel to sort out appropriate applications for many life situations. Paul might have stopped his letter to the Romans at 12:2, and we still would have had sufficient theological insight to put the patterns of Christian living together.

But Paul does not end his letter with the act of consecration. **By the grace** [we might add "and inspiration"] **given me** (v. 3) suggests that Paul wanted to flesh out in some detail his own understanding of how a renewed Christian deals with the complexities of life in Rome. In the succeeding verses, Paul does not cover all the bases of human behavior. But, he does give us powerful examples for dealing with some of the more difficult areas of interpersonal relationships.

Paul opens his discussion of practical matters by addressing the diversity that exists in the human family and in the body of Christ. Equality and its corollary, humility, would be much easier to attain if every person was stamped out of the same mold. We would not waste nearly as much time trying to assess who is more qualified, more talented, or more gifted than another if we all were identical. But quick observation reveals that differences do abound. There are clearly differences in **the measure of faith** (v. 3), **function** (v. 4), and **gifts** (v. 6) within the community of faith. "The pattern of this world" (v. 2) would be to make personal judgments concerning who is more gifted and, thus, better than others.

Paul lays out in basic form his idea of a holistic body in which all parts do their respective tasks without competing with or opposing each other. (A more detailed explanation of this concept appears in 1 Corinthians 12.) The **measure of faith** given to Paul enables him to disregard petty distinctions as irrelevant and counterproductive to the work of the Kingdom. The less mature believers in Rome are directed to at least minimize such comparisons, using **sober judgment** (Rom. 12:3) in order to avoid inflated views of themselves.

If Jesus' disciples were repeatedly tempted to argue among themselves concerning who was the greatest, we cannot assume that this pattern of thinking has disappeared within the household of faith. But Paul gives sound advice for avoiding dissension in the ranks: First, don't waste time making comparisons. Recognize that roles, abilities and gifts come from God; leave the assessing of worth to Him. Second, focus on the abilities you have been given, and enhance each gift with the appropriate spiritual grace.

At times, Paul appears to state the obvious in this passage—let prophets prophecy; let teachers teach. But at the close of his list of gifts (vv. 6-8), he suggests that the *quality* of one's contribution is more significant that its nature or quantity. Thus, giving should be done **generously,** leadership performed **diligently**, mercy demonstrated **cheerfully** (v. 8).

In several of his letters, Paul identifies various "gifts of the Spirit" (Romans 12; 1 Corinthians 12; Ephesians 4). Some of these gifts suggest a more supernatural endowment (apostleship, knowledge, discernment); others seem quite human in their origin and expression (leadership, giving, serving). The gifts outlined here in Romans tend to be more natural abilities than divine bestowments. But, even at the level of these mundane activities, Paul suggests that God is the source of all our endeavors and that even simple tasks can be accomplished **according to the grace given us** (v. 6). For Paul, the distinctions between human talent and divine gifts are lost in a unified body whose members have become living sacrifices.

3. THE BELIEVER WHO CARES 12:9-21

Paul follows with a cluster of ten maxims for Christian living. It is difficult to develop any logical sequence or groupings of these meaty statements. Each stands by itself and is largely self-explanatory. In the

English text, all ten appear as imperative statements. In the Greek, only the first (**Love must be sincere,** [v. 9]) is a statement; the remaining nine are expressed using adjective phrases (with gerunds—a gerund being the *-ing* form of a noun). Paul thus suggests that a "sincere" love is crucial and the other items are all manifestations of this type of love. A more literal rendering of the first part of verse 9 would then be, "Let love be without hypocrisy,

hating what is evil,

clinging to what is good,

devoting to one another in brotherly love,

honoring one another above yourselves,

never lacking in zeal, but keeping your spirit fervent,

serving the Lord [some manuscripts read "serving the time"],

rejoicing in hope, enduring in affliction,

continuing in prayer,

sharing with believers in need,

practicing hospitality."

The individual who renews his or her mind with these principles and then lives them out before other human beings would be easily recognized as a person with genuine love.

The acid test for genuine love of the kind manifested by Christ is discovered in one's relationship with those who are enemies. In Romans 12, Paul progresses from loving relationships within the body of Christ to genuine love in the marketplace and public square, and then to love toward those who are adversaries. Here Paul suggests an extraordinary love that is astounding—not so much because of its actions, but because of its resilient ability to direct itself toward those who would be considered our foes.

The actions seem harmless enough, especially if they are exchanged between friends and good neighbors. Who would not rejoice or weep with friends? Who would not want to live in harmony with neighbors? Who would not want an associate who avoided pride and conceit? And, living at peace with everyone would certainly make the world a better place.

All of these commands are given in one brief paragraph of Paul's letter. However, Paul is not urging this type of behavior between friends and bosom buddies. Rather, he indicates that this is appropriate behavior for the Christian to demonstrate toward **those who persecute** us (v. 14), toward those who pay us with evil (v. 17), and toward our **enemy** (v. 20).

How contrary such actions are to the pattern of the world! How transformed and transforming is this ethic to a world of get-even people! Experience has shown time after time that a strategy of settling scores and holding grudges only leads to an escalation of the problem. In such a state of affairs, evil invariably wins.

Thus, Paul offers the Christian counteroffensive: **Do not be overcome by evil, but overcome evil with good** (v. 21). The instinctive response of self-preservation cries back, "Absurd! That's the quickest way to get taken or, worse yet, get killed!" But, from the early Christians who prayed for their tormentors who cast them to the lions, to the Anabaptists in the sixteenth century who went to the stake without resistance, to the nonviolent movements of our modern era, there comes ample evidence that such gentle actions motivated by a sincere heart of love can overcome evil.

Bless and do not curse (v. 14), **live at peace with everyone** (v. 18), **do what is right** (v. 17), and you will exhibit the nonconforming and transformed life that reveals to the world the "good, pleasing and perfect will" of God (v. 2).

ENDNOTE

[1]Wesley, *Works,* vol. 8, p. 286.

INTEGRITY IN THE WORLD

Romans 13:1-14

L ike a pebble dropped in a pond, Paul's description of the Christian lifestyle moves outward, from the relatively secure environment of the body of believers to the more threatening realm of a community that is often hostile to believers. The discussion of one's enemies at the close of Romans 12 would lead Paul naturally to a discussion of the believer's attitude toward government, since in Paul's day, Rome was "no friend of grace," as preachers used to say.

Given the pagan and barbaric nature of the Caesars during this era (Caligula and Nero, to name the most infamous rulers), one might expect Paul to allow for some level of resistance to the state. In Palestine, there were zealots who actively plotted the overthrow of Rome in the name of religious and patriotic passion. Paul maintains his mandate to "overcome evil with good" (12:21) as he proceeds to a discussion of the state.

Obligations to one's government leads Paul to discuss the more general obligations of society—paying one's taxes and debts. But these debts are material and temporal; there is a higher accountability—the debt of love owed to all persons. Paul uses his comments on this highest good to make his final observations in this letter regarding the law.

To close out his discussion of the Christian in the marketplace, Paul introduces an element of urgency based upon his expectation of the soon return of Christ. He returns to the themes of chapters 6 and 8 regarding the mind-set of Christ in a final challenge to clothe oneself with the very character and being of Christ. In this chapter of Romans, Paul describes Christianity in the crucible. Here is how to live by faith in a world that seeks to squeeze us into its patterns. To resist such pressure, Paul calls us again to live transformed lives—lives of love.

1. OBEDIENCE TO RULERS 13:1-5

Before dealing with this matter in its contemporary application, we must capture its full significance for the believers in Rome. For them, the government was not a guarantor of their religious freedom, nor was it the benefactor of the church, as it was after the conversion of Constantine, the emperor in 312 A.D. Rome was the adversary, the enemy of the gospel. How could Paul's readers not think of their Savior flogged by Roman whips, fastened to a cross by Roman nails, pierced by a Roman spear, entombed by a Roman seal? If Paul's letter was written after 57 A.D., the church in Rome had to recall the expulsion of Christians from the city by the emperor, Claudius.

Already the "present sufferings" (8:18) suggested the tribulation to come for these believers. It was one thing to live at peace with personal foes. But certainly Paul did not expect the believers in Rome to exhibit such a gracious spirit toward the political forces that opposed the kingdom of Christ!

Paul's response to such hypothetical questions is direct and unsettling: **Everyone must submit himself to the governing authorities** (13:1). There are no qualifiers, no exemption clauses to make this passage easier to swallow. The command is inclusive; it is to everyone. The instructions are clear: we **must submit** (literally, "place oneself under"). The authority is specific—we are to submit to higher powers (i.e., those having supervisory roles over the believer).

Paul's rationale for such submission to authority is equally unsettling to our ears: **For there is no authority except that which God has established. The authorities that exist have been established by God** (v. 1). For a moment, we must become rather technical and examine not only the words of the original language, but their position in the sentence. In translation, we observe the precise arrangement of the wording in the latter part of verse 1: "[and] those being authorities by God have been established."

Where one attaches the words "by God" makes a significant difference in the interpretation of this passage. If the phrase is linked to "those being authorities" *by God,* then we can assume that some authorities do not exist by the hand or blessing of God, and therefore are not worthy of our submission. On the other hand, if one links "by the God" with the latter phrase, the reading suggests that authorities which exist have been established *by God.* In this view, any and all existing powers gain their legitimacy from God and demand the submission of believers, no matter how difficult that might be.

The ambiguous wording of the Greek text along with the serious theological reflections of Christians have led to several differing opinions concerning the obligation of the Christian to the state. We will look briefly at four alternatives:

a. God in His sovereign power has willed the existence of each and every government that exists. Therefore, believers must submit willingly to the powers over them, no matter how godless or demonic those powers might be.

Supporters of this position point to the corrupt and hostile nature of the Roman Empire in Paul's day. They remind us that the Christians in Rome were commanded to submit to the government, even though, in less than a decade, that government would hunt them down and feed them to lions in the arena! This position is more often held by Calvinists, who see God as determining and controlling every facet of human existence. In such a deterministic theology, one can more easily accept the idea that Christians must resign themselves to present circumstances, since God has willed it to be that way.

Critics of this view point to repeated instances in the Bible where God's people resisted the government, particularly when the political powers defied the law of God. Moses' mother hid him from Pharaoh, Daniel prayed when it was against the law, the three young Israelites refused to bow down to the king's image. Even the early apostles defied the powers in Jerusalem, declaring, "We must obey God rather than men!" (Acts 5:29). The New Testament closes with high praise given to those who would not comply with the law, which told them to have their foreheads marked with the number of the Beast. Certainly, there must be situations where obedience to God allows, if not requires, defiance of the ruling powers.

b. The opposing alternative to the first view is held by those Christians who consider all earthly governments to be tainted with evil. Thus, these Christians consider their only ruler to be God himself, and the only law that binds them to be the divine Word of God. While they agree that wicked people need to be restrained by laws and rulers, they withdraw from that society and consider themselves to be an entity separate from the land where they reside.

It is difficult to find a biblical example of this view. However, the monastic communities of the ancient church and the Amish communities in our own society illustrate this view. Expecting no benefits or protection from the secular powers, they claim they have no obligation to submit to secular laws and authority. Citing the words of Jesus—"all who draw the sword will die by the sword" (Matthew 26:52)—they turn to the simple truths of the Sermon on the Mount and the teachings of the early apostles to define their relationships with each other.

It is not difficult to find biblical support to refute this view. Throughout history, God's people have lived under the authority of secular powers, from Abraham's sojourn in Egypt to the early Christians' citizenship in the Roman Empire. Both by example and by direct command, God's people are urged to respect, pray for and obey rulers, even when these rulers are not believers. Jesus paid the Temple tax and urged His hearers to "give to Caesar what is Caesar's" (Matt. 22:21). Paul used his rights as a Roman citizen to gain a hearing in the courts of Rome. To suggest that believers can simply "check out" of the society in which they live is both unrealistic and inconsistent with the biblical message as a whole.

c. Another alternative is to suggest that God has ordained *certain* governments as instruments of His righteousness. In this view, other political powers are so alien to His kingdom as to disqualify themselves from such authority. Those who hold this view believe that the task of a discerning Christian is to decide whether a particular government merits submission or not. Such an attitude appears to be surfacing in our culture among radical conservative groups who, in the name of loyalty to God, have assumed an adversarial role toward governments which they consider to be secular and opposed to God. Individuals in these groups are not opposed to civil government. However, they are willing to submit only to political authorities which meet *their* criteria of what the state should be.

The weakness of such a view seems obvious. Any time individuals who are called to be subject to higher powers have the privilege of "checking out" of the system, abuses will likely occur. If a state must be "Christian" in order to be obeyed, who will determine what constitutes "Christian"? If believers can exempt themselves from unpleasant duties (paying taxes, obeying laws) by appealing to immoral or unscriptural aspects of the government, society soon will approach chaos.

d. A final view acknowledges that government (authority) is established and ordained by God. From the earliest period of the human race, God allowed kings and rulers to bring order and justice to society by establishing civil rule. When persons are allowed to determine their own morality, chaos results. The book of Judges closes with this insightful commentary on the need for government: "In those days Israel had no king; everyone did as he saw fit" (Judges 21:25).

To prevent such lawlessness and wicked behavior, God instituted the concept of government. He has allowed this authority of one human over another to take many forms in different times and places. God's approval of laws and rulers does not mean, however, that He endorses every political leader and every policy that legislators create. The Bible, and particularly this passage in Romans, calls Christians to recognize the need and value of political authority, even when it is less than perfect.

Paul could not endorse all the actions of Roman government, but he did place himself under its authority, nonetheless. He spoke with respect to rulers during his trial; he recognized the authority of his jailer, even when escape from prison might have been possible (Acts 16:25-28). He never spoke in negative terms of the soldiers who guarded him in Rome. But, at the same time, Paul had a clear sense of where his ultimate allegiance was placed. In an age when it was popular, even mandated, to declare Caesar as Lord, Paul reminded the Philippian Christians that "Jesus Christ is Lord" (Phil. 2:11).

Here is a view that calls believers to stick with the society in which they are placed, to obey the established laws whenever possible, to offer appropriate respect for what that government seeks to do in its most enlightened moments. At the same time, a Christian must be willing to resist evil, even when evil wraps itself in the cloak of civil law. The Christian must be willing to maintain loyalty to Christ in the face of unjust or even wicked laws, and pay the full penalty of the law when the kingdoms of God and humans clash. The same Romans who were urged by Paul to submit to Rome would also be willing to die for their faith in the arena, rather than submit to the demands of worship Caesar.

The principles used to decide when submission to authority is appropriate and when it is contrary to the gospel are complex. They are difficult to apply to every person in every case. We can conclude, however, the following:

- God has ordained human government as a means of restraining wickedness and promoting the common good.
- Individual governments are an expression of God's plan, and to the degree that they advance the good of humanity they are to be respected and obeyed.
- Governments, like individuals, may act contrary to the laws of God. In such cases, these governments stand under His judgment and condemnation.

- The believer is commanded to respect and obey the civil authorities who serve as God's agents for justice and righteousness.
- Christians must maintain final allegiance to God. When the specific commands of God contravene the laws of government, Christians must obey God, while still maintaining a respect for the unrighteous government that rules them.

In this passage, 13:1-5, Paul presents the most explicit teaching on this complex issue to be found anywhere in the Bible. Without allowing all the "buts" and "what ifs" to overwhelm us, we must look for his central teachings on this most practical matter.

Although Paul addresses this command to **everyone,** he has particularly in mind those Christians in Rome who are wrestling with issues of ultimate allegiance. It is easy enough to declare that believers should obey God *and* country when the objectives and commands of both coincide. For the believers "being" in Rome, (1:7) the issue was becoming increasingly problematic. No doubt there were those who suggested, if not openly advocated, defiance of Roman authority in the name of allegiance to Christ. Paul's response is to remain in submission to Roman authority. For Paul, the alternative is almost unthinkable.

Paul chooses to associate all authority with God. While the passage here speaks directly of political power, Paul will appeal for the same attitude of submission when the authority is spousal (Ephesians 5:22-33), parental (6:1-4), social (6:5-9), or ecclesiastical (Phil. 2:29). Paul's appeal to "submit to one another out of reverence for Christ" (Eph. 5:21) is not an appeal for believers to be the "doormats" of society, but is rather a solid recognition of the value of respecting and using authority for the good of the whole.

Paul then states the same thing in its contrary form: **He who rebels against the authority is rebelling against what God has instituted** (Rom. 13:2). Again, we suggest that the issue here is more an attitude toward authority in general, rather than an attitude toward specific rulers or laws.

We can hardly look at our own history in North America without giving some justification for sincere Christians to rebel against the stated authorities—even in an era when the ruling powers were at least nominally Christian. The eighteenth-century American revolution against British taxation, and the abolitionist's defiance of United States slave laws would illustrate the point that Christians *may* at times be justified in resisting the existing government.

These circumstances notwithstanding, Paul's point is that defiance of constituted authority is a serious matter and cannot be undertaken without careful reflection and reasoning by the believer. We also should keep in mind that Paul is operating under the assumption that the governing powers are just and good. He is assuming that both citizens and rulers are **those who do right** (v. 3). In an ideal situation, the ruler has the best interests of the citizen in mind, and the citizen has no fear of such authority. The ruler in such a scenario can even be viewed as **God's servant to do you good** (v. 4).

Here Paul uses the word *diakonos,* the same word he uses elsewhere in his letters to describe those who serve within the church as ministers. Without ignoring the possibility that rulers can oppose the gospel and kingdom of Christ, Paul suggests an ideal society where church and state exist in separate realms of authority, while sharing a common ministry of "doing good." It would be difficult to make a case from this passage for unqualified hostility to all civil authority as a Christian response, just as it would be impossible to construct a case from other biblical passages for unquestioning obedience to the state.

What is the range of authority that God has granted to these civil authorities? Paul uses the phrase **bear the sword** (v. 4) when describing the ruler's authority to punish evildoers. There is no question that a sword is an instrument designed to inflict injury and pain. Does Paul justify such treatment of criminal offenders?

Here again, we struggle with matters of historical context or timeless truths. In Paul's day, the sword was used frequently and vigorously to impose the government's will upon the people and to punish those who resisted. If tradition is correct, Paul eventually would feel the blade of such a sword in the final moment of his own life. One could assume that Paul's use of the term in a passage commending a ruler as **God's servant. . . . to bring punishment on the wrongdoer** (v. 4) would justify harsh treatment of those criminal elements in our society today.

But, throughout the New Testament, a different attitude surfaces concerning physical means of authority. We have already cited Jesus' comment that those who take the sword will perish by it. In the Sermon on the Mount, Jesus addresses the ancient law of justice—"eye for eye and tooth for tooth" (Matthew 5:38; Exodus 21:24)—and offers a new covenant alternative: "Love your enemies, do good to those who hate you" (Luke 6:27). Even Paul seems to present a nonviolent approach to dealing with settling the accounts of social injustices: "'It is mine to avenge; I will repay,' says the Lord. . . . Overcome evil with good" (Rom. 12:19, 21).

How do we resolve this tension? Is the "sword" an instrument of God's righteous standard, or is it a violent and counterproductive means of resolving social problems? It might be helpful to remember that Paul is speaking to believers *in Rome*. In that circumstance, they were prime examples of Jesus' observations concerning His disciples being *in,* but not *of* the world. In a perfectly Christian society, one would hope that problems, even those involving violations of the law, could be resolved by nonviolent means of rebuke, instruction and prevention. But, believers do not yet live in such a society. The powers and authorities are too often from outside the circle of faith. They operate on different principles and use methods such as Roman swords to accomplish their purposes.

The difficult task of the Christian is to work to bring about God's kingdom righteousness "on earth as it is in heaven" (Matt. 6:10), while learning to live and function in a world that is not yet redeemed. Paul acknowledges the authority and even the methods of a pagan state, while appealing to the believers in Rome not to succumb to these patterns. Instead, the transforming reality of Christ must renew our minds . . . and, by God's grace, impact the world in which we live.

Paul combines two elements in his closing comment: accommodation to the authorities of this world, and inner sensitivity to the Spirit. The bottom line is to submit to the authorities. The Christian's motivation for such a response is twofold. As a citizen of Rome (or anywhere else in the world), one must respect and fear the sword of punishment. The Christian, however, also submits **because of conscience** (v. 5), recognizing that God's standard of what is right, and not the rules and regulations of the state, is the primary determinant of one's conduct.

2. PAYMENT OF OBLIGATIONS 13:6-7

The discussion of obedience to the laws of the ruler leads Paul along a path which will once more bring him back to the believer's conduct in the normal relationships of society. He shifts first to a discussion of taxes. Arguing once again that the authorities who impose these taxes are **God's servants** (v. 6), Paul urges compliance with the tax codes of his day.

This call for submission to authority is all the more striking when we recall the widespread corruption that characterized tax collectors in New Testament times. These revenue agents were the subject of deep scorn in the outlying provinces of the Empire. Jesus' willingness to even associate with them led to considerable criticism from the Jews (Matthew 11:19; Mark 2:16). The crowds once tried to manipulate Jesus into granting them an exemption for paying Caesar's due—a ploy He skillfully dodged. Even with a compelling argument that Rome did not deserve the exorbitant tax they demanded, Jesus and Paul alike indicate that the believer must respect the authority of the state and **give everyone what you owe him** (v. 7), whether that obligation be monetary amounts or simple respect for the official's role and duties.

3. LOVE FOR NEIGHBORS 13:8-10

Having discussed in detail the relationship of the believer to the state, Paul now lets his mind meander through several related topics before giving serious attention to another problem of Christian conduct in Romans 14. It is difficult to identify a common theme or logical progression in the closing verses of chapter 13. However, Paul is still dealing with the very practical dimensions of the believer's life, particularly as it relates to moral right and wrong.

He places side by side the best of the Mosaic law, the Ten Commandments, and the worst of moral lawlessness. He endeavors to avoid returning to the legalism of the people of Israel, in which adherence to rules defined one's right relationship with God. Yet, Paul refuses to release the believer from moral accountability; there is a lifestyle that is demanded of one who claims to have abandoned the past life of sin and "put . . . on the Lord Jesus Christ" (v. 14 KJV).

The question of the believer and the law has been a recurring theme in this letter. In the earlier sections of Romans, Paul dealt with God's moral law of righteousness as it is revealed in conscience and Scripture. In this chapter (13:1-7), Paul has dealt with political law and the believer's relationship to the state. Although we can distinguish between these two understandings of law, we also must acknowledge the interconnection between the two. Both moral and political law are concerned with conduct among human beings. Both presume to set a standard that constitutes the fabric of societal relations. Good political law seeks the same ends of justice and equity that are found in the moral commandments of God.

Thus, Christian scholars often have combined the two aspects of law and have debated what purpose *law* in general has for human society. Christians can quite readily agree on the nature and validity of two distinct functions of law. The first purpose of law is to restrain wicked persons. Whether we are talking of the Ten Commandments or the banking regulations of the Federal Reserve, they share a common goal of keeping individuals just and honest in their dealings with each other. This first purpose of the law is the reason Paul can urge Christians to support rulers who might be godless individuals. Despite these rulers' lack of faith, they still have the good sense to prevent moral chaos and anarchy.

But for the Christian, a deeper, more spiritual purpose for the law exists. This second purpose has been a common theme in the early chapters of Paul's letter to the Romans. The law condemns the unrighteous person and drives the sinner to the gospel. Paul has indicated that "I would not have known what sin was except through the law" (7:7). While emphasizing that obedience to the law cannot make one right with God, Paul stresses the value of the law in bringing one to the act of faith.

These two uses of the law are endorsed by the great body of Christians. However, some Christians have proposed a "third use of the law" which has resulted in a parting of company with other believers. John Calvin and the Anabaptist reformers of the sixteenth century suggested that the law was beneficial not only for the restraint of the wicked and the condemnation of sinners; it also served as the moral code for believers. While the law could not save a person, it was essential for defining the conduct and moral standards for Christians.

Martin Luther, the great Reformation advocate of Paul, balked at such a view. Luther did not deny that the Christian was bound to a high standard of righteousness; he did oppose any suggestion that such righteousness could be arranged as a system of commandments or rules. He contended that Christ had released the believer from the law (7:6), so that the person who lived by the Spirit was not bound by any law. To support such a radical view, Luther appealed to Paul and especially to Romans 7. As we look at Paul's discussion of the "law of love," we should keep in mind the debate concerning the uses of the law.

The discussion of obligations owed to the state takes Paul logically to other financial obligations—debts owed to other individuals. The Old Testament law had forbidden usury—the practice of loaning money at interest—no doubt because the rates were almost always excessive. However, the practice of lending and borrowing money was common in both Roman and Jewish circles. Jesus told several parables, in which one of the principal characters was a debtor. Paul's instructions to the Roman Christians was direct: **Let no debt remain outstanding** (v. 8).

We need to notice first what Paul does *not* say in this passage. He does not forbid the lending or borrowing of money. Rather, he urges the quick and conscientious payment of obligations that one has incurred with other individuals. We might well ask whether Paul would want a believer to go out at a later date and borrow money again. Is Paul urging new converts to clear previous obligations so they can pay as they go during the rest of their Christian lives? Or might Paul allow a person to incur indebtedness, so long as that believer demonstrated good stewardship both in entering into and exiting from debt?

The text does not give us sufficient data to make a final judgment. There are well-known Christians who use this passage to condemn any borrowing of money beyond one's ability for *immediate* repayment. Others will use this passage to encourage wise financial planning, particularly where investment necessitates owing money to someone else.

The point Paul really wants to make is in the concluding half of verse 8: **except the continuing debt to love one another.** Paul contrasts the quick payment of financial obligations with the ongoing and unpayable debt of love which believers owe to each other, in and out of the community of faith.

In our modern "charge it" society, this is a powerful image. Many of us know what it means to struggle to reduce the credit balance on that charge account to the point where we are debt free. But, given the grace that God has bestowed upon us in Christ, and the love which He has poured into our hearts (5:5), we can only come close to fulfilling the "charges" of His law of righteousness by continually expending love to others.

We have discovered already in this book that human beings can never fulfill all the demands of the law as a means to standing justified before God. God's grace demonstrated in Christ is the only way to find that right standing. But, as transformed individuals, we are now capable of expressing divine love to others. In those expressions of love, we become capable of meeting the demands of the law.

Paul argues this point by making several assumptions—some expressed directly and some indirectly. These assumptions include the following:

a. We are limiting our discussion to the law as it relates to human relationships. Notice that Paul cites only those commandments which deal with *human-to-human* responsibilities (what we term "the second table" of the law, since they would have been on the second stone tablets that Moses received from God). Paul makes no mention of the first four commandments (Exodus 20:3-11), which deal with one's relationship to God. These commandments are summed up in the great commandment, which Paul does not mention either: "Love the LORD your God with all your heart and with all your soul and with all your strength" (Deuteronomy 6:5).

b. Loving one's neighbor is the essence of all God's commandments concerning human relationships. Paul sees no need for keeping detailed rules of conduct or elaborate explanations of what each commandment entails. If genuine love (equal or surpassing the love one has for himself or herself) is manifested, the expectations of the law have been met.

c. Loving one's neighbor fulfills the demands of God's moral standard for human relationships, *but it does not save a person.* It would be unthinkable for Paul to revert to a Jewish understanding that claims a right standing simply on the basis of works of righteousness. Love of God and faith in Christ are what justify one before God, not keeping the law. If a "third use of the law" means that keeping commandments, no matter how noble and lofty they might be, is the determining factor in sustaining one's justification, Paul would reject it immediately. Salvation must always be by grace and through faith.

d. However, the person transformed by grace through faith is capable of loving others in such a way that the standard of God's law can be met in real persons living in a real world. **Love is the fulfillment of the law** (Rom. 13:10). If a "third use of the law" means that believers are capable of loving others and are expected to do so, then Paul could affirm that this *fulfilled* law is still operational in the life of believers.

As followers of Christ, we must walk the narrow path of His grace and our response of love. To stress God's grace and unconditional love, to the point where we sense no obligation to love others and avoid harming them, is to open the door to moral lawlessness and a life unworthy of God's holy name. To equate the life of grace with *performing* certain behavioral duties is to return to the very law that condemned us. We must walk by faith in God and live a life of love toward others.

4. PURITY OF LIFESTYLE 13:11-14

As Paul moves toward the close of his instructions to the Romans on how to live a transformed life in the world, he shifts his focus from the *location* of that activity to its *timing*. The fact that these believers were "being" in Rome (see comments on 1:7) added a certain urgency to this letter. That urgency was intensified by Paul's conviction that the present age was drawing to a close and a new age was about to break into history. (1 Thessalonians 5:1-4).

The New Testament gives abundant evidence that the believers in Paul's day expected the return of Christ momentarily. Both Peter and Paul alerted their readers that the Lord was "at hand" (Phil. 4:5; 1 Peter 4:7 KJV). Paul's letters to the church at Thessalonica resolved questions about the timing of the Second Coming. Paul assured these Christians that those who had died recently ("fallen asleep" would be included in the hosts who would greet Christ at His return (1 Thess. 4:13-16). The question of what would happen to deceased saints suggests that the Christians at first assumed the end would come before death overtook the saints in the church.

Here in Romans, Paul repeats that theme. He calls for watchfulness on the part of the slumbering believers in Rome, perhaps drawing upon Jesus' comparing His coming to the arrival of a thief at night (Matt. 24:42-44). Daybreak provided an appropriate image for this great prophetic event. Thus, the exhortation, **The night is nearly over; the day is almost here** (Rom. 13:12).

Suddenly, Paul shifts the imagery of light and dark in a new direction. As the passage (vv. 11-14) opens, night represents the present age; light symbolizes the dawning of the Kingdom to come. Now darkness and light become associated with the forces of evil and good.

Here Paul draws upon imagery that was widespread in first-century religious thought. The Jewish Essenes, an early monastic community, wrote of a great conflict between the forces of light and darkness in what we now refer to as the Dead Sea Scrolls. The "mystery religions" that were springing up across the Mediterranean region often referred to a cosmic conflict using these same images. The heresy of "gnosticism," which would be one of the greatest threats to the early church, also played upon a dualistic struggle between spirit and matter, light and darkness.

Paul does not deal so much with a *cosmic* struggle of opposing forces as a *moral* darkness that leads humans to debased actions—"men loved darkness instead of light because their deeds were evil" (John 3:19). The depths of this evil is graphically portrayed in the words Paul uses to describe their behavior: **orgies** (literally, *revelry*), **drunkenness, sexual immorality** *(bedding)*, **debauchery** *(shamelessness)*, **dissension and jealousy** (Rom. 13:13).

Could Paul possibly be describing the behavior of *believers* in Rome? The pronoun used in this verse is "us" (**Let us**), rather than some wicked "them." The appeal is to behave decently—a command certainly appropriate for believers. But, how could one allow for such unchristian conduct among those whom Paul has described as persons who have crucified the sinful nature and risen with Christ? Paul is more likely referring to the culture and immoral influences that surrounded the believers in Rome, the patterns that were always attempting to squeeze the Christians into a different mold.

Now, at the end of his discussion (13:14), Paul re-echoes the themes of 12:2. **Clothe yourselves with the Lord Jesus Christ** parallels the command to "be transformed by the renewing of your mind." **Do not think about how to gratify the desires of the sinful nature** echoes the warning, "Do not conform any longer to the pattern of this world."

Believers today would find the immoral behaviors Paul describes as equally abhorrent to the life of faith. But we must be mindful that the world of darkness which surrounds us is not that different from the corrupt Rome of Paul's time. We can be tempted, as easily as any recipient of Paul's letter, to gratify desires that often lurk in the shadows of our own spirits.

The solution then and now is a proactive stance. Faith requires a deliberate choice of spiritual wardrobe. We must **put on the armor of light** (13:12). But, even prior to donning the armor, we must **clothe [ourselves] with the Lord Jesus Christ** (v. 14) and His righteousness. Why? **Because our salvation is nearer now than when we first believed** (v. 11). With the early church we cry, *"Maranatha!* Come, Lord Jesus!"

15

SENSITIVITY IN DISPUTES

Romans 14:1–15:7

P aul's shift to a new topic of discussion in chapter 14 does not appear to flow out of previous discussions. Although it deals with practical matters related to the Christian life, it has no apparent connection to the end times or Paul's appeal to become persons of light rather than darkness.

In fact, one might suggest that chapter 13 would have made a good concluding point to Paul's treatise on salvation. He has spelled out the nature of sin, faith, and justification. Paul has explored both personal salvation as well as the broader issue of salvation for his people, the Jews. Finally, Paul has spelled out the ramifications of the transformed life as it relates to interpersonal dynamics in the community of faith, one's neighborhood, and civic authorities. The closing paragraph of chapter 13 offers a vision of the approaching dawn of a new age, as well as an appeal for the believers in Rome to live in expectant hope of the salvation that draws nearer every moment.

Wrap it up, Paul! What an appropriate point to offer a final blessing and a few personal remarks. We would expect the passage beginning with 15:13 and extending to the end of the letter to appear right after the close of chapter 13. But, like an appendix in a book or a final digression in a speech, Paul moves to a new theme that deals specifically with the problem of weaker believers in the body of Christ.

While we cannot explain why Paul thought it essential to include this section, or why it is situated in this portion of the letter, we can understand the significance of the issue for the early believers in Rome. We have already noted the tension between Jews and non-Jews in the secular records of this era. And, within the book of Romans, the interrelations of Jews and Gentiles have surfaced directly or by inference at several points. Paul has words of rebuke for the Jews, particularly regarding their misunderstanding of one's justification with God. But Paul also chides the Gentiles for their arrogance and lack of compassion for unbelieving Jews.

The fact that tension surfaced between Jews and Gentiles *within* the body of Christ should not surprise us. The point of tension most likely would be regarding various standards of conduct and religious practice observed by the Jews. As believers who brought a tradition of scrupulous adherence to the law (as they understood it), Jewish Christians would be shocked at the liberal attitude and behavior of the Gentiles.

The Gentiles, on the other hand, came to the faith from morally lax backgrounds. Having previously engaged in the activities Paul describes in 13:13, they no doubt considered the Christian ethic of chastity, honesty and self-control as rigorous enough without adding ceremonial and behavioral technicalities to the list.

Paul's "ministry of reconciliation" (2 Corinthians 5:18) took him beyond drawing unbelievers toward Christ to also unifying a divisive body of believers. Here we see Paul endeavoring to steer an appropriate course between the twin dangers of legalism and license. And we can be grateful that this additional topic made it into the closing portions of his letter. For the issue he addresses here has not yet disappeared from the ranks of the faithful.

Although the issues of the Jewish ceremonial law are no longer the major source of tension, matters related to one's view of scriptural commands and one's own religious heritage make the question of weak and strong Christianity still very relevant to our understanding and expression of the gospel today. We approach Paul's discussion of this with a genuine desire to learn of Christ—and with the expectation that Paul will leave us all a little unsettled with his insightful advice.

1. DIVERSITY SHOWING RESPECT 14:1-12

Without any transitional phrase or bridging of ideas, Paul lays down the main point statement of this discussion: **Accept him whose faith is weak** (v. 1). No place in this entire passage does he identify a specific group who comprise these weak believers, although the context and allusions to specific practices suggest that he is referring to Jewish converts to the faith. It is these individuals who most likely would be concerned with matters of diet (v. 2) and religious observances (v. 5).

But let us commend Paul for his restraint from labeling persons with a particular spiritual lifestyle. We are often less sensitive and charitable than he is. Many of us are quick to brand all persons belonging to a particular denomination or religious tradition with the popular stereotype of that group. Thus, all Methodists become "liberals," all Mennonites become "legalists," all Pentecostals become "holy rollers," and the labeling goes on and on. Better simply to describe the beliefs and practices of individual believers, or to speak in general terms of the doctrinal perspectives of various traditions without stereotyping.

Paul simply acknowledges that in the Roman church there are stronger and weaker Christians. And he uses these contrasting terms in a particular sense. He is not discussing their relationship *with God* in terms of strength or weakness, nor their ability to engage in spiritual warfare against the Enemy, nor their potential for leadership in the church. Paul focuses attention instead on their ability to deal with **disputable matters** (v. 1) relating to Christian conduct.

Before discussing how various believers deal with these matters of conscience, we must be clear about the limits of the topic. Not every aspect of Christian conduct is a matter for personal conviction. No place in this discussion does Paul allow for Christians to debate the Ten Commandments. The individual who has no deep convictions about sexual relationships out of marriage is hardly the "strong" Christian. The person who totally disregards the Sabbath (no matter how he or she understands the term) is not a stronger Christian than one who is scrupulous about keeping it holy! We cannot take this passage to mean that Paul commends those who have few, if any, convictions about how to live the Christian life.

But, neither is Paul dealing with matters that are purely of personal taste and preference. This is not a passage about differences between eating broccoli or carrots! This is not a passage on whether one likes choruses or hymns in Sunday morning worship. Too often we want to spiritualize every matter of personal taste and make it a deep religious conviction. That is not what Paul is wrestling with in these verses.

The specific area Paul addresses is **disputable matters**—those *religious* convictions that often divide sincere Bible-believing Christians, who interpret the meaning of scripture passages in different ways. The early Reformers, particularly the Lutherans, quickly encountered these disputable matters as they attempted to remove those aspects of Roman Catholicism which they considered unbiblical, while retaining elements of worship and conduct that were legitimate expressions of their understanding of the faith. Very quickly, debates arose about ministerial attire, the use of candles, and statues of the saints. One person's rich tradition of spirituality was another person's demonic practice.

Luther himself had to enter the fray. He proposed that there were elements of Christianity which were essential (we would say "fundamental" today) to the faith. Other issues were altogether irrelevant to debate in the context of what was right for a Christian to do. Luther then proposed a third category, the *adiaphora,* from the Greek word meaning "indifferent" or "inconsequential." This category included those things that did matter to some Christians, but not to others, or those issues on which conscientious believers could not come to agreement concerning the biblical view.

These disputable matters, or *adiaphora,* still abound in Christian circles. Unfortunately one cannot always clearly label issues that belong in this category. While evangelical Christians all agree that adultery is sinful and contrary to the gospel, these same Christians differ on whether other actions and attitudes toward the opposite sex are appropriate for the Christian (e.g., social dancing, or mixed swimming at public beaches). Christians agree that the Sabbath should be holy, but differ extensively on what activities are appropriate for Sunday. Paul offers the following principles to guide believers through this behavioral mine field:

a. The weaker person is the one who has the greater scruples concerning religious matters. This statement jars many believers who have considered themselves the strong ones because they have stringent standards regarding behavior. In their eyes, the weak are those who have few convictions and appear to take the easy route of lax behavior on disputed matters. Paul reverses the conventional wisdom of the church and proposes that those who maintain strict codes have not learned the deeper lessons of faith, where the Spirit's direction and biblical *principles* govern one's behavior, rather than rules and regulations.

Paul is no doubt thinking back to his earlier experiences in Pharisaism, where well-meaning students of the law endeavored to protect their traditions ("Fencing the Torah," it was called) by detailed codes of conduct. But in Christ he had found a freedom from such a restrictive view of righteousness. Paul's concept of Christian liberty was so expansive that it led him to propose that "love is the fulfillment of the law" (13:10). With such a view of the gospel, Paul could only look at those who relied on specific regulations as "weak."

By contrast, the person who lives in the broader context of freedom (**to eat everything** [14:2]) is judged to be stronger. But, notice that it is a person's **faith** (v. 2) which allows him freedom, not his insensitivity to the Scriptures or his disregard of the Spirit's leading. Paul is not contrasting a person who is "more spiritual," and thus eats vegetables, with a person who is "less spiritual" and eats anything. Both persons are operating out of their faith, but each comes to a different understanding of what is appropriate behavior for the believer.

b. Rather than scorning or even criticizing the weaker Christian for such scrupulous behavior, Paul urges the strong believer to **accept him . . . without passing judgment** (v. 1). It is apparent that Paul's sympathies lie with the stronger believer, but he does not use this position to look down upon his brother and label him a "legalist." Furthermore, the person of high religious standards must not condemn his "laid-back" brother and label him as worldly or unspiritual (v. 3). The love which "does no harm to its neighbor" (13:10) compels both parties to accept each other as sincere members of the family of faith.

Paul considers both the weak and the strong to be valid in their convictions because **God has accepted [them]** (v. 3). Furthermore, the final determination of who is "right" will be made by God, and not by any human judgment. In regard to both the weak and the strong, **to his own master he stands or falls** (v. 4).

Even when making that powerful affirmation of God's right to judge the matter, Paul avoids any hint that it is the *behavior* of these believers that will justify them. Yes, God will have to determine the integrity and appropriateness of their conduct, but if either or both stand righteous before God, it will be through their faith and not their works that His "Well done, good and faithful servant!" (Matthew 25:23) will come. **For the Lord is able to make him stand** (Rom. 14:4). No one stands on his own merits or works.

c. Paul suggests that two believers can differ on a disputable matter, and both may be right. The question is not who has the most verses to back up his position or who can present the best logical arguments. The question is one of honest integrity before God. **Each one should be fully convinced in his own mind** (v. 5). Augustine, the great bishop of the church in ages past, confessed that as a young Christian he loved to argue doctrine with other people, not because he was convinced that he was right, but purely for the joy of arguing and because he *wanted* to be right! He is not the last believer whose mind is already made up and does not want to be confused with the facts.

It is interesting that Paul does not urge the Romans to come to an agreement or to work toward some position of compromise. The unity of the body of Christ does not require unity on all matters of doctrine and practice. It demands love and acceptance of those who, in good faith, have become convinced in their own minds that their view is consistent with Scripture and God's "good, pleasing and perfect will" for their lives (12:2).

A personal conviction, however, must be balanced with a life directed toward God. Paul allows believers either to partake or abstain, so long as both actions are **to the Lord** (14:6). One can all too easily turn the passion of personal convictions into an ego trip of self-righteousness: "I would never be caught doing . . ." or, "It doesn't bother me in the least to. . . ."

The bottom line on these disputed matters is not what *I* think; it is whether I have been convinced by His Spirit in my mind, and whether I do all things "in the name of the Lord" (Colossians 3:17). In living and in dying, in eating and in abstaining, **we belong to the Lord** (Rom. 14:8). A Christian does not always have to be right, but a Christian should always be convinced and committed to Christ.

Paul makes more than an incidental reference in this passage to living and dying. He sustains the image for three verses (7-9) and even ties it to the death and resurrection of Christ. Apparently, Paul has more than the natural process of death in mind when he speaks of one dying to himself or dying to the Lord. Already, at this early point in the history of the church, faith in Christ entailed a certain risk of persecution or even martyrdom.

Paul himself had to be very much aware of the possibility of premature death because of his faith in Christ. This passage in Romans is very reminiscent of Paul's mental tug-of-war in 2 Corinthians concerning remaining in the body with the church or being absent from the body with the Lord (2 Cor. 5:6-10). There he also determines, "We make it our goal to please him, whether we are at home in the body or away from it" (v. 9). And he concludes that God's "judgment seat" is where the final resolution of our actions will be evaluated (v. 10; cf. Rom. 14:10), and not in the heated debates of disputing Christians.

In Paul's reference to living and dying, he may be addressing the first hints of a concept that came to have widespread acceptance in the early church—that dying for one's faith was the ultimate proof of one's commitment to Christ, and thus guaranteed the martyr a sure place in heaven. The very word *martyr* is an English word taken directly from the Greek word for "witness." What greater witness of one's faith could a believer give than to die for his Lord? And what greater indication of spiritual cowardice could one demonstrate than to run from persecution?

Thus, another comparison between weak and strong Christians surfaces. Perhaps already in Paul's day, some Christians were claiming spiritual high ground by their willingness to die for the Lord. Others no doubt offered sound reasons for avoiding persecution in order to live for the Lord and the fledgling church. Would there have been discussions in Rome at this early date about living or dying for the Lord? No matter, says Paul. The same issue applies here as it does with personal convictions. We do not live or die to ourselves; we do not suffer or avoid suffering based on our self-interest. **Whether we live or die, we belong to the Lord** (v. 8).

The conclusion of the matter is clear. We must accept each other in love, recognizing that matters of *adiaphora* exist in the body of Christ. Our final accountability is not to each other; **each of us will give an account of himself to God** (v. 12). We must cease judging our brothers and sisters, and leave that task to a righteous God.

2. FREEDOM SHOWING RESTRAINT 14:13-23

In this age of tolerance and respect for the diversity of our society, one would think Paul has done very well to urge Christians in Rome not to judge each other. At this point, he has proposed a "live and let live" approach to a very complex problem. Yes, he has identified the scrupulous believer as weak in comparison to the one who governs his life by the freedom of the Spirit's leading. However, Paul has cautioned the stronger Christian not to look down on the weaker, but rather to accept him as also directed by the Spirit.

But in this passage, Paul offers an even greater challenge to the believer who lives in the freedom of conscience. Paul proposes that there are instances where one might restrict behavior—not for the sake of conscience, but for the sake of love.

Actions of self-restraint are almost always difficult. Paul tells the Galatians that one of the fruits of the Spirit is self-control (Gal. 5:23). Elsewhere he indicates that he makes his body his slave, even beating it, so he "will not be disqualified for the prize" (1 Cor. 9:27). This sort of mastery is to be expected in areas where the believer is tempted to act contrary to God's commands or desires.

Now Paul is suggesting that restraint to the point of *not* doing what conscience allows is permissible, even when a believer feels no conviction or condemnation for a particular action. It may be the *right* response. That such restraint might be difficult is suggested by Paul's command to **make up your mind** (Rom. 14:13). The same mind that is "fully convinced" (v. 5) that an act is acceptable must now inform the will that it ought not to be done! If believers are expected to choose this difficult path of love, they ought to take careful notice of when it is or is not expected of them.

a. This action is appropriate when dealing with members of the family of faith. Throughout the remainder of Romans 14, Paul refers to the relationship between a believer and a **brother** (vv. 15, 21; see also v. 13—by inference, he refers to one's sister, too). Paul is not dealing with our conduct before unbelievers in the world. Certainly there is call for restraint in how one behaves in such circumstances as well, but Paul will address those situations elsewhere. Here he focuses on the tensions that exist *within* the community of faith. But the sensitivity is directed toward a member of the community who is close enough relationally to be identified as a sibling—**a brother.**

Certainly other voices clamor for attention and control within the church. One can imagine preachers who, "lording it over those entrusted to [them]" (1 Peter 5:3), take it upon themselves to define the moral standard for the entire body. A visiting evangelist can preach his convictions without any regard for the real-life context of his hearers. The argumentative neighbor from another denomination can give his opinions on moral conduct at will. The self-righteous Pharisee can set himself up as the standard for everyone else to follow. These are not the persons Paul tells us to accommodate for love's sake. It is the brother, and a weak brother at that.

b. Furthermore, restraint is necessary in situations where the strong believer's freedom would result in spiritual harm to the weaker individual. Believers must be sensitive to the person who **is distressed** (Rom. 14:15) by some action of theirs to the degree that it causes the weaker brother **to stumble** (v. 20) or **fall** (v. 21) in his spiritual walk. This action would be one of enough significance that it puts the weaker brother's relationship with God in jeopardy, and creates the possibility that one person's freedom might **destroy the work of God** (v. 20) in another and, thus, ultimately **destroy [that] brother for whom Christ died** (v. 15).

In other words, Paul is speaking of serious damage control for a believer whose moral sensitivity is weak. He is not advocating that Christians must accommodate their behavior to all the pet peeves and personal tastes that are expressed among the faithful.

Paul's parallel passage on this topic in 1 Corinthians has resulted in considerable misunderstanding and unwarranted browbeating in conservative areas of the church. His statement, "If meat make my brother to offend, I will eat no flesh" (1 Cor. 8:13 KJV), has been interpreted to mean that believers must refrain from doing those things that other believers find offensive. And "offensive" has been given a wide range of meaning! The New International Version more correctly translates the verse to read, "If what I eat causes my brother to fall into sin. . . ."

One can now better understand the motivation that prompts Paul to suggest personal sacrifice on behalf of another believer. The law of love would constrain followers of Christ from doing anything that would threaten the spiritual well-being of a brother or sister in Christ, particularly if that individual were already weak in the faith. It does not compel a believer to change behavior like a chameleon with every new opinion that is expressed in the congregation.

For example, I have adorned my face with a beard for many years. On several occasions I have had dear saints tell me they did not like my beard and thought it was unbecoming for a minister. I have graciously smiled and thanked them for their opinion. I have never shaved my beard out of duty to those who are offended to see me with one. However, if a young Christian would inform me that her confidence in the gospel was deeply shaken by my facial hair and that she was seriously considering leaving the faith because of my beard, for her sake and for my commitment to the gospel, I would go looking for a razor.

c. The decision of the stronger believer to refrain for the sake of love does not require a change in the inner convictions. Paul is not requiring the person who lives in freedom to develop more strict rules for living. For the sake of love, the strong brother need not agree with one who views his actions as inappropriate for the believer. In fact, Paul states, **Do not allow what you consider good to be spoken of as evil** (Rom. 14:16).

He only asks that, out of love, the stronger Christian not flaunt that freedom in the face of a weaker brother, either by doing what distresses the weaker one, or by scorning the strict standards he maintains. While allowing the more liberated Christian the right to freedom, Paul cautions, **Whatever you believe about these things keep between yourself and God** (v. 22).

d. Paul's ultimate objective is the unity of the body and the furthering of Christ's kingdom—**peace and . . . mutual edification** (v. 19). But both of these objectives could easily be hindered by quarrels over disputed matters.

To define the gospel (or even spirituality) in terms of what a person eats is to negate the far more significant qualities that manifest themselves in the person who lives by faith. Paul's passing reference to these virtues (**righteousness, peace and joy in the Holy Spirit** [v. 17]) takes us back to Romans 5 where the blessings of justification are spelled out in the same terms. Paul's deep-seated concern is that while these tensions in Rome regarding eating and drinking are disputed matters, they easily can become destructive to the gospel of salvation through faith, not works.

Therefore, Paul is far more concerned about the lack of faith and love that accompanies this dispute than the issues of clean or unclean food and the drinking of wine. The greater danger for believers is that doubts concerning their standing with God may arise—doubts based upon inconsequential patterns of behavior. If a believer can be made to question his relationship with God because of guilty feelings over dietary matters, Satan's battle for the soul is half won. If believers judge and condemn each other on the basis of outward works, then faith will be abandoned and the sin of pride and self-righteousness will rear its ugly head again.

Paul urges the Gentile believers to stay with faith, while treating the weaker members of the body with love; to do anything less in this situation leads to sin. His concluding observation, **Everything that does not come from faith is sin** (v. 23), must be kept in the context of this passage. Although the statement has a pleasing and very theological ring to it, one ought not wrench these words from the passage and apply them to all the generic dimensions of life.

There are a myriad of things in life that cannot be associated directly with faith—but which are not sinful. Hiking in the Rockies, watching a football game on TV, and studying algebra are hardly things of faith. But, to suggest that any dimension of life which cannot be defined by spiritual categories or be directly tied to one's walk with God is sinful is to apply this verse in ways it was never intended.

Paul's point in this passage is strong. When the Christian community shifts its focus and the foundation of righteousness away from faith in God's promise and toward any human effort or standard of measurement, it is departing from the gospel and is displeasing God. Strange irony, indeed, that those who would protect the gospel by their strict standards of spiritual conduct are those most likely to undermine and destroy it.

3. STRENGTH SHOWING GENTLENESS 15:1-7

As Paul moves to the close of his discussion on this matter, he shifts pronouns from the second person "you" to the more inclusive "we," identifying himself clearly with strong believers who govern their outer actions by inner openness to the Spirit. Paul's reference to **the failings of the weak** (v. 1) should not be seen as moral failure on their part.

The King James translation is probably clearer when it says, "infirmities of the weak." The Greek word suggests weakness that comes from lack of use rather than something defective. Paul would then be suggesting that the persons who govern their conduct by rigid rules are not the spiritual "toughies" we think they are. In a sense, they suffer from spiritual atrophy—not using their minds and consciences to sort out the complex dynamics that often affect a moral decision.

Rather than sort out the problem, these weaker Christians depend on quick, black-and-white answers picked up from a popular book, a TV evangelist or an opinionated saint in the church. In contrast, Paul sees spiritual strength arising out of the mind that is renewed (12:2) and is therefore "able to test and approve what God's will is," even in the thorny issues that complicate our lives each day.

But again, Paul does not condemn or belittle these weaker Christians. He urges others to join him in bearing with these persons, even when that action calls for us **not to please ourselves** (15:1). Without caving in to all the rigid rules of our weaker neighbors, we must demonstrate love that will build up these persons and perhaps move them to a deeper insight concerning the walk of faith. And why must strong Christians act so sensitively toward those who do not live in the freedom of the Spirit? Because Jesus would have acted that way (v. 3).

Here Paul gives a hint of the powerful theme expressed in a later letter: "Your attitude should be the same as that of Christ Jesus: Who . . . made himself nothing. . . . and became obedient to death—even death on a cross!" (Philippians 2:5-8). If the Master could demonstrate that level of self-control in order to reach down to our level of understanding, the believer who operates on the level of moral principles ought to be able to enter the world of one who sees things from a much narrower perspective.

To drive home his point, Paul uses a tactic which is puzzling, especially if (as we suggested earlier) he is addressing this portion of Romans to Gentiles. He cites a passage from the Psalms (69:9, quoted in Rom. 15:3) describing David's dejection from the treatment of his

229

enemies. Certainly Paul had heard stories of Jesus' life that would have illustrated his point better than the Old Testament reference, which Paul interprets prophetically! Apparently Paul's devotion to Scripture and its authority prompted him to draw from the holy writings of his own tradition, rather than relate incidents that were not yet accepted as authoritative words by the early church.

That this was Paul's thinking is evident from the next verse, which is more an aside than a further point in his instructions about weaker brothers: **For everything that was written in the past was written to teach us** (v. 4). Paul's high view of Scripture allows him to read the biblical texts with eyes of faith, finding Christ in obscure passages, finding insights for living in the midst of levitical rules and regulations, finding sources of **endurance and . . . encouragement** (v. 4) in Scripture passages, far beyond what the authors had in mind when writing those verses.

Obviously, there are dangers when one takes this approach too far. A charlatan or false teacher can find a scriptural prooftext for almost any belief or behavioral practice (remember David Koresh?). Yet, who can deny the benefit there is in God's Word when it is used properly and *devotionally,* in order to offer words of encouragement so that **we might have hope** (v. 4) in the midst of very stressful circumstances. We can be most understanding when we discover that Paul or other New Testament writers found unlikely passages from the Old Testament to bolster their ideas, because we also have been encouraged by holy words which have strengthened our faith and Christian living as well.

Paul concludes this section with a prayer and a final exhortation. In a situation that must have been tense, if not explosive, for the believers in Rome, Paul prays for **a spirit of unity** (v. 5). Such oneness comes not from winning arguments by destroying the opponent's case. Neither does it come by caving in and compromising one's convictions for the sake of peace. This spirit of unity comes from following Christ and glorifying "your Father in heaven" (Matt. 5:16).

Just as the gift of salvation comes to those who believe in their hearts and confess with their mouths (Rom. 10:9-10), so now the *life* of salvation is expressed in the body of Christ **with one heart and mouth** (15:6). It is not enough for the weaker and stronger believers in Rome to claim unity based solely on the fact that they share the same heart belief; no, they must all take their hymnals and stand and sing the Doxology *together!* That public declaration of their unity in Christ holds them accountable within the body.

Accountable for what? Paul states it in uncompromising terms: **Accept one another, then, just as Christ accepted you** (v. 7). Again and again, the Scriptures instruct us to pattern our lives after the example of our Lord: "Forgive as the Lord forgave you" (Colossians 3:13); "Live a life of love, just as Christ loved us" (Ephesians 5:2). Now we must reach out to brothers and sisters in the faith and accept them as Christ has accepted us.

Christ does not accept us because we are right in all of our actions and ideas. Christ does not accept us by lowering His standards of holiness and righteousness to our flawed judgment of things. He accepts us *in spite* of who we are, not because of who we are.

The ramifications of this passage for Christians who emphasize the holy life is somewhat unsettling. In the early history of the holiness movement, we were more closely equated with those "weaker brothers" who maintained deep convictions concerning the moral and ethical patterns of faith. Whether the issue was hairstyles, the wearing of jewelry, attending movies, or dancing, we knew precisely where we stood and assumed that all believers should have similar strict codes of behavior. We were known in the wider community as Christians of strict standards, and we were proud of that heritage.

In more recent years, our passion for reaching out to those beyond our circle of belief and behavior has resulted in a significant influx of converts to the faith who do not necessarily share those same strong convictions regarding holy living. A new generation uses different scriptures and a different way of thinking to develop standards that seem very strange, even unbiblical, to those who have made rather clear definitions of holy and unholy behavior.

We now find ourselves confronted with much the same tension that faced the believers in Rome. Parties within the movement defend their more conservative lifestyles with deep conviction, and express deep dismay at the lax spirituality of the new generation of believers. The younger converts, liberated by the power of Christ from the enslaving powers of sin, rejoice in their freedom from the condemnation of the law, and wonder why so many believers remain bound by strict rules of conduct that do not seem to connect directly with the great themes of Jesus' teaching.

And so, the disagreement persists after two thousand years of Christianity. The dangers of legalism and liberalism are discussed and debated by parties that have labeled their opponents in exaggerated terms. Somehow we must learn to **accept one another . . . in order to bring**

praise to God (Rom. 15:7), without discrediting the freedom of the strong or despising the scruples of the weak.

THE MINISTRY
OF CHRIST

Romans 15:8-33

Paul's opening to the final section of Romans dealing with moral instruction *(parenaesis)* was a bold appeal to the Roman Christians, challenging them to present themselves as sacrifices to God (12:1-2). Now, as Paul concludes this section on how to reflect God's righteousness in the actions of life, he slips out of the topic almost imperceptibly. His firm advice about accepting those who are weak shifts to the unity that should be present in the body of believers—a unity centered on praise to Christ.

Paul moves in a steady progression from Christ as the example of accepting others to Christ as the light to the Gentiles. Paul then asserts his special commission to serve the Gentiles, and tells how God has blessed those endeavors. But, his ministry to the Gentiles will not be complete until he has reached the western boundaries of the Mediterranean Sea, including a personal trip to Rome.

Paul's letter then comes full circle, back to his desire expressed in the opening verses of Romans to "impart to [them] some spiritual gift to make [them] strong" (1:11). Rather than ending this letter with climactic clashes of powerful truth, like those found in chapter 8, he lets the music of his message fade quietly, ending with an almost whispered benediction: **The God of peace be with you** (15:33).

1. CHRIST'S MINISTRY TO THE GENTILES 15:8-13

Paul concludes his discussion on handling the weaker believer with the firm command: "Accept one another" (v. 7). But, rather than starting off in a totally different vein, as he did to begin this matter in 14:1, Paul now uses his rhetorical skills to build a subtle transition to the theme with which he opened the letter—his special mission to the Gentiles.

Paul reminds the Roman believers that Christ himself demonstrated this accommodating spirit by becoming **a servant of the Jews** [the Greek text reads "of circumcision"] **on behalf of God's truth** (15:8). In our present thinking, we take for granted that Jesus was a Jew, "born under law" (Galatians 4:4) to fulfill all the Old Testament prophecies concerning the Savior coming from the line of David. As to his title of Messiah, there would be no question about His Jewish lineage.

However, there is still something profound about the fact that the Son of God manifested himself among a people who had become locked in the grip of the law. One could make a *logical* case that God might send His Son directly to the unrighteous Gentiles who would more readily accept His claims to divinity. The very narrowness and rigidity of the Jewish people led to their rejection of Jesus' message of love and forgiveness.

Yet, as Paul points out, God chose to send His Son to redeem the world through a nation that had "failed" because they had reduced righteousness to rules and rituals. Rather than ignoring these people or writing them off as divine rejects, Christ was born "a servant of [circumcision]," and from that Jewish origin became "a light for revelation to the Gentiles and for glory to [His] people Israel" (Luke 2:32). Paul seems to suggest to Gentile believers that if God could accomplish His purposes in Christ by accommodating those bound up with the law, He can also use their sensitivity to the weaker believers as a means of furthering His purposes in Rome.

But now the progression of thought has shifted away from weak and strong and has centered upon the recurring theme in this letter of God's great mercy and sovereign plan for redeeming the world to himself. Paul's grasp of the Old Testament is demonstrated as he cites four passages from widely separated sections of the Old Testament which all foretell a time when Gentiles will join with God's people in praising the Lord.

The final prophecy Paul mentions (Rom. 15:12) ties together several strands that appeared earlier in his letter. **The Root of Jesse** takes us back to the description of the olive tree (chap. 11) with its holy root (v. 16) and engrafted branches. The **hope** of the Gentiles (15:12) draws us back to the hope in chapter 8 that causes the whole of creation to groan in expectation for a coming redemption (v. 22).

No place do the echoes of earlier truths resound more than in the benediction of 15:13. All the themes of chapter 5 now resurface in Paul's prayer. Once again, we hear of the faith (trust) that brings **joy, peace** and **hope** which come through the presence of the **Holy Spirit** in the believer's life. Here, as in the earlier reference (5:5), the result is an abundant life that is overflowing because of the love poured out upon us from God.

This abundant life is not a gift once received and then irrevocably ours. Paul brings us back again to the response of faith by stressing that the blessings of joy and peace fill us **as [we] trust in him** (15:13). As branches must keep on abiding "in the vine" in order to bear fruit (John 15:4), so the believer must keep trusting in the grace of God in order to manifest peace, joy and hope to the world.

2. PAUL'S MINISTRY TO THE GENTILES 15:14-22

Paul has been rather pointed in his instructions to the believers in Rome. He has called them to show mutual respect to those in the fellowship, to demonstrate love toward those who are hostile in the marketplace, to respect the authorities of the state, and to accept those of differing moral codes in the church. Although it is safe to assume that specific situations in Rome prompted these instructions, no place in these verses do we hear Paul specifically accusing his readers of living in violation of the "law of love." By contrast, one cannot read Paul's letter to the Galatians without feeling the stinging rebuke that fills the verses of that epistle.

Paul concludes his letter to the Romans by affirming these believers. He perceives them to be persons **full of goodness, complete in knowledge and competent to instruct one another** (15:14). In this verse, he progresses from inner character (goodness) to intellectual comprehension (knowledge) to practical skills (competency in instruction). This same pattern should manifest itself in believers today. It is not enough to develop communication skills if we do not have a solid grasp of the content of what we are communicating.

We are hearing more and more "talk show" chatter in the church that lacks solid content and a firm grasp of Christian truth. Such "instruction" is evidence of lives which echo that of Shakespeare's Lady MacBeth: "full of sound and fury, signifying nothing." We must become complete in knowledge before we open our mouths to teach others.

But we cannot be complete in knowledge simply by reading books, taking notes and accumulating degrees after our names. The completeness of our knowledge relies on our developing an inner life that is **full of goodness.** When we have established our spiritual priorities, grasping the spiritual significance of what we proclaim will come naturally. Goodness, an inner quality based on a right standing with God, will lead to complete knowledge (the ability to grasp all the dimensions of God's grace and love [Ephesians 3:18-19]), which will foster competence in sharing that truth with others.

Paul acknowledges that he has competence and confidence to teach these matters because of his divine commission **to be a minister of Christ Jesus to the Gentiles** (Rom. 15:16). Here Paul departs from his normal term for "minister" or "servant" *(diakonos)* to describe his role, and instead uses a term for "civil servant"—one who volunteers to work on behalf of the people for no remuneration. These ambassadors of goodwill were highly respected in the community and were considered above reproach due to their selfless labor. Paul views in a similar way his untiring labors to win the Gentiles to Christ. He serves under the authority of the King, yet *offers* his services willingly, rather than out of compulsion or for material gain.

Paul identifies his ministry further with the priestly function of offering sacrifices which are **acceptable to God, sanctified by the Holy Spirit** (v. 16). Here is one of the only allusions Paul makes to the priesthood, no doubt because of the serious distortions that the Temple priests had made of the meaning of worship and faith in the Jewish tradition. Paul will select several other words to describe the vocational tasks of those "set apart for the gospel of God" (1:1). He will find parallels to their roles in shepherds, overseers, civil servants, elders, and even waiters or servants.

But only here, when speaking of the Gentiles as an offering to God, does Paul liken his work to that of the priests. Just as individual believers act as *both* priest and sacrifice when offering their bodies to God (12:1), Paul sees himself in a larger role of offering an entire body of believers (the Gentiles) to God as a sacrifice of gratitude and consecration.

No doubt Paul already had some inkling of the significant role he was playing in the transformation of the gospel from a small messianic sect of Judaism to the world-changing religion it would become in just a few centuries. His special commission to the Gentiles, authorized by the church in Jerusalem (Acts 15:22f.) was already revolutionizing the church. In the face of his critics, Paul boldly asserted his right to preach this new word as an apostle of Christ.

The very interplay of authority and humility that opened this letter to the Romans now reappears in the closing section. Despite Paul's unique role as **a minister of Christ Jesus to the Gentiles** (15:16), Paul gives the credit for his accomplishments to Christ, and refuses **to speak of anything except what Christ has accomplished through [him]** (v. 18). Who among us could exercise such confidence in doing the task to which God has called us, while demonstrating the humility of Paul?

Paul defines his accomplishment in terms of what he has done and what the divine Spirit has done. For his part, Paul offers what he has said and done—the actions of a person allowing Christ to live in and through him (Gal. 2:20). For His part, God has empowered Paul's ministry through the presence of the Spirit and with **signs and miracles** (Rom. 15:19).

In the church today, there are those who seem unwilling to allow all these dynamics to coexist in the life of the body. Instead, these people give undue attention to only one or two of these elements. There are large congregations which put emphasis only on what their preacher says. The message is everything, and the communication skills of their leader define the ministry and impact of the church.

Other congregations stress the works of mercy and justice that are done in the name of Christ. They organize agencies, undertake projects and gain considerable notoriety for their efforts on behalf of the needy persons of their community . . . often to the neglect of the other aspects of the life of the church.

Still other churches place great emphasis on the power of the Spirit. Their worship experiences are intense and demonstrative. They characterize the Christian life as an exciting adventure, and they expect every gathering of the faithful to be filled with dramatic episodes of how God intervenes in the everyday activities of the faithful. Preaching and acts of mercy take a backseat to this enthusiasm of the Spirit.

And, more recently, we have seen a movement of "signs and wonders" springing up in the church. Discontent with the "ho-hum" routines of many believers, this group emphasizes the supernatural work of God. These Christians expect and often experience the spectacular work of God in their lives, including divine healing and deliverance from evil powers that enslave and oppress. Many Christians are attracted to these worship services in order to witness or hear of these miracles. The danger of such a movement is that the sound teaching of the Word and the daily disciplines of the Christian life are often lost in the search for the supernatural.

Which of these groups has discovered the true gospel? "All of them . . . and none," Paul would likely reply. A healthy church values all of these elements, and combines **what [is] said and done—by the power of signs and miracles, through the power of the Spirit** (vv. 18-19), into a unified and balanced whole. Although these "one-focus churches" attract considerable attention and thrive for a time, the solid work of God's kingdom goes on in congregations that have found, like Paul, the value of all these dimensions in the work of ministry.

The effectiveness of such a ministry for Paul is demonstrated by the size of his parish. His "parish" stretched for over fifteen hundred miles along the Mediterranean coasts. Congregations were found in towns and cities **from Jerusalem all the way around to Illyricum** (a province in Greece that bordered on the provinces of Italy with its capital city of Rome [v. 19]). This vast spread of Christianity was fresh and new. Paul was the missionary pioneer, pressing forward into new territories with his message, rather than **building on someone else's foundation** (v. 20).

Paul was no doubt thinking of the Jewish Christians who frequently arrived in town shortly after his departure, and who endeavored to persuade new converts to follow "their gospel" of Jesus *and* the Jewish laws. Paul's passion was to preach the good news to the unreached, and not to set straight all the misunderstandings of the disciples of other evangelists. His challenge to move out to a lost world, rather than to rearrange denominational statistics, is as valid today as it was when he wrote this letter.

3. PAUL'S MINISTRY TO THE ROMANS 15:23-33

Over the course of Romans 15, Paul has gradually moved away from his teaching to a more personal description of his ministry to the Gentiles. Now he closes with direct remarks about his hope for a future visit to Rome—a desire he expressed in his introductory remarks to the letter (1:10-11). One can now grasp the trajectory of Paul's lifetime of mission work. Beginning on the eastern shores of the Mediterranean Sea, Paul has pushed farther and farther to the west (as far as Illyricum), with intermittent trips back to his base of operations in Antioch of Syria. Now, he shares with the Romans his dream of spanning the full length of the Mediterranean and preaching the gospel in Spain, including a visit to Rome on his way through (15:24).

Whether or not Paul fulfilled that dream is a matter of debate among historians. There is reference in some of the earliest Christian writings, outside of the New Testament canon, that Paul preached the gospel in the westernmost regions of the Empire (Spain?) before his martyrdom in Rome. Fitting that reference into the chronology of Paul's life, as recorded in Acts, requires Paul's release from arrest in Rome prior to his final sentencing and death. Such a parole seems plausible, given the freedom Paul was given by the Romans during his time in Rome (Acts 28:30-31).

Other scholars find such a trip out of the vicinity of Rome unlikely for one who was awaiting trial in the courts. They suggest that Paul's desire, expressed here in Romans, became a "fact" after his death by the statements of well-meaning admirers. But the trip to Spain will have to remain a matter of conjecture. We know that Paul finally did meet the believers in Rome, but under far different circumstances than he imagined when writing this letter from Corinth.

In this letter, Paul corroborates the account of a special fund collected for the famine-ravished believers in Jerusalem (2 Corinthians 8). His intention was to deliver this gift from the Gentiles to the Jewish congregation in Jerusalem and then launch another missionary tour extending to Italy and Spain. His arrest in Jerusalem and subsequent appeal to Caesar resulted in a very different, but no less effective, ministry to the believers in Rome. Despite the fact that Paul went to Rome in chains, his arrival was no less **in the full measure of the blessing of Christ** (Rom. 15:29).

Paul ends the body of his letter with a prayer request. The apostle who constantly remembered the church in Rome "in [his] prayers at all times" (1:10) feels no hesitation in asking these persons of faith to reciprocate by praying for him as well. He must have sensed that the impending trip to Jerusalem was filled with risks. He might have anticipated a hostile reception by his former associates, the unbelievers in Judea, who still viewed Christians (and especially Paul) as enemies of their religious traditions.

But, he also sensed a more subtle threat. The saints in Rome could be equally cool in their reception. Here was Paul coming back to proclaim the success of his controversial work among the Gentiles. Here was Paul bringing gifts from believers about whom the Jerusalem Jews had expressed grave reservations in previous times. Here was Paul providing sustenance to those who once had been the very pillars of the church. His concern that his **service in Jerusalem [might] be acceptable to the saints there** (15:31) was certainly legitimate.

For all of his brash methods and bold confidence, Paul remained a person desiring reconciliation. He wanted peace with his enemies outside the church and peace among the brothers and sisters within the congregation as well. What fitting words to close these personal remarks: **The God of peace be with you all. Amen** (v. 33).

17

CONCLUDING REMARKS

Romans 16:1-27

Having ended the body of his letter with a *shalom,* the Jewish blessing of peace, Paul now turns to less theological tasks—a letter of commendation and personal greetings. Whether the text of chapter 16 was added to the end of the parchment (the treated animal skin used for writing in the first century) or was included as a separate document, we do not know. In either case, we can be grateful that some well-meaning copyist or editor in the early church did not delete this material, thinking it irrelevant to the great themes Paul has presented in the first fifteen chapters. This final chapter, though not as theological, tells us much of the spirituality of Paul and the early congregation at Rome.

1. GREETINGS TO ACQUAINTANCES 16:1-16

This great letter to the Romans was hand-delivered from Paul to the church in Rome by a woman who lived in Cenchrea (v. 1), a town not far from Corinth. Paul identifies this woman, Phoebe, as a minister *(deaconos)* of the church. This may simply refer to the helping actions of this woman, as we are still talking about the early stages of the church's organization. On the other hand, the word *minister* in other New Testament passages is already used as a designation for a particular office held by individuals. The fact that a woman is given this designation, is described as a "sister," and is given the task of bearing this letter, suggests that the role of women in the New Testament church was significant and welcomed. (Note how often in the following verses Paul will speak words of praise for women and their labors in the body of Christ.)

Since Phoebe comes to Rome as a stranger, Paul encourages the believers there to welcome her and offer her the same degree of assistance she has offered **many people, including [him]** (v. 2). She is no doubt a woman both of means and abilities who has served Paul and the church well. The frequent suggestion by some today that Paul was a misogynist—one who despises women—cannot be supported when looking at this and other references to particular women in his writings.

Paul then proceeds to offer personal greetings to twenty-six individuals, identifying twenty-four of them by name. Scholars have endeavored to give more detailed identities and biographical details for many of these. A few, like Priscilla and Aquila, are clearly associated with other references in the New Testament. Others have been linked to nonbiblical references in the historical records of Rome and in the early legends of the saints passed down through the Roman Catholic Church.

The fact is that many of the names mentioned in this passage were common names in Paul's day. To identify these persons with every other similar name is largely speculative. We will assume for the most part that these are persons who are little more than a name—their stories lost in the great ocean of history.

But, if we knew nothing about these persons other than what Paul tells us, there is still a rich meaning to this account. We discover, first of all, the significance of individual persons in the fellowship of the saints. Paul did not settle for saying "hello" to all the folks in the First Church of Rome. His relationship with them was too intimate and personal to lump them all together. These were individuals with unique personalities and particular stories of divine grace in their lives. Paul wanted to salute them by name.

So it is with our Heavenly Father. It is perfectly valid to describe God's relationship with His creatures in terms of the group. We acknowledge Him to be the God of Israel, the God of the United States (and other nations too!), the God of Wesleyans (and other theological traditions too!) and even the God of the little body of believers who worship in the building down the road.

But the miracle of divine grace is a salvation that is offered to individuals. Little children utter deep theological insights when they sing "Jesus Loves Me." Isaiah recounts God's own words when he says, "Fear not, for I have redeemed you; I have summoned you by name; you are mine" (Isa. 43:1). Why should Paul not salute the family of God in Rome with deeply personal references? There is for example, **Epenetus, who was the first convert to Christ in the province of Asia** (Rom. 16:5). What memories of Paul's sharing the faith and seeing lives won to Christ would that name evoke? **Persis** was a **dear friend** (v. 12), suggesting that there were deeper bonds for Paul than simply of pastor and parishioner.

Priscilla and Aquila appear first in the list of greetings. In this case, we do have considerable information about their lives and can understand why Paul pauses to salute them. Paul met these two during his first visit to Corinth (Acts 18:2). They had previously lived in Rome, but were no doubt among the Jews who were banished from that city by the emperor, Claudius, in 52 A.D. Since Paul shared their trade of weaving canvas for sails and tents, they took up residence together in Corinth. And together they moved on to Ephesus, where they included greetings along with Paul's greeting to the church in Corinth (1 Corinthians 16:19).

Now they reside in Rome, where a church has begun in their house. Certainly this couple was pivotal in the establishing of a body of believers in the capital city. We catch one final hint of them when Paul greets them, now residents of Ephesus, at the end of his second letter to Timothy (2 Tim. 4:19). Deep friendship indeed!

But, in Paul's greeting to them in the book of Romans lies a curious compliment: **They risked their lives** [literally, "laid down their necks"] **for me** (16:4). We cannot identify the particular incident in Paul's life that would have prompted these words. Nevertheless, this is descriptive of the wonderful ties that bind believers together in Christian love.

How many of us are able to recall a saint in our past experience who reached out on our behalf at some risk to themselves? Unexpected funds have kept students in college and missionaries on the field. Older believers have dared to believe in new converts, even when their conduct would not warrant such confidence. History records those who have actually given up their lives for others—all in the name of Christ's love. Paul closes his letter to this church by celebrating the individual lives who make up that body of believers and give it the richness of the family of God.

A second feature of Paul's personal greetings is the value he places on laboring together in the Kingdom. The most frequent characteristic of these believers is their willingness to **work hard in the Lord** (v. 12). Paul has discovered that difficult experiences are often made tolerable, if not enjoyable, by **fellow workers** (vv. 3, 9) who share the burden and effort. We should note that the reference to working, and especially working hard, is most frequently attached to the women that Paul greets in this letter. No less than ten women are acknowledged in this list. Again, one has difficulty making Paul out to be a chauvinist in this context!

Two references to these fellow workers bear special note. Paul greets **Andronicus and Junias, . . . who have been in prison with me** (v. 7). One modern paraphrase renders this verse to say, ". . . who did time with me." The translation is less than accurate, but the idea conveyed is powerful and very true. How much would it have meant to Paul just to have Christian friends with him in a time of distress. Although we have not likely been imprisoned, who among us have not found our lives enriched by Christian brothers or sisters who "did time" with us in an hour of need?

One of the most tender relationships in the New Testament is buried in Paul's greeting to **Rufus . . . and his mother, who has been a mother to me, too** (v. 13). Scholars agree that Paul is not referring to a biological parent here, but to a woman who treated Paul with the love and care that can only be described as maternal in its character. Again, we think of the host of Christians who have discovered a familial relationship (brother, sister, father, mother) within the household of faith. The almost trite designations of "brother" or "sister" still used in some Christian circles suggest a deep bonding that occurs as we work together for the gospel. Paul pays tribute to all the fellow workers in the Kingdom by his greetings to his friends in Rome.

Finally, we observe the significance of these apparent "nobodies" in the kingdom of God. Despite our attempts to give these persons importance by linking them to obscure references in the first century, they remain less than household names for most of us. We know of St. Paul, St. Peter, and the other "greats" of the New Testament church. However, apart from their mention here in Romans, most of these persons would have passed into the annals of history totally unknown and unremembered if Paul had not paused for a moment to send his hello. We give great honor to Paul, and rightly so. He would remind us that his life and ministry were shaped by these "insignificant" persons who, in the Kingdom to come, may be considered the greatest by a God who sees things differently than we do.

In other lists—some written, and others only in the mind—appear thousands and thousands of names of Christian "nobodies" who, as instruments of God's grace, have proclaimed and lived the gospel for two thousand years. With Paul, "the churches of Christ salute you" (v. 16 KJV).

2. PRAISES TO GOD 16:17-27

When reading the book of Romans, one suspects that Paul has trouble getting through his farewells. There are at least five places where one might think Paul is wrapping up his epistle: 8:39; 11:36; 13:14; 15:13, 33. Apparently his deep commitment to his ministry, and his compassion for the believers in Rome prompts Paul to add "just one more thought" to his letter.

Having commended the believers in Rome for their faith (1:8), and having given specific compliments for their hard work (16:3-16), Paul now offers a word of caution. Even in the church at Rome, there are persons **who cause divisions** and offer ideas **contrary to the teaching [the Romans] have learned.** The proper response? **Keep away from them** (16:17).

It is interesting that Paul has urged the believers in Rome to *accept* weaker Christians who differ on matters of religious convictions. But here he is addressing those who differ on matters of teaching and have a personal agenda in what they are doing. These persons act in service of themselves, not Christ. There is a place in the body of Christ for honest disagreement and debate over matters, so long as all persons are seeking the "good, pleasing and perfect will" of God (12:2). However, when deceptive strategies of **smooth talk and flattery** (16:18) replace the sincere search for truth, that is no time to speak of tolerance and acceptance!

The difficult question, of course, is how does one distinguish between deceptive error and honest disagreement? Paul does not spell out in detail how to discern the difference. He offers instead some rather common-sense advice: **Be wise about what is good, and innocent about what is evil** (v. 19). Well-intended believers have more than once felt they needed to know all the details and innuendoes of some particular evil—whether the matter dealt with false doctrine or immoral behavior. In the name of becoming "experts" on the matter, they have risked their spiritual well-being and sometimes "have shipwrecked their faith" (1 Tim. 1:19) by probing the depths of matters where ignorance (or at least innocence) might have been more advised.

At the same time, many Christians take righteousness for granted and do not explore the significance of goodness and the disciplines that foster holy living. To be wise about what is good requires "the renewing of [one's] mind" (Rom. 12:2) and a thought life oriented toward "whatever is true . . . noble . . . right . . . pure . . . lovely . . . [and] admirable" (Philippians 4:8). Paul notes that the believers in Rome have earned a reputation for their **obedience** (Rom. 16:19) that corresponds to a similar reputation for their faith (1:8). If only congregations of believers today would be noted above all for these two qualities—obedience and faith.

In a stand-alone verse, Paul offers yet another benediction to this epistle. The "good words" are filled with ironic twists. First, **the God of peace will soon crush Satan.** The great cosmic struggle, first mentioned in the Garden of Eden (Genesis 3), will result in the destruction of "the dragon, that ancient serpent, who is the devil, or Satan" (Revelation 20:2). Rather than describing the Destroyer in terms of power and divine wrath, Paul indicates that **the God of peace** (Rom. 16:20) will accomplish this task. Ernest W. Shurtleff reminds us again in his hymn, "Lead On O King Eternal," that "not with swords' loud clashing, nor roll of stirring drums; with deeds of love and mercy, the heavenly kingdom comes."

One would expect God to crush Satan under *His* feet. But, in another twist in the text, Paul informs the believers in Rome that it will be *their* feet that God will use to bring about this great end to evil. The mystery of the gospel is that God chooses to use fallen (and redeemed) creatures to accomplish His plan for the ages. Jesus heard the accounts of the disciples he had sent out to share the good news and revealed to them that he "saw Satan fall like lightning from heaven" (Luke 10:18). What power God is willing to divest into the hands of His followers when they live by faith and obedience!

Finally, Paul introduces a time element that could puzzle the reader. **Soon** Satan will be crushed (Rom. 16:20). Is this another case of Paul's uninformed belief that Christ would return momentarily? Or does Paul grasp a deeper meaning of God's purposes, realizing that no matter when the end of history might occur, the power of Satan has been broken in the Cross, and that in the power of the Spirit, believers are *now* "more than conquerors through him who loved us" (8:37)?

Victory for the future—praise God! And **the grace of our Lord Jesus** (16:20) for the here and now. In a letter loaded with deep theological truths, Paul offers very few details concerning the end times and God's final plan for history. Instead, Paul gives the ultimate assurance we need to walk with God—grace for today and a glorious hope for the future.

Having sent greetings to his believing friends in Rome, Paul now lets his colleagues in Corinth pass along their personal regards. Without speculation on the details of these persons' lives, we learn that Paul was supported in his endeavors (perhaps even in his writing) by a group of colleagues whom he valued. We also learn the name of Paul's scribe— **Tertius**—who wrote down Paul's words and slipped in a greeting of his own (v. 22).

In all, Paul singles out thirty-five individuals in his concluding remarks. In most instances, he describes them with a single word or brief phrase. What rich "epitaphs" to the faithful are found in these compliments: "fellow worker[s]," "a mother to me," "my dear friend," "tested and approved in Christ," "outstanding among the apostles," and the list goes on. What brief phrase would our fellow Christians (or the world) attach to our name? Would the distinguishing feature of our lives bring glory to Christ, as do the titles of these long-ago saints?

How does one end such a powerful expression of the gospel of Christ? Paul endeavors to sum up the heart of his letter to the Romans by directing their thoughts to God. In the closing benediction, he outlines salvation history one final time:

    a. God's eternal plan of love is ultimately a **mystery hidden for long ages** (v. 25).

    b. He has chosen to reveal aspects of that mystery through the prophets of the Old Testament (v. 26).

    c. The good news of salvation has been proclaimed by Jesus Christ and declared to the church at Rome by Paul himself (v. 25).

    d. The great truth of God's righteousness through faith (the gospel) can establish believers—even those in Rome (v. 25).

    e. The purpose of this gospel is **that all nations might believe and obey him** (v. 26).

    f. All **glory** for this great reality of life in Christ must be returned to the Giver, **the only wise God . . . through Jesus Christ** (v. 27).

The Apostle Paul has no need to be ashamed. God has chosen him for salvation. Jesus Christ has reconciled him to God. The Holy Spirit transforms his mind and conduct. He stands in God's righteousness—not by virtue of his own endeavors, but by the ever-repeated response of faith, "from first to last." This salvation is not for Paul alone; the good news is for "everyone who believes. . . . Just as it is written: 'The righteous will live by faith'" (1:16-17). Thanks be to God!